ECONOMICS

OTHER ECONOMIST BOOKS

Guide to Analysing Companies
Guide to Business Modelling
Guide to Business Planning
Guide to Economic Indicators
Guide to the European Union
Guide to Financial Markets
Guide to Investment Strategy
Guide to Management Ideas
Numbers Guide
Style Guide

Dictionary of Business
Dictionary of Economics
International Dictionary of Finance

Brands and Branding
Business Consulting
Business Ethics
Business Strategy
China's Stockmarket
Emerging Markets
The Future of Technology
Globalisation
Headhunters and How to Use Them
Successful Mergers
The City
Wall Street

Essential Director
Essential Economics
Essential Investment
Essential Negotiation

Pocket World in Figures

ECONOMICS

Making Sense of the Modern Economy

Edited by Simon Cox

THE ECONOMIST IN ASSOCIATION WITH

PROFILE BOOKS LTD

Published by Profile Books Ltd
3A Exmouth House, Pine Street, London EC1R OJH
www.profilebooks.com

The greatest care has been taken in compiling this book.
However, no responsibility can be accepted by the publishers or compilers
for the accuracy of the information presented.

Where opinion is expressed it is that of the author and does not necessarily coincide
with the editorial views of The Economist Newspaper.

Typeset in EcoType by MacGuru Ltd
info@macguru.org.uk

Printed in Great Britain by
Clays, Bungay, Suffolk

A CIP catalogue record for this book is available
from the British Library

HARDBACK
ISBN-10: 1 86197 545 7
ISBN-13: 978 1 86197 545 4

PAPERBACK
ISBN-10: 1 86197 606 2
ISBN-13: 978 1 86197 606 2

The paper this book is printed on is certified by the © 1996 Forest Stewardship
Council A.C. (FSC). It is ancient-forest friendly. The printer holds FSC chain of
custody SGS-COC-2061

FSC

Mixed Sources
Product group from well-managed
forests and other controlled sources

Cert no. SGS-COC-2061
www.fsc.org
© 1996 Forest Stewardship Council

Contents

Contributors   vii
Introduction   viii

Part 1 The new liberalism
1   The case for globalisation   3

Part 2 The lopsided world economy
2   The phoney recovery   55
3   America's imbalances   67
4   China's rise   87
5   The underachievers   103

Part 3 The arteries of capitalism
6   Finance   135
7   Central banks   173
8   Global capital   197

Part 4 Worldly philosophy
9   The uses and abuses of economics   235

Index   304

Contributors

Brian Barry is *The Economist's* business correspondent based in Chicago. He contributed articles to Chapters 5 and 9.

Simon Cox is *The Economist's* economics correspondent. He contributed to Chapter 9. He is also the editor of this book.

Clive Crook was deputy editor of *The Economist*. He wrote Chapters 1 and 8, and contributed to Chapter 9.

Robert Guest was Africa editor of *The Economist* and is now the paper's Washington correspondent. He contributed to Chapter 9.

Patrick Lane is the finance editor of *The Economist*. He contributed to Chapter 9.

Marc Levinson was finance editor of *The Economist*. He wrote Chapter 6.

Zanny Minton-Beddoes is Washington economics editor of *The Economist*. She wrote Chapter 3, and contributed to Chapter 9.

David Shirreff is *The Economist's* finance and business correspondent based in Frankfurt. He contributed to Chapter 5.

John Smutniak was *The Economist's* economics correspondent. He contributed to Chapter 9.

Paul Wallace is *The Economist's* UK economics correspondent. He contributed to Chapter 9.

Pam Woodall is economics editor of *The Economist*. She wrote Chapters 2 and 4. She also contributed to Chapters 7, 5 and 9.

Introduction

Economists attract ridicule and resentment in equal measure. People mock them, in the same way they poke fun at all eggheads and number-crunchers. But for everyone who scoffs, there is someone (perhaps the same person) who secretly fears that economists are the unacknowledged legislators of the world, purveyors of dangerous ideas that are filling the heads and turning the minds of the political leaders who claim to be in charge.

If only. Protectionism, populism and paternalism still hold great sway over human affairs, their appeal seemingly impervious to centuries of economic logic. *The Economist* was founded in 1843 in opposition to an infamous piece of protectionist folly, Britain's Corn Laws, which propped up the price of wheat to the great benefit of landlords and the severe detriment of anyone trying to buy a loaf of bread. Those laws were eventually repealed. But similar policies still thrive over 160 years later, and *The Economist* regularly enters the lists against them.

Some causes and questions endure. This is one reason why the articles in this book, all written by journalists at *The Economist* in recent years, can claim to have a useful life beyond the week in which they were published and the immediate events that prompted them. The protagonists may change – Alan Greenspan has handed over the chairmanship of the Federal Reserve to Ben Bernanke; Gerhard Schröder has lost Germany's chancellery to Angela Merkel – but the dilemmas that defined their years in power outlive them. As a result, the pieces in this book have been only lightly edited to remove passages overtaken by events; and a short endnote has been added to some of them for those curious to know what happened next.

There is a second reason why the pieces in this book are worth revisiting: the laws of economics do not change from week to week. If you have ever wondered why America's trade deficit attracts so much fuss, why central bankers enjoy so much deference, whether stockbrokers earn their commissions, or why we cannot solve unemployment by sharing work out more evenly, the articles in this book provide answers based on economic principles of lasting relevance.

Those principles can be found in many a dry and scholarly textbook. But textbooks lack bite. *The Economist*, however, has a point of view, and is not shy of an argument. Its opponents, those who inveigh against the evils of capitalism and the iniquities of trade, do not have a monopoly on moral passion. *The Economist*'s combativeness can be an aid, not a bar, to understanding. Explaining an issue and making a point often go hand in hand. And one does not have to agree with something to profit from reading it. The articles in this book succeed if they are worth arguing with.

The nine chapters in this book are divided into four parts. Chapters 2–5 track the fortunes of the world economy. This decade started badly, but at its mid-point the economic scene appears unusually tranquil. Inflation is subdued, despite high oil prices. America's economy stuttered in the last three months of 2005, but was in good voice for the preceding nine. Spirits are rising in Germany, and, after a decade of debilitating deflation, prices are starting to rise in Japan. Lest you be lulled into complacency, however, these chapters look at the powerful economic undertow beneath this placid surface: overstretch in America; an industrial revolution in China; and chronic underachievement in Japan and Germany.

The "capital" in capitalism is the subject of Chapters 6–8. Most books on finance claim to tell you how to make money. This book has a different ambition. It asks not what the financial system can do for you, but what finance does for the economy. Contrary to popular belief, the moneymen and stockjobbers, "their brains full and throbbing with greedy hopes or bare fears" as Walt Whitman memorably described them, can perform a useful economic function, even if that is not part of their intention. This part of the book explains how money and credit are created, regulated and circulated. It also takes an extended look at what happens when capital spills across national borders, sometimes with overwhelming force.

The last chapter of this book looks at how economics is applied and misapplied to many questions of practical importance, from trust busting to garbage collecting, from saving for retirement to saving the planet. People often assume that economists give only one kind of advice: leave it to the market. Certainly, economists have a healthy respect for what the market can achieve. But they are often at their most creative when showing how the market can fail, and how it can be harnessed for social purposes everyone holds dear.

Two ugly neologisms supposedly define our age: globalisation and neo-liberalism. The first is a buzzword, the second a boo-word. *The Economist* has been around since an earlier era of globalisation, brought to an end by the first world war, when liberalism did not need a prefix. In the intervening years, its guiding philosophy has suffered some cataclysmic setbacks as nations turned to statism and economic isolationism. Seen from this long perspective, the recent prominence of liberal ideas is not something that can be taken for granted. And so the first chapter of this book makes the case for globalisation, and the new, or renewed, liberalism that underpins it.

PART 1

THE NEW LIBERALISM

1

THE CASE FOR GLOBALISATION

Globalisation is the remarkable result of innocuous choices. Companies in one nation choose to employ workers in another, and consumers in a third country choose to buy the stuff they make. To put it this way is not to diminish the technological innovations – from high-speed internet links to standardised shipping containers – that have made such choices possible and affordable. Nor is it to ignore the legislative effort – the lowering of import tariffs and the lifting of foreign-ownership restrictions – that has allowed these choices freer expression. But it is to emphasise that globalisation, a phenomenon that has generated such controversy and ire, is not the result of a low conspiracy or a grand design. It is rather the aggregate result of lots of people getting by, doing what they judge to be in their best interest given their circumstances.

This simple observation is the starting point for the articles that follow. They argue that globalisation is worth defending for the same reason that people's choices are worth respecting. Despite the vast energies spent extolling globalisation's virtues and excoriating its sins, this point is often missed.

It is missed because globalisation has the wrong advocates, speaking the wrong language. The case for tighter economic integration is most often put by businessmen, eager to avail themselves of a world of cheap workers and new consumers. The argument is then taken up by politicians, who portray globalisation as an irresistible force they can blame for their own unpopular decisions. We must adapt to the world economy, they say. There is no alternative. But it would be equally true to say that the world economy has adapted to us, our choices of whom to work for and what to buy.

Amartya Sen, one of the few economists respected on both sides of the globalisation barricades, puts it like this: "To be generically against markets would be almost as odd as being generically against conversations between people." Markets, like conversations, are a form of exchange. And globalisation is what results when that exchange extends across national borders. This chapter worries that the policies favoured by many of globalisation's critics would end up excluding some players from the conversation. They would close markets to firms in poor countries that could not meet the minimum wages or environmental standards critics favour.

Globalisation did not invent developing-country poverty. But it has awoken many people to it. The forces of trade and investment have drawn the poor into the economic orbit of the rich, making their plight harder to ignore. Hard-pressed people in faraway countries have entered the life of rich consumers in intimate ways, stitching the shirt on their back and sewing the shoes on their feet. Some conscientious shoppers feel sullied by the whole process. Their compunctions are understandable: a sweatshop is an ugly thing. But how they feel vanishes into insignificance compared with how poor workers fare. The evidence in this chapter suggests that the world's poor stand to gain from jobs serving rich consumers. That is why they choose them. And their choices deserve a measure of respect.

Globalisation and its critics

Globalisation is well worth defending. But neither governments nor businesses can be trusted to make the case

The strongest case for globalisation is the liberal one. It is almost never heard, least of all from governments or businessmen. International economic integration, on the liberal view, is what happens when technology allows people to pursue their own goals and they are given the liberty to do so. If technology advances to the point where it supports trade across borders, and if people then choose to trade across borders, you have integration, and because people have freely chosen it this is a good thing. Also, again because people have freely chosen this course, you would expect there to be economic benefits as well.

By and large, theory and practice confirm that this is so. Adam Smith's invisible hand does its work. People choose what serves their own self-interest, each of them making that judgment for himself. The result is that society as a whole prospers and advances – spontaneously, not by design of any person or government.

All kinds of qualifications and elaborations are needed, obviously, to fill out the argument properly. Some of them will be offered in due course. But it is essential to understand one point from the outset. The liberal case for globalisation is emphatically not the case for domestic or international laisser-faire. Liberalism lays down no certainties about the requirements of social justice in terms of income redistribution or the extent of the welfare state. It recognises that markets have their limits, for instance in tending to the supply of public goods (such as a clean environment). A liberal outlook is consistent with support for a wide range of government interventions; indeed a liberal outlook demands many such interventions.

But the starting point for all liberals is a presumption that, under ordinary circumstances, the individual knows best what serves his interests and that the blending of these individual choices will produce socially good results. Two other things follow. The first is an initial scepticism, at least, about collective decision-making that overrides the individual kind. The other is a high regard for markets – not as a place where profits are made, it must be stressed, but as a place where society advances in the common good.

Why then are governments and business leaders rarely heard to put this case? Because for the most part they are not liberals. Perhaps it goes with the job that politicians of left and right, traditional and modern, have an exaggerated view of their ability to improve on the spontaneous order of a lightly governed society.

It would be even more naive, and contrary to all experience, to expect business itself to favour a liberal outlook. Businesses are ultimately interested in one thing: profits. The business-bashing NGOs are right about that. If businesses think that treating their customers and staff well, or adopting a policy of "corporate social responsibility", or using ecologically friendly stationery will add to their profits, they will do it. Otherwise, they will not.

Does that make market capitalism wrong? On the contrary, the point of a liberal market economy is that it civilises the quest for profit, turning it, willy-nilly, into an engine of social progress. If firms have to compete with rivals for customers and workers, then they will indeed worry about their reputation for quality and fair dealing – even if they do not value those things in themselves. Competition will make them behave as if they did.

Here, then, is where the anti-business NGOs get their argument completely upside down – with genuinely dangerous consequences for the causes, sometimes just, which they hope to advance. On the whole, stricter regulation of international business is not going to reduce profits: the costs will be passed along to consumers. And it is not going to diminish any company's interest in making profits. What it may well do, though, by disabling markets in their civilising role, is to give companies new opportunities to make even bigger profits at the expense of society at large.

For example, suppose that in the remorseless search for profit, multinationals pay sweatshop wages to their workers in developing countries. Regulation forcing them to pay higher wages is demanded. The biggest western firms concede there might be merit in the idea. But justice and efficiency require a level playing-field. The NGOs, the reformed multinationals and enlightened rich-country governments propose tough rules on developing-country factory wages, backed up by trade barriers to keep out imports from countries that do not comply. Shoppers in the West pay more – but willingly, because they know it is in a good cause. The NGOs declare another victory. The companies, having shafted their developing-country competition and protected their domestic markets, count their bigger profits (higher wage costs notwithstanding). And the developing-country workers displaced from locally owned factories explain to their children why the West's new deal for the victims of capitalism requires them to starve.

If firms ruled the world

A fashionable strand of scepticism argues that governments have surrendered their power to capitalism – that the world's biggest companies are nowadays more powerful than many of the world's governments. Democracy is a sham. Profits rule, not people. These claims are patent nonsense. On the other hand, there is no question that companies would run the world for profit if they could. What stops them is not governments, powerful as they may be, but markets.

Governments have the power, all right, but they do not always exercise it wisely. They are unreliable servants of the public interest. Sometimes, out of conviction, politicians decide to help companies reshape the world for private profit. Sometimes, anti-market thinking may lead them to help big business by accident. And now and then, when companies just set out to buy the policies they want, they find in government a willing seller. On all this, presumably, the sceptics would agree.

But they miss the next crucial step: limited government is not worth buying. Markets keep the spoils of corruption small. Government that intervenes left and right, prohibiting this and licensing that, creating surpluses and shortages – now that kind of government is worth a bit. That is why, especially in developing countries with weak legal systems, taming capitalism by regulation or trade protection often proves such a hazardous endeavour.

If NGOs succeeded in disabling markets, as many of them say they would like to, the political consequences would be as dire as the economic ones. It is because the sceptics are right about some things that they are so wrong about the main thing.

Profits over people

Critics argue that globalisation hurts workers. Are they right?

THE LIBERTY that makes economic integration possible is desirable in itself. In addition, advocates of globalisation argue, integration is good for people in material terms – that is why free people choose it. Sceptics disagree on both points: globalisation militates against liberty and democracy, they say, and while it makes some people who are already rich even richer, it does this by keeping the poor in poverty. After all, globalisation is merely capitalism writ large. A later part of this chapter deals with the implications of globalisation for democracy. But first, is it true that globalisation harms the poor?

In a narrow sense, the answer is yes: it does harm some of the poor. Free trade and foreign direct investment may take jobs from workers (including low-paid workers) in the advanced industrial economies and give them to cheaper workers in poor countries. Thanks to the North American Free-Trade Agreement (NAFTA), for instance, there are no tariffs or investment restrictions to stop an American manufacturer closing an old factory in the United States and opening a new one in Mexico.

Sceptics score this strategy as a double crime. The rich-country workers, who were probably on low wages by local standards to begin with, are out of work. That increase in the local supply of labour drives down other wages. Meanwhile, the poor-country workers are drawn into jobs that exploit them. How do you know that the poor-country workers are being exploited? Because they are being paid less, often much less, than their rich-country counterparts got before trade opened up – and in all likelihood they are working longer hours in shabbier premises as well. The only gain from this kind of trade, the indictment continues, accrues to the owners of the companies who have shifted their operations from low-wage factories in industrialised countries to poverty-wage factories in the south.

Some of this is true. Trade displaces workers in the industrialised countries; other things being equal, this will have some depressing effect on the wages of other workers; and pay and conditions in developing-country factories are likely to be worse than in their rich-country counterparts. But whereas the displaced rich-country workers are plainly worse off than they were before, the newly employed poor-country workers are plainly better off. They must be, because they have chosen to take those jobs.

As for profits, yes, that is the spur for moving production to a lower-wage area. But no company can expect to hang on to this windfall for long, because it will be competed away as other companies do the same thing and cut their prices. That lowering of prices is crucial in understanding the broader benefits of the change. It is what makes consumers at large – including poor consumers – better off, raising real incomes in the aggregate.

What about the rich-country workers who are not displaced, but whose wages may nonetheless come under downward pressure? It is hard to generalise. On the one hand, their wages may fall, or fail to rise as quickly as they would have done otherwise; on the other, they benefit from lower prices along with everybody else. On balance, you would expect that some will lose, some will gain, and some will be about as well off as they were before. In developing countries, the labour-market side of this process will tend to work in the other direction. The increase in demand for poor-country labour ought to push up wages even for workers who are not employed in the new trade-related jobs.

So capitalism-globalisation is not mainly concerned with shifting income from workers to investors, as the sceptics maintain. Rather, it makes some workers worse off while making others (including the poorest ones of all, to begin with) better off. And in the aggregate it makes consumers (that is, people with or without a job) better off as well. Altogether, given freer trade, both rich-country and poor-country living standards rise. That gives governments more to spend on welfare, education and other public services.

Changing gear

Note that all this counts only the so-called static gains from trade: the effects of a once-and-for-all shift in the pattern of production and consumption. Modern economics also emphasises the importance of dynamic gains, arising especially from the economies of scale that freer trade makes possible. The aggregate long-term gain for rich and poor countries alike is likely to be far bigger than the simple arithmetic would suggest.

Moreover, few displaced rich-country workers are likely to be permanently out of work. Most will move to other jobs. Also, new jobs will be created by the economic opportunities that trade opens up. Overall, trade neither reduces the number of jobs in the economy nor increases them. In principle, there is no reason to expect employment or unemployment to be any higher or lower in an open economy than in a closed economy – or, for that matter, in a rich economy as compared to a poor economy. Still, none of this is to deny that the displaced rich-country workers lose out: many, perhaps most, of those who find alternative work will be paid less than they were before.

In thinking through the economic theory of liberal trade, it is helpful to draw a parallel with technological progress. Trade allows a country to shift its pattern of production in such a way that, after exporting those goods it does not want and importing those it does, it can consume more without there having been any increase in its available resources. Advancing technology allows a country to do something very similar: to make more with less. You can think of trade as a machine (with no running costs or depreciation): goods you can make cheaply go in at one end, and goods that would cost you a lot more to make come out at the other. The logic of protectionism would demand that such a miraculous machine be dismantled and the blueprint destroyed, in order to save jobs.

No question, technological progress, just like trade, creates losers as well as winners. The Industrial Revolution involved hugely painful economic and social dislocations – though nearly everybody would now agree that the gains in human welfare were worth the cost. Even in far milder periods of economic transformation, such as today's, new machines and new methods make old skills obsolete. The Luddites understood that, which made them more coherent on the subject than some of today's sceptics, who oppose integration but not technological progress. Logically, they should oppose both or neither.

Politically, of course, it is essential to keep the two separate. Sceptics can expect to win popular support for the view that freer trade is harmful, but could never hope to gain broad backing for the idea that, so far as possible, technological progress should be brought to a halt. Still, it might be better if the sceptics concentrated not on attacking trade as such, but on demanding help for the workers who suffer as a result of economic progress, whether the cause is trade or technology.

Winners and losers

So much for the basic theory. What does the evidence say? For the moment, concentrate on the prospects for workers in rich countries such as the United States (the next chapter will look in more detail at workers in poor countries). By and large, the evidence agrees with the theory –

though things, as always, get more complicated the closer you look.

A first qualification is that most outward foreign direct investment (FDI) from rich countries goes not to poor countries at all, but to other rich countries. In the late 1990s, roughly 80% of the stock of America's outward FDI was in

Where the money goes
America's stock of direct investment overseas, 2000

	$bn	% of total
High-income countries	982.8	81.0
Middle-income countries	218.1	18.0
Low-income countries	12.2	1.0
All countries	1,213.1	100.0

Sources: Edward M. Graham, Institute for International Economics; *The Economist*

Canada, Japan and Western Europe, and nearly all of the rest was in middle-income developing countries such as Brazil, Mexico, Indonesia and Thailand. The poorest developing countries accounted for 1% of America's outward FDI (see Chart 1.1). Capital is hardly flooding to the world's poorest countries – more's the pity, from their point of view.

The notion that outward FDI reduces the demand for labour in the sending country and increases it in the receiving one needs to be revised as well. It was based on the assumption that when rich-country firms invest in poor countries, rich-country exports (and jobs) are replaced by poor-country domestic production. In fact, evidence from the United States and other countries suggests that outward FDI does not displace exports, it creates them: FDI and exports are, in the jargon, net complements. This is because the affiliates of multinationals trade with each other. Figures for 1995 show that America's exports to its foreign-owned affiliates actually exceeded its imports from them (see Chart 1.2 on the next page).

Before FDI, the companies exported finished goods. After FDI, they ship, let us suppose, a mixture of finished goods and intermediate goods. The intermediate goods will be used to make finished goods in the FDI-receiving country. The corresponding increase in exports of intermediate goods outweighs the fall, if any, in exports of finished goods. Overall, then, exports from the FDI-sending country rise. At the same time, the sending country's imports rise as well, partly because the affiliate sells goods back to the sending country. Exports rise, which increases the demand for labour; and imports rise, which decreases the demand for labour.

What does all this mean for the labour markets of the rich, FDI-sending countries? Jobs are created in exporting industries which will tend to be relatively high-paying, but overall employment will not rise,

Keeping it in the family 1.2

American exports to, and imports from, American-owned affiliates abroad, 1995, $bn

	Intra-company	Inter-company	Total
All countries			
Exports	145.5	24.5	170.0
Imports	123.9	19.4	143.3
Balance	21.6	5.1	26.7
High-income countries			
Exports	129.0	20.8	149.9
Imports	94.0	15.1	109.1
Balance	35.0	5.7	40.7
Middle-income countries			
Exports	28.9	5.4	34.3
Imports	31.5	1.9	33.4
Balance	-2.6	3.5	0.8
Low-income countries			
Exports	1.6	0.2	1.8
Imports	1.8	0.4	2.2
Balance	-0.2	-0.2	-0.4

Source: Edward M. Graham, Institute for International Economics

for reasons explained earlier. For every job created, another one somewhere else will be destroyed. The jobs that go will tend to be in industries that compete with imports. On average, studies suggest, those jobs pay lower wages.

On balance, then, you could say that the economy has gained: it now has more higher-paying jobs and fewer lower-paying jobs. A policy which attempted to resist a shift like that would be difficult to defend on its merits. Unfortunately, though, the people getting the higher-paying jobs are not necessarily the ones who have lost the lower-paying jobs. Because of the boost to exports, the overall effect of outward FDI on jobs and wages in the sending country is more benign than the simple theory suggests – but some people still lose.

Another implication of the shift in the demand for labour in the rich, FDI-sending countries is a possible widening of income inequality. In a country such as the United States, the combined action of trade and capital flows is likely to raise the demand for relatively skilled labour and lower the demand for relatively unskilled labour. Some hitherto low-wage workers may succeed in trading up to higher-paid jobs, but many others will be left behind in industries where wages are falling. In this scenario, high and average wages may be rising, but wages at the bottom may be falling – and that means greater inequality.

You would expect to see a similar pattern in an economy that was undergoing rapid technological change. So in the United States, which fits that description better than most in the 1990s, you could say that economic integration may have added to the already powerful pressures that were acting to increase inequality. Since those same pressures were raising living standards in the aggregate – not just for the very rich – it would be a misleading summary, but not a false one.

Explaining inequality

Of these two unequalising forces, economic integration and technological progress, which is likely to be more powerful? If it were the latter, that would raise doubts over the sceptics' focus on globalisation as the primary cause of social friction. The evidence suggests that technology is indeed much the more powerful driver of inequality. One study, by William Cline, estimated that technological change was perhaps five times more powerful in widening inequality in America between 1973 and 1993 than trade (including trade due to FDI), and that trade accounted for only around six percentage points of all the unequalising forces at work

Getting less equal	1.3
Illustrative sources of increase in the ratio of skilled to unskilled wages in the United States 1973–93, %	

A. Equalising forces	
Increase in stock of skilled relative to unskilled labour	-40

B. Unequalising forces	
Trade:	7
Lower transport and communication costs	3
Liberalisation	3
Outsourcing	1
Immigration	2
Falling minimum wage	5
De-unionisation	3
Skill-biased technological change	29
Other unexplained	29
TOTAL	97
C. Net effect	18

Note: Percentages for unequalising forces must be chained, not added, to equal total unequalising effect. Similarly, "A" and "B" must be chained to calculate "C".

Source: William R. Cline, Institute for International Economics

during that period. That is just one study, but it is not unrepresentative. The consensus is that integration has exerted a far milder influence on wage inequality than technology.

Mr Cline's study in fact deserves a closer look. It found to begin with that the total increase in the ratio of skilled to unskilled wages in the two decades to the early 1990s was 18%. This was the net result of opposing influences. An increase in the supply of skilled labour relative to the supply of unskilled labour acted to equalise wages, by making unskilled labour relatively scarce. By itself, this would have driven the wage ratio down by 40% (see Chart 1.3). But at the same time a variety of unequalising forces pushed the ratio up by 97%, resulting in the net increase of 18%. These unequalising forces included not just trade and technology, but also immigration, reductions in the real value of the minimum wage, and de-unionisation.

Two things strike you about the numbers. First, trade has been relatively unimportant in widening income inequality. Second, this effect is overwhelmed not just by technology but also by the main force operating in the opposite, equalising, direction: education and training.

This means that globalisation sceptics are missing the point if they are worried mainly about the effect of integration on rich-country losers: trade is a much smaller factor than technology. Some people in rich countries do lose out from the combination of trade and technology. The remedy lies with education and training, and with help in changing jobs. Spending in those areas, together perhaps with more generous and effective help for people forced to change jobs by economic growth, addresses the problem directly – and in a way that adds to society's economic resources rather than subtracting from them, as efforts to hold back either technological progress or trade would do.

Grinding the poor

Sceptics charge that globalisation especially hurts poor workers in the developing countries. It does not

FOR THE MOST PART, it seems, workers in rich countries have little to fear from globalisation, and a lot to gain. But is the same thing true for workers in poor countries? The answer is that they are even more likely than their rich-country counterparts to benefit, because they have less to lose and more to gain.

Orthodox economics takes an optimistic line on integration and the developing countries. Openness to foreign trade and investment should encourage capital to flow to poor economies. In the developing world, capital is scarce, so the returns on investment there should be higher than in the industrialised countries, where the best opportunities to make money by adding capital to labour have already been used up. If poor countries lower their barriers to trade and investment, the theory goes, rich foreigners will want to send over some of their capital.

If this inflow of resources arrives in the form of loans or portfolio investment, it will supplement domestic savings and loosen the financial constraint on additional investment by local companies. If it arrives in the form of new foreign-controlled operations, FDI, so much the better: this kind of capital brings technology and skills from abroad packaged along with it, with less financial risk as well. In either case, the addition to investment ought to push incomes up, partly by raising the demand for labour and partly by making labour more productive.

This is why workers in FDI-receiving countries should be in an even better position to profit from integration than workers in FDI-sending countries. Also, with or without inflows of foreign capital, the same static and dynamic gains from trade should apply in developing countries as in rich ones. This gains-from-trade logic often arouses suspicion, because the benefits seem to come from nowhere. Surely one side or the other must lose. Not so. The benefits that a rich country gets through trade do not come at the expense of its poor-country trading partners, or vice versa. Recall that according to the theory, trade is a positive-sum game. In all these transactions, both sides – exporters and importers, borrowers and lenders, shareholders and workers – can gain.

What, if anything, might spoil the simple theory and make things go awry? Plenty, say the sceptics.

First, they argue, telling developing countries to grow through trade, rather than through building industries to serve domestic markets, involves a fallacy of composition. If all poor countries tried to do this simultaneously, the price of their exports would be driven down on world markets. The success of the East Asian tigers, the argument continues, owed much to the fact that so many other developing countries chose to discourage trade rather than promote it. This theory of "export pessimism" was influential with many developing-country governments up until the 1980s, and seems to lie behind the thinking of many sceptics today.

A second objection to the openness-is-good orthodoxy concerns not trade but FDI. The standard thinking assumes that foreign capital pays for investment that makes economic sense – the kind that will foster development. Experience shows that this is often not so. For one reason or another, the inflow of capital may produce little or nothing of value, sometimes less than nothing. The money may be wasted or stolen. If it was borrowed, all there will be to show for it is an insupportable debt to foreigners. Far from merely failing to advance development, this kind of financial integration sets it back.

Third, the sceptics point out, workers in developing countries lack the rights, legal protections and union representation enjoyed by their counterparts in rich countries. This is why, in the eyes of the multinationals, hiring them makes such good sense. Lacking in bargaining power, workers do not benefit as they should from an increase in the demand for labour. Their wages do not go up. They may have no choice but to work in sweatshops, suffering unhealthy or dangerous conditions, excessive hours or even physical abuse. In the worst cases, children as well as adults are the victims.

Is trade good for growth?

All this seems very complicated. Can the doubters be answered simply by measuring the overall effect of openness on economic growth? Some economists think so, and have produced a variety of much-quoted econometric studies apparently confirming that trade promotes development. Studies by Jeffrey Sachs and Andrew Warner at Harvard, by David Dollar and Aart Kraay of the World Bank, and by Jeffrey Frankel of Harvard and David Romer of Berkeley, are among the most frequently cited. Studies such as these are enough to convince most economists that trade does indeed promote growth. But they cannot be said to settle the matter. If the application of econometrics to other big, complicated questions in economics is any guide, they probably never will: the precise economic linkages that underlie the correlations may always be too difficult to uncover.

This is why a good number of economists, including some of the most distinguished advocates of liberal trade, are unpersuaded by this kind of work. For every regression "proving" that trade promotes growth, it is too easy to tweak a choice of variable here and a period of analysis there to "prove" that it does not. Among the sceptics, Dani Rodrik has led the assault on the pro-trade regression studies. But economists such as Jagdish Bhagwati and T.N. Srinivasan, both celebrated advocates of trade liberalisation, are also pretty scathing about the regression evidence.

Look elsewhere, though, and there is no lack of additional evidence, albeit of a more variegated and less easily summarised sort, that trade promotes development. Of the three criticisms just stated of the orthodox preference for liberal trade, the first and most influential down the years has been the "export pessimism" argument – the idea that liberalising trade will be self-defeating if too many developing countries try to do it simultaneously. What does the evidence say about that?

Pessimism confounded

It does not say that the claim is nonsense. History shows that the prediction of persistently falling export prices has proved correct for some commodity exporters: demand for some commodities has failed to keep pace with growth in global incomes. And nobody will ever know what would have happened over the past few decades if all the developing countries had promoted trade more vigorously, because they didn't. But there are good practical reasons to regard the pessimism argument, as applied to poor-country exports in general, as wrong.

The developing countries as a group may be enormous in terms of geography and population, but in economic terms they are small. Taken together, the exports of all the world's poor and middle-income countries (including comparative giants such as China, India, Brazil and Mexico, big oil exporters such as Saudi Arabia, and large-scale manufacturers such as South Korea, Taiwan and Malaysia) represent only about 5% of global output. This is an amount roughly equivalent to the GDP of Britain. Even if growth in the global demand for imports were somehow capped, a concerted export drive by those parts of the developing world not already engaged in the effort would put no great strain on the global trading system.

In any event, though, the demand for imports is not capped. In effect, export pessimism involves a fallacy of its own – a "lump-of-trade" fallacy, akin to the idea of a "lump of labour" (whereby a growing population is taken to imply an ever-rising rate of unemployment, there being only so many jobs to go round). The overall growth of trade, and the kinds of product that any particular country may buy or sell, are not preordained. As Mr Bhagwati and Mr Srinivasan argued in a review of the connections between trade and development, forecasts of the poor countries' potential to expand their exports have usually been too low, partly because forecasters concentrate on existing exports and neglect new ones, some of which may be completely unforeseen. Unexpected shifts in the pattern of output have often proved very important.

Pessimists also make too little of the scope for intra-industry specialisation in trade, which gives developing countries a further set of new opportunities. The same goes for new trade among developing countries, as opposed to trade with the rich world. Often, as developing countries grow, they move away from labour-intensive manufactures to more sophisticated kinds of production: this makes room in the markets they previously served for goods from countries that are not yet so advanced. For example, in the 1970s, Japan withdrew from labour-intensive manufacturing, making way for exports from the East Asian tigers. In the 1980s and 1990s, the tigers did the same, as China began moving into those markets. And as developing countries grow by exporting, their own demand for imports rises.

It is one thing to argue that relying on trade is likely to be self-defeating, as the export pessimists claim; it is another to say that trade actually succeeds in promoting growth. The most persuasive evidence that it does lies in the contrasting experiences from the 1950s onwards of the East Asian tigers, on one side, and the countries that chose to discourage trade and pursue "import-substituting industrialisation" (ISI) on the other, such as India, much of Latin America and much of Africa.

Years ago, in an overlapping series of research projects, great effort went into examining the developing countries' experience with trade policy during the 1950s, 1960s and early 1970s. This period saw lasting surges of growth without precedent in history. At the outset, South Korea, for instance, was a poor country, with an income per head in 1955 of around $400 (in today's prices), and such poor economic prospects that American officials predicted abject and indefinite dependence on aid. Within a single generation it became a mighty exporter and world-ranking industrial power.

Examining the record up to the 1970s, and the experience of development elsewhere in East Asia and other poor regions of the world, economists at the OECD, the World Bank and America's National Bureau of Economic Research came to see the crucial importance of "outward orientation" – that is, of the link between trade and growth. The finding held across a range of countries, regardless of differences in particular policies, institutions and political conditions, all of which varied widely. An unusually impressive body of evidence and analysis discredited the ISI orthodoxy and replaced it with a new one, emphasising trade.

The trouble with ISI

What was wrong with ISI, according to these researchers? In principle, nothing much; the problems arose over how it worked in practice. The whole idea of ISI was to drive a wedge between world prices and domestic prices, so as to create a bias in favour of producing for the home market and therefore a bias against producing for the export market. In principle, this bias could be modest and uniform; in practice, ISI often produced an anti-export bias both severe and wildly variable between industries. Managing the price-rigging apparatus proved too much for the governments that were attempting it: the policy produced inadvertently large and complex distortions in the pattern of production that often became self-perpetuating and even self-reinforcing. Once investment had been sunk in activities that were profitable only because of tariffs and quotas, any attempt to remove those restrictions was strongly resisted.

ISI also often had an even more pernicious consequence: corruption. The more protected the economy, the greater the gains to be had from illicit activity such as smuggling. The bigger the economic distortions, the bigger the incentive to bribe the government to tweak the rules and tilt the corresponding pattern of surpluses and shortages. Corruption and controls go hand in hand. ISI is not the only instance of this rule in the developing countries, but it has proved especially susceptible to shady practices.

Today, developing-country governments are constantly, and rightly, urged to battle corruption and establish the rule of law. This has become a cliché that all sides in the development debate can agree on. But defeating corruption in an economy with pervasive market-suppressing controls, where the rewards to illegality are so high, is extraordinarily hard. This is a connection that people who favour closed or restricted markets prefer to ignore. Limited government, to be sure, is not necessarily clean; but unlimited government, history suggests, never is.

Remember, remember

On the whole, ISI failed; almost everywhere, trade has been good for growth. The trouble is, this verdict was handed down too long ago. Economists are notoriously ignorant of even recent economic history. The lessons about what world markets did for the tigers in the space of few decades, and the missed opportunities of, say, India (which was well placed to achieve as much), have already been forgotten by many. The East Asian financial crisis of 1997–98 also helped to erase whatever lessons had been learned. And yet the prosperity of East Asia today, crisis and continuing difficulties notwithstanding, bears no comparison with the economic position of India, or Pakistan, or any of the other countries that separated themselves for so much longer from the international economy.

By and large, though, the governments of many developing countries continue to be guided by the open-market orthodoxy that has prevailed since the 1980s. Many want to promote trade in particular and engagement with the world economy in general. Even some sceptics might agree that trade is good for growth – but they would add that growth is not necessarily good for poor workers. In fact, it is likely to be bad for the poor, they argue, if the growth in question has been promoted by trade or foreign capital.

Capital inflows, they say, make economies less stable, exposing workers to the risk of financial crisis and to the attentions of western banks and the IMF. Also, they argue, growth that is driven by trade or by FDI gives western multinationals a leading role in third-world development. That is bad, because western multinationals are not interested in development at all, only in making bigger profits by ensuring that the poor stay poor. The proof of this, say sceptics, lies in the evidence that economic inequality increases even as developing countries (and rich countries, for that matter) increase their national income, and in the multinationals' direct or indirect use of developing-country sweatshops. So if workers' welfare is your main concern, the fact that trade promotes growth, even if true, is beside the point.

Yet there is solid evidence that growth helps the poor. Developing countries that have achieved sustained and rapid growth, as in East

Asia, have made remarkable progress in reducing poverty. And the countries where widespread poverty persists, or is worsening, are those where growth is weakest, notably in Africa. Although economic policy can make a big difference to the extent of poverty, in the long run growth is much more important.

It is sometimes claimed that growth is less effective in raising the incomes of the poor in developing countries than in rich countries. This is a fallacy. A study confirms that, in 80 countries across the world over the past 40 years, the incomes of the poor have risen one for one with overall growth (see Chart 1.4).

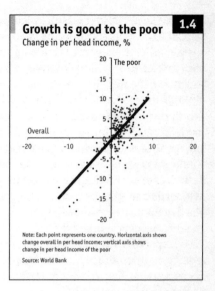

Growth is good to the poor 1.4
Change in per head income, %

Note: Each point represents one country. Horizontal axis shows change overall in per head income; vertical axis shows change in per head income of the poor
Source: World Bank

The sceptics are right to be disturbed by sweatshops, child labour, bonded labour and the other gross abuses that go on in many poor countries (and in the darkest corners of rich ones, too). But what makes people vulnerable to these practices is poverty. It is essential to ask if remedial measures proposed will reduce poverty: otherwise, in attacking the symptoms of the problem, you may be strengthening their underlying cause. It is one thing for the sceptics to insist, for instance, that child labour be prohibited; it is quite another to ensure that the children concerned go to school instead, rather than being driven to scrape a living in even crueller conditions.

The barriers to trade that many sceptics call for seem calculated to make these problems worse. Some sceptics want, in effect, to punish every export worker in India for the persistence of child labour in parts of the Indian economy. This seems morally indefensible as well as counter-productive in economic terms. The same goes for the campaign to hobble the multinationals. The more thoroughly these companies penetrate the markets of developing countries, the faster they introduce their capital and working practices, the sooner poverty will retreat and the harder it will be for such abuses to persist.

This is not to deny that the multinationals are in it for the money –

and will strive to hire labour as cheaply as they can. But this does not appear to be a problem for the workers who compete to take those jobs. People who go to work for a foreign-owned company do so because they prefer it to the alternative, whatever that may be. In their own judgment, the new jobs make them better off.

But suppose for the moment that the sceptics are right, and that these workers, notwithstanding their own preferences, are victims of exploitation. One possibility would be to encourage foreign firms to pay higher wages in developing countries. Another course, favoured by many sceptics, is to discourage multinationals from operating in these countries at all. But if the aim is to help the developing-country workers, this second strategy is surely wrong. If multinationals stopped hiring in the developing world, the workers concerned would, on their own estimation, become worse off.

Compared with demands that the multinationals stay out of developing countries altogether, the idea of merely shaming them into paying their workers higher wages seems a model of logic and compassion. Still, even this apparently harmless plan needs to be handled cautiously.

The question is, how much more is enough? At one extreme, you could argue that if a multinational company hires workers in developing countries for less than it pays their rich-country counterparts, it is guilty of exploitation. But to insist on parity would be tantamount to putting a stop to direct investment in the developing world. By and large, workers in developing countries are paid less than workers in rich countries because they are less productive: those workers are attractive to rich-country firms, despite their lower productivity, because they are cheap. If you were to eliminate that offsetting advantage, you would make them unemployable.

Of course you could argue that decency merely requires multinationals to pay wages that are "fair", even if not on a par with wages in the industrial countries. Any mandatory increase in wages runs the risk of reducing the number of jobs created, but you could reply that the improvement in welfare for those who get the higher pay, so long as the mandated increase was moderate and feasible, would outweigh that drawback. Even then, however, two difficult questions would still need to be answered. What is a "fair" wage, and who is to decide?

What fairness requires
A "fair" wage can be deduced, you might argue, from economic principles: if workers are paid a wage that is less than their marginal produc-

THE CASE FOR GLOBALISATION

The lure of multinationals

1.5

Average wage paid by foreign affiliates and average domestic manufacturing wage by host-country income, 1994

	All countries	High-income	Middle-income	Low-income
Average wage paid by affiliates, $'000	15.1	32.4	9.5	3.4
Average domestic manufacturing wage, $'000	9.9	22.6	5.4	1.7
Ratio	1.5	1.4	1.8	2.0

Source: Edward M. Graham, Institute for International Economics

tivity, you could say they are being exploited. Some sceptics regard it as obvious that developing-country workers are being paid less than this. Their reasoning is that such workers are about as productive as their rich-country counterparts, and yet are paid only a small fraction of what rich-country workers receive. Yet there is clear evidence that developing-country workers are not as productive as rich-country workers. Often they are working with less advanced machinery; and their productivity also depends on the surrounding economic infrastructure. More tellingly, though, if poor-country workers were being paid less than their marginal productivity, firms could raise their profits by hiring more of them in order to increase output. Sceptics should not need reminding that companies always prefer more profit to less.

Productivity aside, should "good practice" require, at least, that multinationals pay their poor-country employees more than other local workers? Not necessarily. To hire the workers they need, they may not have to offer a premium over local wages if they can provide other advantages. In any case, lack of a premium need not imply that they are failing to raise living standards. By entering the local labour market and adding to the total demand for labour, the multinationals would most likely be raising wages for all workers, not just those they hire.

In fact, though, the evidence suggests that multinationals do pay a wage premium – a reflection, presumably, of efforts to recruit relatively skilled workers. Chart 1.5 shows that the wages paid by foreign affiliates to poor-country workers are about double the local manufacturing wage; wages paid by affiliates to workers in middle-income countries are about 1.8 times the local manufacturing wage (both calculations exclude wages paid to the firms' expatriate employees). The numbers come from calculations by Edward Graham at the Institute for International Economics. Mr Graham cites other research which shows that wages in Mexico are highest near the border with the United States, where the operations of American-controlled firms are concentrated. Separate studies on Mexico, Venezuela, China and Indonesia have all found that foreign investors pay their local workers significantly better than other local employers.

Despite all this, you might still claim that the workers are not being paid a "fair" wage. But in the end, who is to make this judgment? The sceptics distrust governments, politicians, international bureaucrats and markets alike. So they end up appointing themselves as judges, overruling not just governments and markets but also the voluntary preferences of the workers most directly concerned. That seems a great deal to take on.

Is government disappearing?

Not as quickly as one might wish

ECONOMISTS ARE OFTEN ACCUSED of greeting some item of news with the observation, "That may be so in practice, but is it true in theory?" Sceptics too seem much more interested in superficially plausible theories about the diminishing power of the state than in the plain facts.

In practice, though perhaps not in theory, governments around the world on average are now collecting slightly more in taxes – not just in absolute terms, but as a proportion of their bigger economies – than they did at the beginning of the 1990s. This is true of the G7 countries, and of the smaller OECD economies as well (see Chart 1.6 on the next page). The depredations of rampant capitalists on the overall ability of governments to gather income and do good works are therefore invisible. These findings are so strange in theory that many economic analysts have decided not to believe them.

Tax burdens vary a lot from country to country – something else which is wrong in theory. Despite the variations, governments in all the advanced economies are well provided for. The United States is invoked by some European anti-globalists as the land of naked capitalism, the nadir of "private affluence and public squalor" to which other countries are being driven down. Well, its government collected a little over 30% of GDP in taxes in 2000: an average of some $30,000 per household, adding up to roughly $3 trillion. This is a somewhat larger figure than the national income of Germany, and it goes a long way if spent wisely.

At the other extreme is Sweden, despite its celebrated taxpayer revolt of the early 1990s. In 2000 its taxes came to 57% of GDP, a savage reduction of three percentage points since 1990. Next comes Denmark, on 53%, fractionally higher than in 1990. And here's a funny thing. Sweden and Denmark are among the most open economies in the world, far more open than the United States. Denmark's ratio of imports to national income is 33%, compared with America's 14%. And in common with other advanced economies, neither of these Scandinavian countries has capital controls to keep investment penned in.

Harvard's Dani Rodrik, one of the more careful and persuasive globalisation sceptics, has written: "Globalisation has made it exceedingly

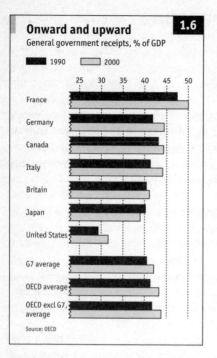

Onward and upward 1.6

General government receipts, % of GDP

■ 1990 ☐ 2000

25 30 35 40 45 50

France

Germany

Canada

Italy

Britain

Japan

United States

G7 average

OECD average

OECD excl G7, average

Source: OECD

difficult for government to provide social insurance ... At present, international economic integration is taking place against the background of receding governments and diminished social obligations. The welfare state has been under attack for two decades." Sweden, admittedly, is reeling, its government now able to collect only 57% of GDP in tax. But plucky Denmark is resisting these attacks well, and so is most of the rest of Europe.

Money isn't everything

Even if taxes were falling precipitously, it would be absurd to claim, as many globalisation sceptics do, that companies are nowadays more powerful than governments. It is routine to be told, as in *The Silent Takeover*, by a Cambridge University academic, Noreena Hertz, things like this: "51 of the 100 biggest economies in the world are now corporations." Quite what that implies is never explained: readers are invited to draw their own conclusion about the relative power of governments and companies.

Before you even think about whether it makes sense to weigh corporate power against state power, you can see that this particular comparison, which measures the size of companies by their sales, is bogus. National income is a measure of value added. It cannot be compared with a company's sales (equal to value added plus the cost of inputs). But even if that tiresome, endlessly repeated error were corrected, there would be no sense in comparing companies with governments in terms of their power over people.

The power of even the biggest companies is nothing compared with that of governments – no matter how small or poor the country concerned. The value added of Microsoft is a little over $20 billion a year, about the same as the national income of Uruguay. Does this make it remotely plausible that Bill Gates has more sway over the people of

Uruguay than their government does? Or take Luxembourg – another small economy with, presumably, a correspondingly feeble state. Can Microsoft tax the citizens of Luxembourg (whose government collected 45% of GDP from them last year), conscript them if it has a mind to, arrest and imprison them for behaviour it disapproves of, or deploy physical force against them at will? No, not even using Windows XP.

But those are specious comparisons, you might reply. Of course Mr Gates is less powerful than the government of Uruguay in Uruguay, but he exercises his power, such as it is, globally. Well then, where, exactly, is he supposed to be as powerful in relation to the government as the alarming comparison between value added and national income implies? And if he does not have this enormous power in any particular country or countries, he does not have it at all. In other words, the power that Mr Gates exercises globally is over Microsoft. Every government he ever meets is more powerful than he is in relation to its own citizens.

In a war between two countries, national income is relevant as a measure of available resources. If companies raised armies and fought wars, their wealth would count for something. But they don't, and couldn't: they lack the power. Big companies do have political influence. They have the money to lobby politicians and, in many countries, to corrupt them. Even so, the idea that companies have powers over citizens remotely as great as those of governments – no matter how big the company, no matter how small or poor the country – is fatuous. Yet it is never so much as questioned by anti-globalists.

Any power to tax, however limited, gives a country more political clout than Microsoft or General Electric could dream of. But how can a small, exceptionally open economy such as Denmark manage to collect more than 50% of GDP in taxes, in utter defiance of the logic of global capitalism? The answer seems inescapable: Denmark no longer exists, and questions are starting to be asked about the existence of many other European countries. At least, that is how it looks in theory; in practice, the theory needs to be looked at again.

The limits of government

The alleged squeeze on government arises from the fact that, in a world of integrated economies, again in Mr Rodrik's words, "owners of capital, highly skilled workers, and many professionals ... are free to take their resources where they are most in demand". The people Mr Rodrik refers to have high incomes. Through the taxes they pay, they make an indispensable contribution to the public finances. If economic integration allows capital and skills to migrate to low-tax jurisdictions, the tax base will shrink. Governments will find themselves unable to finance social programmes, safety nets or redistribution of income. Anticipating this flight of capital and skills, governments have to cut taxes and dismantle the welfare state before the migration gets under way. Markets triumph over democracy.

That is the theory. Experience largely refutes it, but it is not entirely wrong. In a variety of ways, economic integration does put limits on what governments can do. However, some of those constraints are eminently desirable. Integration makes it harder to be a tyrant. Governments have been known to oppress their subjects. Oppression is more difficult with open borders: people can leave and take their savings with them. In such cases, global markets are plainly an ally of human rights.

The affinity of totalitarianism and economic isolation was obvious in the case of the Soviet Union and communist eastern Europe; it is still plain today in the case of North Korea, say. But democracies are capable of oppression too. It would therefore be wrong to conclude that integration is undesirable merely because it limits the power of government, even if the government concerned is democratic. One needs to recognise that some constraints on democracy are desirable, and then to ask whether the constraints imposed by markets are too tight.

These issues are rarely, if ever, addressed by the critics of globalisation: it is simpler to deplore the notion of "profits before people". The sceptics either insist, or regard it as too obvious even to mention, that the will of the people, democratically expressed, must always prevail. This is amazingly naive. Even the most elementary account of democracy recognises the need for checks and balances, including curbs on the majoritarian "will of the people". Failing those, democracies are capable of tyranny over minorities.

The sceptics are terribly keen on "the people". Yet the idea that citizens are not individuals with different goals and preferences, but an undifferentiated body with agreed common interests, defined in opposition to other monolithic interests such as "business" or "foreigners", is not just shallow populism, it is proto-fascism. It is self-contradictory, as well. The sceptics would not hesitate to call for "the people" to be overruled if, for instance, they voted for policies that violated human rights, or speeded the extermination of endangered species, or offended against other values the sceptics regard as more fundamental than honouring the will of the majority.

The possibility that people might leave is not the only curb that economic integration puts on government. The global flow of information, a by-product of the integration of markets, also works to that effect. It lets attention be drawn to abuses of all kinds: of people especially, but also of the environment or of other things that the sceptics want to protect. Undeniably, it also fosters a broader kind of policy competition among governments. This works not through the sort of mechanical market arbitrage that would drive down taxes regardless of what citizens might want, but through informing voters about alternatives, thus making them more demanding.

The fashion for economic liberalisation in recent years owes something to the remarkable success of the American economy during the 1990s: a success which, thanks to globalisation, has been seen and reflected upon all over the world. Growing knowledge about the West helped precipitate the liberation of eastern Europe. But information of this kind need not always favour the market. For instance, the failure of the American government to extend adequate health care to all its citizens has been noticed as well, and voters in countries with universal publicly financed health-care systems do not, on the whole, want to copy this particular model. The global flow of knowledge creates, among other things, better-informed voters, and therefore acts as a curb on government power. This does nothing but good.

The anti-globalists themselves, somewhat self-contradictorily, use the information-spreading aspect of globalisation to great effect. Organising a worldwide protest movement would be much harder without the world wide web, but the web itself is merely one dimension of globalisation. The economic integration that sceptics disapprove of is in many ways necessary for effective resistance to the more specific things they object to – not all of which, by any means, are themselves the products of globalisation.

Still, all this is to acknowledge that economic integration does limit the power of government, including democratic government. The question is whether it limits it too much, or in undesirable ways. So far as far public spending is concerned, the answer seems clear. Given that even in conditions of economic integration people are willing to tolerate tax burdens approaching 60% of GDP, and that tax burdens of between 40% and 55% of GDP are routine in industrial economies other than the United States, the limits are plainly not that tight. These figures say that democracy has plenty of room for manoeuvre.

The mystery of the missing tax cut

One puzzle remains: why are taxes not coming down? There are several answers. One is that international integration is far from complete, and is likely to remain so. Technology has caused distance to shrink, but not to disappear. National borders still matter as well, even more than mere distance, and far more than all the interest in globalisation might lead you to expect. For all but the smallest economies, trade and investment are still disproportionately intranational rather than international. Especially in the developed world, borders still count not so much because of overt protectionist barriers, but because countries remain jurisdictionally and administratively distinct. This is not likely to change in the foreseeable future.

For instance, if a supplier defaults on a contract to sell you something, it is much easier to get legal redress if your seller is in the same country (and subject to the same legal authority) than it would be if you had to sue in a foreign court. Because of these difficulties in contracting, trading across borders still calls for much more trust between buyers and sellers than trading within borders – so much so as to rule out many transactions. This remains true even in systems such as the European Union's, where heroic efforts have been made to overcome inadvertent obstacles to trade, suggesting that they will prove even more durable everywhere else.

You would expect the international mobility of capital to be especially high, given that the costs of physically transporting the stuff are virtually zero, yet it is surprising just how relatively immobile even capital remains. In the aggregate, the flow of capital into or out of any given country can be thought of as balancing that country's saving and investment. If the country invests more than it saves (that is, if it runs a current-account deficit), capital flows in; if it saves more than it invests (a current-account surplus), the country must lend capital to the rest of the world. Perfect capital mobility would imply that, country by country, national saving and investment would move freely in relation to each other. Very large inflows or outflows of capital in relation to national income would be the order of the day. In fact they are not. Nowadays, a surplus or deficit of just a few percentage points of GDP is regarded as big.

Still, capital is much more mobile than labour – and mobile enough, to be sure, to have given rise to some tax competition among governments. So far this competition has affected the structure of tax codes rather than overall tax burdens; total yields have been unaffected. In an effort to attract inflows of capital, and especially inflows of foreign direct investment, governments have been lowering their tax rates for corporate income and raising them for personal income, or relying more on a variety of indirect taxes, or both (see Chart 1.7). But it is easy to exaggerate the extent even of this structural shift, never mind the effect on total taxation. This is because taxes on corporate income were small to begin with, so not much was at stake. In fact, heavy reliance on corporate taxes is bad policy even in a closed economy. Indeed, in a closed economy, you can make

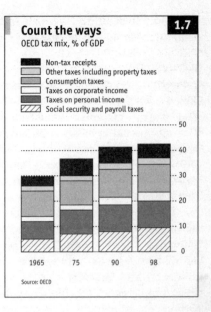

Count the ways   1.7
OECD tax mix, % of GDP

- Non-tax receipts
- Other taxes including property taxes
- Consumption taxes
- Taxes on corporate income
- Taxes on personal income
- Social security and payroll taxes

Source: OECD

a respectable case on efficiency grounds for excluding corporate income from taxes altogether.

Taxes on company profits, the argument goes, are taxes on shareholders' income – ultimately, that is, taxes on a particular category of personal income. In the end, although it is politically convenient to pretend otherwise, "the people" pay all the taxes: companies are mere intermediaries. There is no reason to tax the income people receive as shareholders any differently from the income they receive as owners of bank deposits or as workers. In a closed economy, you might as well abolish the corporate-income tax and instead tax profits when they turn up as dividends in the incomes of individual taxpayers: it is simpler, and it is less likely to affect investment decisions in unintended ways.

In an open economy, however, company ownership is to some extent in the hand of foreigners, not just the citizens of the country where the company is based. This makes it more tempting to tax corporate income, because this allows the government to bring foreigners within the scope of its tax base. Seen this way, it is odd to blame globalisation for downward pressure on corporate-tax rates. Were it not for globalisation, there would be no reason to have corporate taxes in the first place. But it is true that once you are collecting corporate taxes, greater capital mobility limits your take.

Economic integration rationalises, and at the same time limits, reliance on corporate-income taxes. The issue is subtler than it seems.

Staying put

But what matters far more than corporate tax policy is that most people, skilled as well as unskilled, are reluctant to move abroad. Since workers tend to stay put, governments can tax them at surprisingly high rates without provoking flight. In all but extreme cases, the democratic constraint (the need to secure a broad measure of popular support for tax increases) binds governments long before the economic constraint imposed by international integration (the risk that groups facing very high taxes will leave). In the case of taxes on profits, it is true that the economic constraint will bind before the democratic one, and that globalisation serves to tighten the economic constraint further – but this does not matter. There is no need for high taxes on profits if people are willing to hand over 50% or more of what they produce in the form of taxes on income and consumption.

To simple-minded believers in the most desiccated branch of neoclassical economics, all this may seem surprising. Their theories regard people as "rational economic men", narrow utility-maximisers with no ties to family, place or culture. Presumably, these ciphers would shop around for low-tax jurisdictions. Oddly, the same benighted view of human nature must be shared by many globalisation sceptics – otherwise, why would they fear taxpayer flight on a scale sufficient to abolish the European welfare state? But in real life, it is better to take a fuller, broader view of the human condition. Since people seem to choose to be tied down, indeed to relish it, governments, within broad limits, can carry on taxing them regardless of globalisation. If it seems prudent to cut taxes on profits in order to attract inflows of foreign investment, no problem. Taxes on people will still be sufficient to finance generous public spending of every kind.

Be very afraid

Many anti-globalists have strangely little confidence in the merits of the policies they are anxious to sustain. Fearing what may be lost if globalisation continues uncurbed, Mr Rodrik writes:

> If it was the 19th century that unleashed capitalism in its full
> force, it was the 20th century that tamed it and boosted its
> productivity by supplying the institutional underpinnings of

market-based economies. Central banks to regulate credit and
the supply of liquidity, fiscal policies to stabilise aggregate
demand, antitrust and regulatory authorities to combat fraud
and anti-competitive behaviour, social insurance to reduce
lifetime risk, political democracy to make the above
institutions accountable to the citizenry – these were all
innovations that firmly took root in today's rich countries only
during the second half of the 20th century. That the second
half of the century was also a period of unprecedented
prosperity for Western Europe, the United States, Japan and
some other parts of East Asia is no coincidence. These
institutional innovations greatly enhanced the efficiency and
legitimacy of markets and in turn drew strength from the
material advancement unleashed by market forces ... The
dilemma that we face as we enter the 21st century is that
markets are striving to become global while the institutions
needed to support them remain by and large national ... The
desire by producers and investors to go global weakens the
institutional base of national economies.

The argument, presumably, is that international capital will flow
away from countries with the high public spending and taxes that these
highly developed institutions involve. One answer is that international
investment, as already noted, is much less important in most countries
than domestic investment. But a more fundamental question is this:
why should foreign capital flow away from countries that have
equipped themselves with these institutions, if, as Mr Rodrik emphasises, those arrangements have "boosted ... productivity" and "greatly
enhanced the efficiency ... of markets" – so much so that the most ambitious period of national institution-building was also a time of growing
and "unprecedented" prosperity for the nations that joined in?

If public spending boosts productivity, then competition among governments for inward investment is likely to favour more public spending (and the taxes needed to pay for it), not less. Suppose, as seems
plausible, that public spending on education raises productivity by
increasing the supply of skilled workers. Then you would expect international investment to be drawn to countries that invest heavily in top-
quality schools and universities. Suppose, as may also be true, that
public spending on social programmes such as health and welfare raises
productivity, by producing a healthier and more contented workforce,

with better labour relations and greater labour mobility. If so, again international capital will be drawn to countries that spend money on those things. Globalisation, surely, will not frown on policies whose net effect is to foster productivity and efficiency.

But what about policies that do not serve those goals? Many would argue, for instance, that welfare policies, especially if too generous, encourage idleness and reduce economy-wide productivity. Suppose that is true. Also suppose that, knowing it to be true, most people want such policies anyway. You might feel that they are entitled to that opinion, and in a democracy they are entitled to get their way. Another example might be policies to limit working hours. Suppose that they reduce productivity, but that people vote for them anyway. Must globalisation overrule democracy?

Globalisation v democracy

The answer even in this case is no – and to see why is to understand why so many of the fears about globalisation and democracy are groundless. Policies that reduce productivity do, in the first instance, cut a country's feasible standard of living, narrowly defined in terms of GDP per head. But what happens after that? If a country that is open to international trade and capital flows adopts some such policies, perhaps on the ground that they will raise living standards according to some broader definition, wages and profits will fall relative to what they would otherwise have been. Next, investment will fall and the capital stock will shrink, again compared with what they would otherwise have been. This will continue until the scarcity of capital drives the rate of profit back up, at the margin, to the rate prevailing in the global capital market.

All this time the economy will grow more slowly than if the policies had not been followed. Once the economy has adjusted, however, it remains as "competitive" as it was at the outset: lower wages have restored labour costs per unit of output, and a smaller stock of capital has restored the return on capital. The economy has grown more slowly for a spell. It is less prosperous than it would have been. But in due course, once wages and profits have adjusted, the economy will again be as attractive, or unattractive, to foreign investors as it was at the outset. The government's adoption of policies that compromise efficiency is not punished by excommunication from the global economy, or with an accelerating spiral of decline; the only penalty is compromised efficiency and lower measured incomes, which is what the country chose in the first place.

Would the economy have fared any better without globalisation? Had it been closed to international flows of goods and capital, could it have adopted those productivity-cutting policies and paid no price at all? The answer is no. Even in a closed economy, policies that reduce productivity would cause wages and profits to fall, as in the open-economy case. The return on capital would be lower, so saving and investment would decline, relative to what they would have been (there would be no cross-border capital flows in this case, so saving and investment must always be equal). The capital stock would shrink and growth would be held back until the scarcity of capital drove the return back up. As in the open-economy case, the result would be a spell of slower growth and a standard of living permanently lower than it would otherwise have been.

The main difference is probably that in the closed-economy case, the losses would be subtracted from an economy that is already very much poorer than its open-economy counterpart, because it is closed. Conceivably, this would make further losses politically easier to sustain. But that is the most you can say in defence of the view that globalisation forbids social policies which jeopardise productivity. "Stay poor, because once you start to get rich you may find that you like it." Not exactly compelling, is it?

You might well conclude from all this that globalisation, if anything, will lead to higher rather than lower social spending. As argued earlier, globalisation raises aggregate incomes but at the same time increases economic insecurity for certain groups. Both of these consequences tend to raise social spending. Generous social spending is a "superior good": as countries grow richer, they want to spend more of their incomes on it, and can afford to. At the same time, quite separately, greater economic insecurity directly spurs demand for social spending.

Given that globalisation increases the demand for social spending; given that it does not rule out any decision to increase such spending which harms productivity, any more than a closed economy would; given that increases in social spending which raise productivity will be rewarded with inflows of capital; given all this, should globalisation and the generous social spending that democracies favour not go hand in hand? They should, and indeed rising social spending alongside faster, deeper globalisation is exactly what the figures for the past several decades show.

Governments in rich countries need to look again at their social policies, partly to make sure that temporary and longer-term losers from globalisation, and from economic growth in general, get well-designed help. But there is no reason whatever to fear that globalisation makes social policies more difficult to finance. In the end, by raising incomes in the aggregate, it makes them easier to finance. It creates additional economic resources, which democracies can use as they see fit.

A plague of finance

Anti-globalists see the "Washington consensus" as a conspiracy to enrich bankers. They are not entirely wrong

W HEN THEY CRITICISE GLOBALISATION, sceptics are not just talking about economic integration across borders, or about the particular economic policies, such as liberal rules on trade and international investment, that directly facilitate it. They have in mind a much larger set of economic nostrums and institutions: the policies of the "Washington consensus", as it is known, and the international bodies, notably the International Monetary Fund and the World Bank, that strive to put it into effect.

The term "Washington consensus" was coined by the economist John Williamson in 1989. He called it that because of the support it enjoyed from the American government and (not coincidentally) from the Fund and the Bank, the big Washington-based institutions. He said it stood for ten policies. Measures to promote trade and FDI were high on the list, but the new orthodoxy, as he described it, also ran to the following: fiscal discipline (ie, smaller budget deficits), fewer subsidies, tax reform, liberalised financial systems, competitive exchange rates, privatisation, deregulation and measures to secure property rights.

In the view of many sceptics, this broad "neo-liberal" agenda has been deliberately designed to serve the needs of the rich at the expense of the poor. The sceptics' thinking on trade and foreign investment has already been discussed; their view of the rest of the formula is just as scathing. Fiscal discipline, curbs on subsidies and increases in taxes – measures long emphasised by the IMF in its dealings with distressed developing-country borrowers – directly hurt the poor, they say. Privatisation, financial liberalisation and industrial deregulation work to the same effect, by delivering windfall profits to domestic and foreign speculators, by stripping the state of its assets and by weakening rules that protect consumers and workers from abuse.

These policies are forced on poor-country governments regardless of their own views and priorities, incidentally undermining democracy in the developing world. In the longer term, this kind of development – in effect, on terms dictated by the rich countries – saddles the developing countries with crippling debts. It also exposes them to the crazy fluctuations of the global business cycle. East Asia, one-time exemplar of the Washington model, discovered that to its cost; Argentina, another darling of the Washington development establishment, has made the same discovery. Insupportable debts and chronic instability worsen the developing countries' dependence on aid, and allow the IMF to tighten the screws even more vigorously next time, at the direction of American bankers. In every way, sceptics believe, the Washington consensus is a calculated assault on the weak.

Extreme as this caricature may be when taken as a whole, it contains some truths – which is why, for all its absurdity, it is recognisable. The idea that the Washington establishment is engaged in a deliberate conspiracy to oppress developing countries may be nonsense, but there have been mistakes, big and small, and unintended consequences aplenty. The problem is that the valid criticisms are buried under a heap of error, muddle and deliberate distortion. The IMF, the Bank and America's Treasury Department would all feel much more threatened if the shards of intelligent criticism could be filtered from all the rubbish and gathered together.

Beware foreign capital

One of the clearest lessons for international economics in the past few decades, with many a reminder in the past few years, has been that foreign capital is a mixed blessing. This stricture does not apply so much to FDI because, unlike debt, FDI does not need to be serviced and cannot flee at short notice.

But other forms of foreign capital, and especially short-term bank debt, have led many a developing country into desperate trouble. Because of the debt crisis, the 1980s were a lost decade for Latin America; in different ways, Argentina and Brazil have both found themselves in difficulty again because of debt. The financial crisis of the late 1990s set back even the East Asians, up to then the best-performing of all the developing countries. Why has this happened – and why so often?

Borrowers, obviously, have to take their share of the blame for borrowing too much, though that is rarely the whole explanation. Governments that borrow heavily in order to finance recklessly large budget deficits are plainly at fault. There was a lot of that in the 1970s and early 1980s. The case of corporate borrowers in developing countries is more complicated. They may sometimes borrow amounts which seem individually prudent given certain macroeconomic assumptions – such as no devaluation of the currency – but which become collectively insupportable if those assumptions turn out to be wrong. This happened in East Asia in the 1990s, with the further complication that much of the borrowing was channelled through domestic banks, meaning that the ultimate borrowers were unaware of the system-wide exchange-rate risk.

Sometimes, therefore, developing-country banks have been at fault as well – and their governments too, for failing to regulate them effectively. But at least as much of the blame for the developing world's recurring debt traumas lies with rich-country lenders and, at one remove, rich-country governments. Modern banking operates, notoriously, under the persistent influence of moral hazard. This arises because deposit-taking banks are intrinsically fragile operations – and because governments are reluctant to let them fail. Banks are fragile because they promise depositors to repay deposits on demand and in full, even though they are unable to keep that promise if a significant number of depositors decide to exercise their right all at once. To avoid the risk of bank runs, which is high given the design of the contract with depositors, governments arrange deposit-insurance schemes, and other forms of assurance, including the doctrine of "too big to fail".

There are good reasons for this. If a bank fails, it may take other banks and enterprises, not to mention depositors' savings, with it; the broader payments system may also be imperilled. Historically, bank failures are associated with economy-wide recessions; for example, they helped to bring on the Depression of the 1930s (which was the inspiration for the modern deposit-insurance model). But the upshot is that banks are systematically protected from the consequences of their reckless behaviour.

Modern banks keep a far smaller fraction of their deposits as reserves than their historical forebears. Depositors have no incentive to supervise the banks by keeping an eye on reserves or by withdrawing money from the ones that are taking too many risks: their deposits are protected in any case. And banks have a correspondingly big incentive to compete aggressively for deposits which they can lend at high interest rates to risky projects. It is a formula for ruin – and, despite the efforts of regulators to measure and curb those risks, it keeps on working exactly as you would expect. In almost every case of spectacular boom and bust in recent years, in rich and poor countries alike, an exaggerated cycle of banking greed and fear has been a principal cause.

Too big to fail

So when sceptics accuse rich-country governments of being mainly concerned with bailing out western banks when financial crisis strikes in the developing world, they have a point. The pernicious logic of "too big to fail" applies in the international context as well as the domestic one. If you are going to go bust, make sure you are a big developing country rather than a small one, with debts large enough to threaten catastrophic damage to America's financial system. That way you can be assured of prompt attention.

In many other respects, however, the sceptics' attacks on the Fund and the Bank are ill-conceived. The IMF, especially, is criticised for sending its experts into developing countries and commanding governments to balance the budget in ways that assault the poor – by cutting spending on vital social services, ending subsidies or raising taxes on food and fuel, levying charges for use of water, and so on down the list of shame.

Measures to curb budget deficits are often unavoidable by the time the Fund is called in. The only way to reduce a budget deficit is to raise taxes or cut public spending. In many developing countries, where tax systems are narrowly based and unsophisticated, governments may have few options in deciding how to go about it. It would not be in the political interests of the Fund or the Bank to recommend measures that fall heavily on the poor if there were an obvious alternative.

However, the Fund, especially, may have invited much of the criticism it receives in this respect because it specifies policy changes in such detail. The IMF should strenuously avoid letting itself be seen as running the country, giving the government instructions and telling workers and voters to get lost. On the other hand, many sceptics seem to be under the impression that all was well in the countries concerned until the Fund barged in. The Fund turns up only when things have already gone very wrong indeed – and only when the government in question has asked for its help. That last point is surely worthy of more attention than the sceptics pay to it. If governments find the Fund's conditions so oppressive, they always have the option of refraining from asking for its help.

Governments know that the alternative to the Fund's intervention would usually be an even sharper contraction of public spending (including on social services) and/or an increase in taxes (including on things the poor need to buy). By the time the IMF is called in, the question whether to curb government borrowing is not so much a matter of weighing, as sceptics suppose, the case for laisser-faire against the demands of social justice. Often, in the good-faith judgment of the IMF's officials, it is just an inescapable necessity if the economy is to be stabilised. And at times of impending economic collapse, stabilisation is very much in the interests of the poor, who suffer most during slumps.

In fact, most of the policies of the Washington consensus serve, or are capable of serving, the interests of the poor directly, not merely by promoting growth. If governments have been at fault in defending that agenda, it has mainly been in failing to emphasise this. The centrepiece of these policies, fiscal discipline, is sometimes necessary to avert an economic calamity; but even in more normal times, the alternative to steady control of government borrowing is usually high inflation. That, all the evidence shows, hurts the poor more than anyone else.

As noted by Mr Williamson back in 1989, the consensus called not just for fewer subsidies, but for new priorities in public spending, especially more effective support for industry and more spending on education and health – priorities intended to help the poor which the Bank has tried hard to put into practice. The need to broaden the tax base, so as to support additional public spending without destabilising the economy, is another idea that favours the poor, because there is no other way to provide the resources necessary to pay for effective safety nets. Deregulation and improved property rights can also make a real difference to the poor. As the work of Hernando de Soto has shown, it is the poor who suffer most from obstacles to small-scale enterprise and insecure titles to land.

Many sceptics might warm to the Fund and the Bank if they paid more attention to the criticisms directed at the two institutions from the political right. Conservatives worry not so much because the Fund is too mean, or the Bank too keen on market economics, but rather the opposite: they complain that both are engaged in throwing good money after bad. Worse than that, critics on the right argue, the two institutions reward the bad policies that got the patients into trouble in the first place, thereby creating their own kind of moral hazard.

If the Fund and the Bank were simply shut down, as many sceptics and many conservatives would wish, the flow of resources to the developing countries would certainly diminish, at least in the short term. The world economy would be a harsher place for the poor countries. The conservatives argue, in effect, that this would be good for them in the longer term. Those sceptics who favour slower economic growth for the developing world would also be gratified, presumably, if the Fund and the Bank packed up. But it is hard to see what those who are not opposed to development as such see in this course.

Trying to get it right

The IMF and the Bank have certainly made mistakes. They have had spells of over-confidence, though they cannot be accused of that at the moment. Noted scholars such as Joseph Stiglitz, a former chief economist at the World Bank, have criticised them for technical incompetence, and for theological devotion to discredited economic theories; but other economists have argued in their defence, saying, plausibly, that they have done their best in difficult circumstances. They have certainly neglected the importance of allowing governments to "own", and take responsibility for, their policies – a mistake which supplicant governments, anxious to deny responsibility, have usually been keen to encourage. But the Fund and the Bank are aware of this criticism, and are trying to do something about it.

Other improvements in the way the international financial institutions work are surely called for. Many different panels of experts have produced countless proposals, big and small, and some of these are being taken up. Overall, a shift of emphasis is needed. Now that many developing countries have access, for good or ill, to the global capital markets, the Bank needs to focus on disseminating knowledge rather than money. And for both political and economic reasons it would be better if the Fund, for its part, specialised in providing liquidity during emergencies, rather than development finance, subject to simple financial conditions rather than immensely detailed policy blueprints.

The institutions themselves have gone far to acknowledge their mistakes, and the need for reform. In view of this, the ability of the sceptics to maintain their hysterical animosity toward the institutions is surprising. In its way, it demands a measure of respect.

Who elected the WTO?

The WTO is no would-be tyrant. It is democratic to a fault, and has few powers of its own

UNSURPRISINGLY, sceptics extend many of the criticisms they make of the IMF and the World Bank to the World Trade Organisation as well. If anything, they detest the WTO even more. Perhaps this is because, unlike the Fund and the Bank, the WTO brings what many critics regard as the most objectionable aspects of globalisation home to the rich countries, where most of those critics live.

The IMF undermines democracy in the developing world, the charge goes, which is bad enough; the WTO does the same thing in America and Europe as well, which is worse. The IMF and the Bank bring financial ruin to the poor countries that turn to them for help; but in the long term, the WTO inflicts even worse damage than that on all countries, rich and poor alike, solvent or otherwise. It does this, sceptics say, not through onerous borrowing conditions but by force of international law. Its prohibitions undermine efforts to protect the environment and eviscerate safeguards developed over decades to protect the health and well-being of consumers and workers.

On top of all this, of course, the specific mandate of the WTO is to promote trade, which many sceptics regard as a bad thing in itself. According to the anti-globalists' world view, it is only logical that much of the threat posed by the WTO to democracy springs from its dedication to trade. As noted earlier, many sceptics regard a liberal regime of international trade and investment as intrinsically hostile to democracy, because it promotes a competition for profits that overrides voters' political preferences.

This is the "race to the bottom" argument once more. The counter-arguments to this mistaken idea so far as it applies to taxes and the welfare state have already been rehearsed. In the regulation of products and processes, with respect either to safety or to environmental impact, signs of a race to the bottom are equally hard to find. All the movement is the other way. Everywhere, the adoption of more demanding environmental standards gathers pace as incomes rise.

But sceptics are also making a separate point that is less easy to dismiss. They say that the WTO is anti-democratic not merely indirectly, because of its devotion to trade, but also directly, as a matter of institutional design. This anti-democratic character, it is alleged, is a deliberate part of the organisation's working methods – and that is unacceptable, full stop.

According to sceptics, the WTO takes powers away from elected governments and grants them to faceless bureaucrats. It can tell America and Europe that rules to protect endangered species or to keep food free of dangerous chemicals are illegal, and that they must abandon these policies. It can stop governments in poor countries providing cheap generic medicines to their people because that would hurt the profits of the drug companies. The sick must pay over the odds for patent-protected branded drugs, or do without – either is fine with the WTO.

In all these cases, sceptics say, the interests of multinational corporations happen to be in conflict with the democratically expressed wishes of the people. Whenever that occurs, the WTO rules against democracy. Moreover, the critics continue, its unaccountable and unrepresentative bureaucrats arrive at their outrageous edicts in secret: the hidden masters of globalisation are not even required to explain themselves. The WTO is a kind of embryonic world government, but with none of the checks and balances that true democratic government requires. In short, it is an embryonic world tyranny. That is why, in the view of many sceptics, it is the most dangerous of all the institutions of globalisation.

True in part

As before, this indictment combines error, gross exaggeration and apparently deliberate distortion – but, as before, it also contains particles of truth.

The WTO's anti-democratic powers are held to reside mainly in the organisation's new dispute-resolution procedures. The strengthening of these arrangements was one of the notable achievements of the Uruguay Round of trade talks which concluded in 1994; they constitute one of the main differences between the WTO and its predecessor, the General Agreement on Tariffs and Trade (GATT). Under the new rules, governments cannot block the findings of a WTO dispute panel: once they have exhausted their right of appeal, countries held to have broken WTO rules must either change their policies so as to comply, or pay compensation to the injured party, or face trade sanctions. This apparent ability to overrule governments lies at the centre of the sceptics' objections to the new system.

It is true that the system is no longer, if it ever was, a mere bundle of agreements with a procedure for arbitration should disputes arise. Even before the new arrangements were adopted, the GATT had developed a partly rule-making, as opposed to strictly rule-clarifying, character: the reforms pushed a bit further in that direction. Even so, it remains highly misleading to talk of the WTO "taking powers" or forcing governments to ignore voters' wishes.

Despite its developing quasi-judicial role, the WTO remains an unambiguously intergovernmental, rather than supragovernmental, entity. Changes to the organisation's rules are proposed by member governments and adopted "by consensus" – which in practice means they require unanimity. As the WTO likes to say, far from being anti-democratic, it is actually hyper-democratic. No government ever had to accept a new WTO rule because it was outvoted, as might happen in the European Union; every one of the organisation's 150 members has a veto.

If the WTO involves any pooling of sovereignty, therefore, it is only in an extremely limited sense. When a dispute arises, the quarrel may be over exactly what a rule means, or how it should be applied in particular, possibly unforeseen, circumstances; a government can never be compelled to obey a rule that it opposed in the first place. This applies to the new dispute-settlement rules as much as to anything else: every member government has agreed to them as well.

Moreover, the idea that the WTO enforces obedience by punishing violators is itself a distortion. Its principal role, once a dispute is under way, is still to act as referee while two or more governments fight it out. Consider a favourite example of European sceptics: the dispute between the European Union and the United States over hormone-treated beef.

Europe first banned imports of such beef from America in 1989, citing health concerns. The United States took the matter to the WTO's dispute-settlement body. Although sceptics often claim otherwise, the WTO's rules (which, to repeat, both Europe and the United States have freely agreed to) do allow countries to ban imports to protect consumers from dangerous products. But they also require governments to show reputable scientific evidence in support of their controls, and insist that measures do not discriminate between suppliers, rather than favouring one country's exports over another's, or domestic production over imports. Without these provisos, countries could ban imports at will, something which the signatories to the agreement presumably considered undesirable.

To the sceptics' horror, Europe was deemed to have violated the rules. This was not because health concerns are routinely set at naught by the WTO, as is often falsely claimed, nor even because the beef-import ban itself was ruled illegal: the issue never got that far. It was because the EU elected to produce scientific evidence in support of its ban and then failed to do so.

To say that the WTO was trying to force Europe to open its markets seems odd. It was the United States, surely, which was doing the forcing. Every case that comes before the WTO is first and foremost a dispute between governments, not a dispute between a government and the organisation itself. Also, whatever the merits of the beef-and-hormones case, America's government claims to be serving its citizens' interests, just as the EU's authorities claim to represent the voters of Europe. So it is hardly a matter of the WTO against democracy, as sceptics would have it; rather, it is a question of one democracy against a union of other democracies – with the WTO in the middle, taking the brickbats for trying to calm things down.

What if the WTO did not exist, as most sceptics seem to wish? Would the EU ban have been sustained without objection, assuring the primacy of health and environmental standards worldwide, and everywhere peace and light? Plainly not. The same trade dispute would simply have been prosecuted through other means: instead of a mediated dispute conducted under agreed rules, there would have been a naked trial of strength between the EU and the United States.

In such a contest, who knows whether Europe's view on beef and hormones would prevail? What is certain is that the costs of conducting the dispute this way, rather than through the WTO's procedures, would have been very much greater. And although the EU might be able to stand up for its interests in an economic fight with America, a small country in a dispute with a much bigger one would have a less good chance. That is why the governments of poor countries have been so eager to join first the GATT and then the WTO. They understand that in trade policy, unless attitudes change a lot, the alternative to the WTO is not "democracy prevails" but "might is right".

Doing good by stealth?

The multilateral approach to trade liberalisation, pursued first through the GATT and now through the WTO, does have a horrible flaw. It espouses the idea that lowering trade barriers is a concession you make to your trading partners; a sacrifice for which you require compensa-tion, or "reciprocity", in the jargon. This mercantilist view of trade –

exports are good, imports are bad – is an economic fallacy. Politically – and this is to endorse a point made by sceptics – it serves to enthrone producer interests, neglecting all others. Trade agreements go forward when exporters on all sides tell their governments that they see something in it for them; the interests of importers (that is, workers and consumers at large) are implicitly regarded as politically insignificant.

The justification for this pact with the devil is that by setting one country's producer interests against another's, it has mobilised big business in support of freer trade, helping to neutralise protectionist sentiment; as a result, trade has in fact been liberalised. Exporters have been pleased with the outcome, to be sure, but that is not the point. Liberal trade is good because it raises the incomes of consumers and workers at large, and especially because it improves the prospects of the poorest countries. It could be argued that this great prize has been well worth the cost in intellectual dishonesty.

If this mercantilist pact breaks down under public scrutiny, as it may, there is a risk that the cause of liberal trade will be set back. Certainly that is what anti-globalists are hoping. But there is also another, more encouraging, possibility. If governments still want to promote liberal trade – and rising incomes, other things equal, are popular with voters – they could try to do so on its economic merits. Being honest would be inconvenient, and after all these years would certainly seem peculiar. Exporters would be displeased to find that governments were listening to them less avidly. But governments would find it easier to be straightforward about the case for trade. Perhaps they could even convince themselves, and enough voters to make the difference, that unilateral, uncompensated trade liberalisation is the best way to serve the public interest.

If they could do that – but only then – the WTO in its present form would no longer be needed at all, and liberals could join sceptics in celebrating its demise. But given the demands this would place on government, that day will not dawn just yet.

A different manifesto

If sceptics could learn to love capitalism, they would still have plenty to complain about

SOME SCEPTICS have recently started to argue that the movement against globalisation dwells too much on what it is against; it must grow up, and start to say what it is for. This is a worthy thought, but tactically ill-advised.

The main things holding the anti-globalist coalition together are a suspicion of markets, a strongly collectivist instinct and a belief in protest as a form of moral uplift. Once upon a time this combination would have pointed to socialism as a coherent alternative to "the system". But socialism, after the unfortunate experiences of the 20th century, is not quite ready yet for release back into the community. The attitudes that support it are still out there, as evidenced by the protesters, and by the sympathy they arouse among the public. But for the moment, as a programme for government, socialism lacks sufficiently broad appeal.

What else is there? The protest coalition can hang together only if it continues to avoid thinking about what it might be in favour of – a challenge it is all geared up to meet. All the same, it seems a pity.

Meanwhile, the champions of globalisation – governments and big business – are also giving a deeply unimpressive account of themselves. Intellectually, their defence of globalisation ("it's good for our exporters and creates jobs") is a disgrace. And governments deserve fierce criticism for many of their policies, not least in areas of particular concern to anti-globalists.

Rich countries' trade rules, especially in farming and textiles, still discriminate powerfully against poor countries. Rich countries' subsidies encourage wasteful use of energy and natural resources, and harm the environment. It is at least arguable that rich countries' protection of intellectual property discriminates unfairly against the developing world. And without a doubt, rich countries' approach to financial regulation offers implicit subsidies to their banks and encourages reckless lending; it results, time and again, in financial crises in rich and poor countries alike.

All these policies owe much to the fact that corporate interests exercise undue influence over government policy. Sceptics are right to deplore this. But undue influence is hardly new in democratic politics; it has not been created by globalisation forcing governments to bow down. On the contrary, special-interest politics is easier to conduct in closed economies than in open ones. If allowed to, all governments are happy to seek political advantage by granting preferences.

It is dispiriting to watch as big companies work out how to maintain their influence nationally and extend it to the global arena, using "civil society" and "corporate social responsibility" as levers. Naturally, in the light of the protesters' concerns, the multinationals are willing to sit down with governments and NGOs – they have lots of ideas for collecting extra subsidies, and piling punitive taxes and regulation on their less responsible competitors.

Barking up the wrong tree

The protesters' main intellectual problem is that their aversion to capitalism – that is, to economic freedom – denies them the best and maybe the only way to attack and contain concentrations of economic and political power. The protesters do not need to embrace laisser-faire capitalism. They need only to discard their false or wildly exaggerated fears about the mixed economy; that is, about capitalism as it exists in the West, with safety-nets, public services and moderate redistribution bolted on.

Under this form of capitalism, economic growth does not hurt the poor, as sceptics allege; indeed, for developing countries, capitalist growth is indispensable if people are ever to be raised out of poverty. Growth in mixed economies is compatible with protecting the environment: rich countries are cleaner than poor ones. And if prices are made to reflect the costs of pollution, or allowed to reflect the scarcity of natural resources, growth and good stewardship go hand in hand. Above all, free trade does not put poor countries at a disadvantage: it helps them.

Try this for size

If some of the protesters could accept these tenets of mixed-economy capitalism, a narrower but far more productive protest manifesto would come into view. Its overriding priority would be to address the scandal of developing-world poverty. To that end, it would demand that rich-country governments open their markets to all developing-country exports, especially to farm goods and textiles. (Concerns about displaced workers would be met not by holding down the poorest countries, but by spending more on training and education in rich countries, and by cushioning any losses in income there.) It would insist that western governments increase spending on foreign aid, taking care that the benefits flow not to rich-country banks or poor-country bureaucrats, but to the poor, and especially to the victims of disease. To protect the environment, it would call for an end to all subsidies that promote the wasteful use of natural resources, and for the introduction of pollution taxes, including a carbon tax, so that the price of energy reflects the risk of global warming.

This programme to accelerate globalisation and extend the reach of market forces – although at first it might be better to put it another way – would also have a good-governance component. Under that rubric, "trade policy" should ideally be abolished outright: governments have no business infringing people's liberty to buy goods where they will, least of all when the aim is to add to corporate earnings. Short of instant abolition, trade policy should at least be brought into the light so that corporate interests find it harder to dictate its terms. Governments should hold themselves accountable to voters at large, not to companies, industry associations, special interests or indeed to any kind of non-governmental organisation, whatever its ideology or dress code.

Among other things, accountability means accepting rather than denying responsibility. Corrupt or incompetent governments in the developing countries deny responsibility when they blame the IMF or the World Bank for troubles chiefly caused by their own policies. Rich-country governments, notably America's, also use the Fund, the Bank and the WTO – institutions which in practice could never defy their wishes – to deflect blame. Globalisation has left the capacity of governments to gather taxes and pay for public spending essentially undiminished. But in all kinds of ways, again and again, governments and their political opponents have used the supposed demands of globalisation to deny responsibility for broken promises, failures of will or capitulations to special interests. That is no harmless evasion, but a lie that rots democracy itself. Critics of economic integration should be striving to expose this lie; instead, they greet it as a grudging endorsement of their own position.

The crucial point is that international economic integration widens choices – including choices in social provision – because it makes resources go further. Policies to relieve poverty, to protect workers displaced by technology, and to support education and public health are all more affordable with globalisation than without (though not even globalisation can relieve governments of the need to collect taxes to pay for those good things). When governments claim that globalisation ties their hands, because politically it makes their lives easier, they are conning voters and undermining support for economic freedom. Whatever else that may be, it is not good governance.

Whenever governments use globalisation to deny responsibility, democracy suffers another blow and prospects for growth in the developing countries are set back a little further. Anti-globalists fall for it every time, seeing the denials as proof of their case. They make plenty of other mistakes, but none so stupid as that.

The material on pages 5–51 was first published in a survey in *The Economist* in September 2001.

PART 2
THE LOPSIDED WORLD ECONOMY

2

THE PHONEY RECOVERY

"It will purge the rottenness out of the system." With these words, Andrew Mellon, America's treasury secretary, greeted the Great Depression as something to be endured, not avoided. His notorious prognosis, quoted in the following article, is often cited by mainstream economists as an example of the dangerous quackery that used to rein in the discipline. Deep economic slumps are not cathartic. To think so is both callous and confused.

Mellon's impassive response could not be further from the fashion of today's economic policymakers. In the wake of the stockmarket collapse of 2000–01, the Federal Reserve cut interest rates promptly, while President Bush pressed on with his long-standing plan to slash taxes. Consumers were invited to spend the tax dollars the government handed back to them – and the fresh money the Fed printed for them.

The strategy worked on its own terms. America's recession was shallow and brief; its growth since then has been impressive. But as this chapter points out, America's recovery still rings hollow. In a healthy economy, households spend the income they earn, less whatever they can set aside for the future. But in this recovery, jobs and pay did not rebound as forcefully as they have in previous upturns. Spending has been strong, but pay cheques have failed to keep pace.

As a result, America's current prosperity depends on unearned wealth, not earned income. For the typical American family, the bulk of that wealth is in housing, which enjoyed big jumps in value in the wake of the Fed's rate-cutting. Households have kept the economy going by borrowing freely against the paper gains in the value of their homes.

But this chapter expresses fears that Americans are placing too much faith in bricks and mortar. A jump in house prices makes homeowners feel richer, but it adds nothing to America's commercial and industrial base. It is simply a redistribution of income from homebuyers to homeowners.

The Fed's supporters may share some of these concerns about the side-effects of its aggressive remedies. But what, they ask, was the alternative? Its strategy spared America a deeper recession. Next to that, any complaints one might have seem churlish.

Is a recession always worse than the alternative? The first article of this chapter bravely poses this question, which is often begged in the debate. It draws on the thinking of the Austrian economists Joseph Schumpeter and Friedrich Hayek, who both argued that downturns were part of capitalism's inherent rhythm. This school of thought fell into long disrepute after the Great Depression, but its themes and preoccupations are coming back into the economic debate. Some academics see the ups and downs of the business cycle as the economy's natural response to spurts and slumps in innovation. Others worry that interest rates, held at unnatural lows for unprecedented periods, have spread a new "rottenness throughout the system", leaving its financial foundations less sturdy than they appear.

There may be limits to what a government or central bank should do to avoid a recession, this chapter argues, giving two reasons. Their efforts might forestall the necessary restructuring that allows an economy to take advantage of innovation. In this case, stability is bought at the price of sterility. Alternatively, their policies might offer a reprieve, but not an escape: by tempting households to keep spending, they merely put off the day when the economy's rate of saving must rise and the economy must learn to get by without adding ever-increasing amounts to an ever-higher pile of debt. Policymakers should do what they can to avert recessions, the chapter concludes, but no more than they can.

A necessary evil

Should we learn to love recessions?

WHEN AMERICA'S BUBBLE BURST in 2001, the Fed swiftly cut inter-est rates. This has become a habit: every time there has been any financial turmoil at home or abroad – such as the crises in East Asia and Russia and the near-collapse of Long-Term Capital Management in 1998 – the Fed has pumped more money into the economy. Low interest rates saved America from a deep recession. But after such a binge, might the economy not benefit from a cold shower?

Most people would consider this a heretical question. They assume that it is a central bank's job to avoid recessions at all cost. According to one survey, four-fifths of Americans believe that preventing recessions is as important as preventing drug abuse. But are recessions always an unmitigated disaster, or do they also offer some economic benefits? And if central banks respond to every danger sign by pumping in more money, does this not risk simply transferring the problem elsewhere? As America's stockmarket bubble has burst, another bubble now seems to be inflating in its housing market. This allows consumers to go on party-ing, but what happens when the drink runs out?

According to the Austrian economic paradigm, recessions are a natu-ral feature of an economy. Joseph Schumpeter argued that recessions are not an evil that should be avoided, but a necessary adjustment to change. Only by allowing the "winds of creative destruction" to blow freely could capital be released from dying firms to new sectors of the economy, thereby boosting future productivity.

Hayek counselled against massive monetary easing to prevent a recession. If unprofitable investments were made during a boom, then it was better to shut those firms down and clear the way for new, more productive investment. For the Austrian economists the policy choice is not between recession or no recession, but between one now or an even nastier one later. A recession is necessary to work off an imbalance between too much investment and too little saving.

Keynes, quite reasonably, ridiculed the idea that in the long run the Great Depression might turn out to have been a good thing. In the early 1930s the Fed and the American Treasury did not pursue expan-sionary policies, precisely because they thought these might hinder the necessary adjustment. Andrew Mellon, the secretary of the Treasury, urged the market to "liquidate labour, liquidate stocks, liquidate the farmers, and liquidate real estate ... It will purge the rottenness out of the system." America's output duly fell by 30% as the Fed sat on its hands.

Today, a slump on that scale would be unlikely even if the Fed had not cut interest rates swiftly. It would have been headed off by a variety of changes made since the Great Depression: higher government spending and hence more powerful automatic fiscal stabilisers; bank deposit insurance; and a stronger commitment by the Fed to its role of lender of last resort. But even the Austrian economists themselves came to reject the idea that faced with a potentially severe recession, policymakers should do nothing. They approved of stimulus measures to stop recessions from turning into deep depressions, but not of preventing recessions altogether.

The case for the defence

Why is economic instability always assumed to be bad? Some economists argue that recessions result in a permanent loss of output. This rests on the notion that there is a fixed ceiling for output, rising over time, so any shortfall against potential is a permanent loss. On this view, demand-management policies can fill in the troughs without shaving off the peaks, thus increasing average growth.

A more realistic way of looking at it, however, is that business cycles are fluctuations in output above and below an equilibrium trend. This suggests that demand-management policies can mitigate recessions only to the extent that they also choke off expansions; they cannot increase the average rate of growth or employment. Admittedly, cyclical increases in unemployment may become permanent if labour-market rigidities, such as strict hiring-and-firing laws, make it hard for the jobless to find work even when the economy recovers, a condition known as hysteresis. If this is present, as it is in many European countries, then recessions can have a permanent cost. But this is really an argument for labour-market reform to minimise the cost of recessions, not one for measures to prevent them altogether.

A second argument against letting recessions rip is that households may value economic stability for its own sake, even if it makes no difference to the average unemployment rate. Justin Wolfers, an economist at Stanford University, has used surveys of consumer satisfaction from several rich economies to estimate the value that households place on stability. He reckons that starting from current levels of volatility, eliminating the business cycle would increase average well-being by the equivalent of a fall in the unemployment rate of only 0.2 percentage points. By contrast, labour-market reforms could reduce unemployment by several percentage points.

A third common claim is that economic instability and uncertainty may discourage investment, thereby reducing long-term growth. Yet the evidence is weak. More volatile economies do not appear to invest less as a share of GDP. Moreover, looking back, the 20 years to 1938 were by far the most volatile in economic history, yet the average growth rate in developed economies was 3.8%, well above the average growth of 2.7% during the past two decades of relative stability. An analysis of 20 developed economies since 1960 by Bill Martin of UBS Global Asset Management finds little evidence that macroeconomic stability promotes faster growth. If anything, he concludes, countries with greater output variability have enjoyed slightly faster growth in productivity.

This is not as odd as it sounds. A perfectly stable economy would miss out on the advantages of booms as well as the alleged disadvantages of slumps. For instance, in boom times, when credit flows freely, it is easier to finance the risky innovations that may boost future productivity growth. Booms also encourage mergers and acquisitions, a powerful tool for restructuring. More important, as Schumpeter argued, recessions are a process of creative destruction in which inefficient firms are weeded out, releasing resources for more productive firms.

But can we be sure that it will be the least productive firms that go bust in recessions, and that they really will be replaced by new, more profitable ones? Awkwardly, work by Ricardo Caballero and Mohamad Hammour, economists respectively at MIT and DELTA, a French research organisation, finds that good times may be more conducive to economic restructuring than bad. The two economists examined gross job creation and destruction in American manufacturing over the period 1972–93 and found that at the onset of a recession job destruction increases, but it then falls below normal levels until well into the recovery. Job creation declines during a recession and remains relatively low during the initial recovery. Adding up the net effect of job destruction and creation, Messrs Caballero and Hammour conclude that the pace of restructuring actually falls during a recession.

The figures on which the study was based are available only for manufacturing, which has a shrinking share of the economy. Once services are added in, the picture might look different. Still, the study does raise the question of why recessions might hinder rather than help

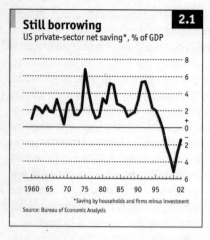

Still borrowing   `2.1`
US private-sector net saving*, % of GDP

*Saving by households and firms minus investment
Source: Bureau of Economic Analysis

industrial restructuring. One answer is that credit markets are imperfect. When credit is tight in a recession, even profitable firms can find it harder to raise money to finance restructuring or new investment.

The dark side of the boom

Even if recessions are not always the most efficient way to reallocate resources, they are necessary to purge the excesses of the previous boom. Stephen King at HSBC argues that a recession should be seen as an unpleasant cleansing experience which leaves the economy in a healthier state: "A bit like taking a cold shower with a lump of carbolic soap." But America's economy has not yet completed this cleansing process: it still has an inadequate savings rate, excessive debt and a huge current-account deficit. The mild recession did little to correct these imbalances, making further pain inevitable.

A good indication of the size of the adjustment yet to be made is the private sector's financial balance (or private-sector net saving, equivalent to saving minus investment), a concept elaborated by Wynne Godley, an economist at Cambridge University. In the United States the private-sector balance shifted from a surplus of 5% of GDP in 1992 to a deficit of 5% of GDP in 2000 as households and firms went on a borrowing spree, an astonishing change after almost four decades when the private sector never ran a deficit at all (see Chart 2.1).

The corporate sector's financial position was not wildly out of line with previous periods of expansion: firms usually run a deficit during booms to finance investment. It was the behaviour of the personal sector that was exceptional, and remains so. The surge in share prices during the 1990s encouraged households to save less and less.

In the past, when a country's private-sector net saving has fallen so sharply, a deep recession or a prolonged period of stagnation has usually followed. Events in Japan, Britain and Sweden after their late 1980s booms are prime examples. Mr Godley has long argued that the same outcome is inevitable in the United States. But America's adjustment still has a long way to go. The private sector's financial deficit narrowed to

1.4% of GDP in 2002, but that still left it well below its 1960–95 average of a surplus of 3% of GDP.

So far, most of the belt-tightening has come from firms. Consumers, on the other hand, have continued to borrow, encouraged by easy money and rising house prices. If the household saving rate rises back to its long-term norm, at the very least a period of slow growth, and perhaps another recession, will surely follow.

Was it a mistake for the Fed to slash interest rates in 2001 and thereby delay this adjustment by households? Some economists believe that a deep but short recession is preferable to a prolonged period of sluggish growth, because recovery comes much sooner, with less damage to the economy's potential growth rate. However, it is arguably better to unwind imbalances gradually to avoid the risk of severe financial problems. Moreover, the Fed has been worried that a deeper recession at a time when inflation is already so low might lead to debt deflation, which central banks should avoid like the plague.

Lower interest rates helped to prop up spending in America largely by fuelling a credit-driven boom in house prices. This fixes one problem but at the risk of creating another.

The great illusion

Spending is increasingly being driven by higher asset values rather than higher incomes

M OST AMERICAN ECONOMISTS will tell you that the Federal Reserve did a brilliant job in preventing a deeper and longer recession after the stockmarket bubble burst. Monetary policy has certainly been successful at keeping up consumer spending, but it has been less good for jobs and incomes. From the trough of the recession in November 2001 to August 2004, America's non-farm payrolls rose by only 0.5%, the weakest jobs recovery on record. Private-sector wages and salaries have risen by only 2.8% in real terms, compared with an average gain of 10.6% in the six previous recoveries (see Chart 2.2). Yet despite this, consumer spending over the same period has surged by 9%. Wages and salaries in America as a proportion of GDP are currently at their lowest level for decades, yet consumer spending relative to GDP is at a record high.

The gap between income and spending has been financed partly by income-tax cuts, but also by saving less and by borrowing. Thanks to low interest rates the price of assets, especially homes, has risen steeply, which has made households feel richer and encouraged them to spend. This is happening not only in America but also in Britain, Australia, New Zealand, Spain and some smaller European economies. Household debt has jumped alarmingly.

Borrowing is not necessarily a bad thing, so long as it does not get out of hand. Household debt in relation to income has steadily risen for at least half a century, largely because financial deregulation has made it easier for households to borrow. However, in the past few years debt has far outpaced its historical trend.

The Fed and others like to explain that there is no need to fret about the recent build-up of debt because it has been matched by big gains in the value of household assets such as shares and homes. President George Bush has boasted that America is enjoying its highest rate of wealth-creation for decades. The snag is that some of the "wealth" being built up by households is phoney. Rising home prices do not increase real wealth for society as a whole. Unlike a rise in equity prices, which in theory (if not always in practice) reflects expectations of higher future profits and an increase in an economy's productive potential, a rise in house prices does not reflect any increase in real productive resources (apart from improvements in the quality of homes); they are a wealth illusion.

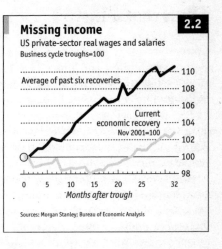

Missing income 2.2
US private-sector real wages and salaries
Business cycle troughs=100

Average of past six recoveries

Current economic recovery
Nov 2001=100

Months after trough

Sources: Morgan Stanley; Bureau of Economic Analysis

Homes are not just assets, they are also a big part of living costs. For a given housing stock, when prices rise, the capital gain to home-owners is offset by the increased future living costs of non-home-owners. Society as a whole is no better off. Rising house prices do not create wealth, they merely redistribute it. Moreover, the prices of assets can fall. Debts, on the other hand, are fixed in value.

American households today are even more addicted to asset appreciation than during the late-1990s stockmarket bubble. Thanks to surging house prices and a partial recovery in share prices, the value of households' total assets rose by a record $6 trillion in 2003, equivalent to 70% of personal disposable income. Increases in property wealth also tend to have a bigger effect on consumer spending than increases in equity wealth. This is because more people own homes than shares and it is easier to convert capital gains on a home into spending power without having to sell the asset, by taking out a bigger mortgage. In 2003 housing-equity withdrawal (the total increase in mortgage debt minus net household investment in housing) rose to 6% of personal disposable income in America and to 8% in Britain. The housing stock has been turned into a gigantic cash machine.

In the long run, the only way to create genuine wealth is to consume less than your income (ie, save), and invest in real income-creating assets. But America and some other economies have been enjoying a very different sort of wealth creation: central banks are, in effect, printing wealth by running lax monetary policies. Illusory paper wealth is boosting consumption at the expense of saving. America's net national saving rate, the share of income that Americans are putting aside for their future, has fallen to a record low, just when they should be saving more to prepare for an ageing society.

Where's my nest egg?

Why bother to save for your retirement when rising home values can do it for you? One good reason is that if the baby-boomers all try to sell their homes at the same time when they retire, house prices will slump. Even if asset prices do not collapse, households' expectations of continuing big gains in the price of houses and shares are highly unlikely to be met, so their nest eggs will be much smaller than they had hoped. For instance, most investors still expect equities to yield double-digit annual returns in the long run. After all, since 1982 the S&P 500 has delivered an average return of 14% a year.

However, a study by Martin Barnes at the Bank Credit Analyst, a Canadian investment-research firm, argues that equity returns over the next decade are unlikely to average more than 5–7% a year. This is because in the long run profits cannot grow faster than nominal GDP, which is now growing more slowly because of lower inflation, and share valuations are already high. If Mr Barnes has got it right, consumers will have to start saving in the old-fashioned way by spending less of their income.

Average house prices in America have risen by 40% in real terms since 1995. That may sound modest compared with gains of 120% in Britain and 80% in Australia, but the increase is twice as big as in America's previous booms in the late 1970s and the late 1980s, making this the country's biggest house-price boom in recorded history. The average ratio of house prices to incomes is already at a record level (see Chart 2.3), yet people are buying homes in the unrealistic hope of large future price rises. That is the definition of a bubble. When two American economists, Robert Shiller and Karl Case, surveyed home-buyers in Los Angeles, Boston, San Francisco and Milwaukee in 2003, the respondents said they expected the value of their homes to rise at an annual average rate of 12–16% over the next ten years.

In the past, housing bubbles have mostly been fairly local affairs, forming in only one or two countries at a time. But now unusually low interest rates around the world may have fuelled the first global property bubble in history. Property prices have been rising briskly not only in America but also in Australia, Britain, China, France, Ireland, New Zealand, Spain and South Africa, among others.

The housing-market analysts trot out all sorts of reasons why houses are not overvalued, such as low interest rates and rapid population growth. However, interest rates are now rising. Not to worry, say the optimists: about 80% of American home-owners have fixed-interest mortgages (unlike most home-buyers in Britain, Australia and Spain, who have variable-rate loans), so they are not at risk. However, in mid-2004 adjustable-rate mortgages accounted for half of all new mortgages in America, leaving households exposed at exactly the wrong time. Despite low interest rates, households' total debt-service

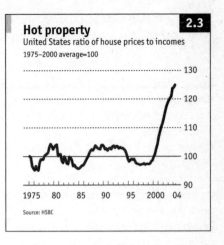

Hot property
United States ratio of house prices to incomes
1975–2000 average=100

Source: HSBC

as a proportion of income is already close to a record high. And even if home-owners with fixed-rate mortgages will not be affected, new home-buyers will face higher mortgage rates. If first-time buyers are squeezed out, the housing market will quickly weaken.

After past booms, inflated house prices typically returned to normal levels by stagnating for a few years as incomes rose. But that is unlikely to work this time. Not only are houses more overvalued than ever before, as measured by the ratios of average home prices to incomes or rents, but inflation is low, so it would take many years of price stagnation for the real price to return to fair value. Over the next few years, house prices in many countries around the world are more likely to fall, leaving some households with homes worth less than their mortgages. The longer that home prices go on rising, the steeper their eventual decline will be.

A fall in house prices would have a much bigger economic impact than a fall in share prices. But even if house prices merely levelled out, consumer spending might slow down sharply because housing-equity withdrawal would decline. Mortgage refinancing in America is already slowing in response to rising mortgage rates. Consumers' ability to turn capital gains into spendable cash has been a lifeline for the economy at a time when real wages were barely rising. That lifeline is now fraying.

Endnote

America grew by a respectable 3.5% in 2005 and the job market improved. But pay lagged behind inflation and the housing market appeared to slow in the second half of 2005.

The material on pages 57–65 was first published in a survey in *The Economist* in September 2002.

3
AMERICA'S IMBALANCES

A closed economy, enjoying no truck with other nations, has no choice but to live within its means. It can consume only what it produces at home, and invest only what it itself saves. An open economy has other options. It can live beyond its means, by consuming what foreigners have made and investing what foreigners have saved.

America does this on an epic scale. Its transactions with the rest of the world are summed up in its balance of payments. This national ledger records both America's trade in goods and services (the main component of the current account) and its trade in assets (the capital account). America's imports vastly exceed its exports. As a consequence, its current account was in the red to the tune of $800 billion in 2005. It makes up this shortfall by selling IOUs to foreigners. Lots of them. In 2005, America borrowed over $90m an hour from the rest of the world.

Eventually, these IOUs must be repaid. According to Warren Buffett, Omaha's richest son, America can look forward to a time when it hands over substantial chunks of its national income each year to foreigners "as tribute for the overindulgences of the past".

The "current-account deficit" is a dry term, drawn from the lexicon of national bean-counters. But there can be drama and some jeopardy behind the phenomenon. The second article in this chapter sets out what is at stake. If the deficit must narrow, there are only three ways it can do so: American spending must fall; foreign spending must rise; or world spending must switch from "foreign" to American production. The quickest way for that to happen is a precipitous fall in the real value of the dollar, which will cut the price of America's exports relative to its imports.

America's current-account deficit cannot be ignored, yet it defies easy characterisation. It has provoked a great deal of debate among economists, but little consensus. They do not agree on how to resolve the problem – or whether it is even a problem at all. A current-account deficit is not, like unemployment or high inflation, always and everywhere a bad thing. Nor is its opposite, a surplus, always a good thing.

The first article in this chapter returns to first principles. For a developing country, which lacks capital but abounds in opportunities for profitable ventures, it is natural to mortgage its future to raise funds for today. That is how the New World built its railways in the 19th century. Likewise, a mature economy that saves more than it can fruitfully invest at home will look abroad for a place to park its money. Germany, for example, has run a big surplus in recent years, largely because rates of investment in the country have waned.

America is a mature economy acting beneath its age. Since 2000, its rates of investment have declined, yet it continues to raise funds abroad at an increasing pace. The sage of Omaha is not the only one to worry that America may eventually pay a price for prolonging the indulgences of youth.

In defence of deficits

Many people regard current-account deficits as dangerous and surpluses as a sign of economic prudence. Yet running a current-account deficit is not necessarily bad

Few bits of economic management sound as irresponsible as running a current-account deficit. Perhaps it is the word "deficit" itself that conjures up notions of profligacy and excess, or it may be the apparent parallel with having an overdraft at the bank. Whatever the reason, many people regard a current-account deficit as self-evidently bad.

A casual glance suggests that such deficits do indeed lurk behind many countries' economic problems. Mexico's bungled devaluation in December 1994 could be traced back to its "unsustainable" current-account deficit of 8% of GDP (see Chart 3.1 on the next page). Other emerging economies with big current-account deficits, such as Hungary or Thailand, have suffered as investors have become fearful of funding such large deficits.

In rich countries, too, current-account deficits often seem to be the source of economic woes. The dollar's headlong decline in the first half of 1995 was blamed on America's hefty external deficit, among other things. Many economists fretted about Australia's current-account deficit, which was estimated at over 5% of GDP in 1995.

Does all this mean countries should as a matter of course aim for a current-account surplus? Even if they could all succeed in doing this, which the laws of arithmetic forbid, it would be a mistake to try.

To see why, remember that the current account is only one part of a country's overall balance of payments, the record of all the transactions between a country and the rest of the world. Put simply, the current account measures mainly trade in goods and services; the capital account measures borrowing and lending.

Like a company's books, the balance-of-payments accounts must balance. A current-account deficit means that more goods and services are flowing into a country than are flowing out. This difference needs to be paid for, so the current-account deficit must be matched by an equivalent amount of foreign borrowing or investment (ie, a capital-account surplus) or by running down reserves of foreign exchange at the central bank.

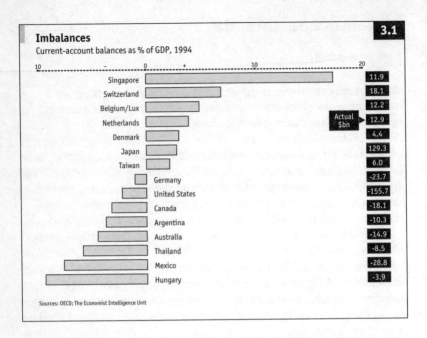

Imbalances
Current-account balances as % of GDP, 1994

Country	Actual $bn
Singapore	11.9
Switzerland	18.1
Belgium/Lux	12.2
Netherlands	12.9
Denmark	4.4
Japan	129.3
Taiwan	6.0
Germany	-23.7
United States	-155.7
Canada	-18.1
Argentina	-10.3
Australia	-14.9
Thailand	-8.5
Mexico	-28.8
Hungary	-3.9

Sources: OECD; The Economist Intelligence Unit

Typically, the biggest components of the current account are the exports and imports of goods. The difference between them is known as the visible-trade balance. The close relationship between this and the current-account balance can lead to confusion. People often suppose that a current-account deficit means that a country is exporting too little because of restrictions in other countries. Many Americans, for instance, are fond of blaming their current-account deficit on Japanese import restrictions.

It is not that simple, because the current-account balance is not just a matter of trade in goods. It also comprises services (such as transport and banking); interest or dividend payments to foreign investors (and receipts on overseas investments); private transfers from workers (such as migrant Turkish workers in Germany sending money home to their relations); and official transfers (such as foreign aid).

Thus a country that has borrowed a lot from abroad in the past, but now has a trade surplus, can still find that the interest payments on its past debts turn the surplus into a current-account deficit (see opposite). A way to avoid confusion is to see the current account as the change in a country's net external financial position. What running a current-account deficit really means is that a country is becoming more indebted to foreigners.

Dissecting the deficit

In mathematics tests at school, achieving full marks means not only getting the answer right, but also showing the right method of getting there. Analysing countries' current-account deficits is similar. Though some information can be gleaned from the overall figure, this can often conceal as much as it reveals. Consider Canada and Mali, two of the countries in Chart 3.2. Both had a current-account deficit of just over 4% of GDP in 1993. But in Canada the visible-trade balance showed a surplus of almost 1.5% of GDP, while Mali's was in deficit by almost 5% of GDP. Canada's interest payments on its large foreign debt, as well as net imports of services, dragged the overall current account into deficit. Mali also had huge net imports of services, of over 12% of GDP: the current-account deficit was saved from exploding only by massive foreign aid from governments overseas, worth 11% of GDP.

Turkey and Australia make another striking pair. Both had similar current-account deficits in 1993, but whereas Turkey had a visible-trade deficit of 8% of GDP, Australia's trade was in balance; again, it was net interest payments which pulled the country into current-account deficit. Proof enough that it is important to look beyond the bottom line.

The devil is in the detail
3.2

As % of GDP, 1993

	Australia	Brazil	Canada	Mali	Turkey
Exports	15.0	8.8	26.1	13.7	8.9
Imports	-15.0	-5.9	-24.7	-18.5	-16.9
Visible-trade balance	nil	3.0	1.4	-4.8	-8.0
Services*	-0.4	-1.1	-2.0	-12.6	3.2
Investment income*	-3.5	-2.4	-3.7	-0.9	-0.9
Private transfers*	0.3	0.4	0.1	3.4	1.7
Official transfers*	-0.2	nil	-0.1	10.8	0.4
Current-account balance	-3.8	-0.2	-4.3	-4.1	-3.6

Source: IMF *Net

Whether this is prudent depends on why this increased indebtedness is occurring. Here again, a bit more national-income accounting is necessary. Assume first that a country has a closed economy: that is, it has no

Open opportunities 3.3

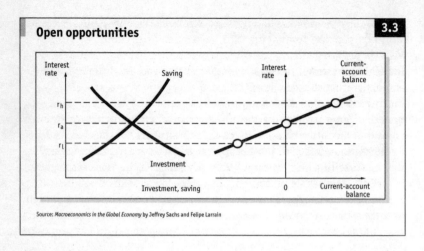

Interest rate / Saving / Investment / Investment, saving

r_h / r_a / r_l

Interest rate / Current-account balance / 0 / Current-account balance

Source: *Macroeconomics in the Global Economy* by Jeffrey Sachs and Felipe Larrain

trade or financial flows with any other country. Its total production must be divided between what is consumed now and what is invested. At the same time the total income received by households (ie, the proceeds from the output) must be either consumed or saved. In such a closed economy the interest rate will be such that total saving equals total investment.

In an open economy, however, investment can be higher or lower than saving, with the current-account deficit (or surplus) being the difference between them. As Chart 3.3 shows, a rise in interest rates is likely to reduce a current-account deficit (or push it into surplus) as saving tends to rise and investment falls.

In principle, for the world as a whole, the current and capital accounts must be in balance. Since the world is a closed economy (we do not, as yet, trade with Mars), world saving must equal world investment. It is logically impossible for every country to run either a surplus or a deficit. (In practice, however, the world ran a current-account deficit of $113 billion in 1994, due to statistical inaccuracies.)

Borrow young, lend later

The fear of current-account deficits stems from an era when economies were relatively closed. Under the post-war Bretton Woods monetary system, most countries fixed their exchange rates and imposed capital controls, making it hard to borrow from abroad. So having a current-account deficit meant drawing down reserves. Eventually these reserves would run out, and there would be a "balance-of-payments crisis".

Nowadays, with capital flowing relatively freely across borders, countries can run current-account imbalances for years. Whether it is wise to do so depends on the circumstances. Is saving too low? Is domestic investment too low? Is the money borrowed being used for productive investment?

On its own, the size of the current-account balance tells you little. Indeed, a large surplus may not always be a sign of strength. It could mean that a country's residents find it more profitable to invest abroad. If this is due to a lack of investment opportunities at home, the country may be forfeiting domestic growth. In Japan's case, its large surplus may be a sign of excessive saving.

Running a sizeable deficit may make sense for a country at a particular stage of development. Poor countries are likely to have accumulated less capital than richer ones. This means that any investment in capital should reap higher returns than in richer countries. So it makes sense for poorer countries to import capital (ie, run a current-account deficit). Examples abound of developing countries borrowing to finance growth: throughout the 1970s, for instance, South Korea's current-account deficit averaged more than 5% of GDP.

Economists have tried to formalise the idea that countries are more likely to be net borrowers or savers at different times. A theory of balance-of-payments stages has it that poor countries begin by running both current-account and trade deficits as they invest heavily. Over time the exports generated by investment generate a trade surplus, but the current account stays in deficit because of the interest due on the debt already accrued. After a while, the country pays off enough of its debt to shift into current-account surplus, and eventually becomes a net creditor to the rest of the world. Finally, at a mature stage, a country runs a trade deficit as it lives off the income from its investments, but it remains a net creditor.

Until recently, America seemed to conform to this view. For most of the 19th century it borrowed from the rest of the world and ran a current-account deficit. By the 1870s it was running a trade surplus, and by 1900 it had managed to notch up a current-account surplus.

During the first half of the 20th century, the United States became the world's biggest net creditor; by the 1970s it was at the mature stage – financing trade deficits with the income from investments abroad. In the late 1970s its current account, too, moved into deficit, although the country remained a net creditor. However, in the 1980s the current-account deficits became so large that America reached a new stage – one not foreseen in theory – of being a net debtor again.

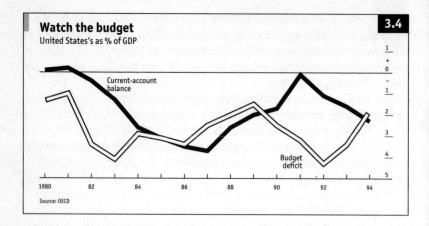

Watch the budget
United States's as % of GDP

3.4

Current-account balance

Budget deficit

1980   82   84   86   88   90   92   94

Source: OECD

Many countries have never followed the pattern. Australia and Canada, for instance, have remained net debtors throughout their history. What matters is not that a country "grows out" of its habit of running current-account deficits, but that it remains capable of servicing its debts. This suggests that the first test of a sensible current-account deficit is that it must be used to finance profitable investment.

Another sensible reason for running a sizeable current-account deficit is to respond to a temporary shock. Consider the impact of a sudden drop in the price of a country's main export products, for instance. If the fall in price is temporary, it makes sense to maintain current consumption and allow the current-account deficit to rise. But if the price fall is permanent, a country needs to reduce its consumption, because it is now (permanently) poorer. So the best course is to finance a temporary shock but adjust to a permanent one – provided it is possible to tell the difference between them.

Blame the budget

It is not always easy to work out exactly what a current-account deficit is financing. One clue comes from overall changes in saving and investment. If the current-account deficit is widening while saving is declining and investment is fairly stagnant, this is worrying. It implies that the borrowed foreign money must be financing consumption rather than investment, which will make it difficult to generate the resources needed to repay the debts later.

A budget deficit and a current-account deficit are closely linked. This is because a country's total investment and saving are each made up of two components: those of the private sector and those of the government. How much does it matter which of these two components, public or private, contributes most to a current-account deficit?

Much of the increase in America's current-account deficit in the 1980s can be explained by the sharp rise in its budget deficit (see Chart 3.4). Since most of the government's expenditure goes on consumption (in the form of subsidies or transfers), a rising current-account deficit fuelled by a rising budget deficit is particularly dangerous.

But sometimes current-account deficits can occur when the government's budget is in balance, or even in surplus. Does this matter?

Many people think not. They argue that a current-account deficit that is driven by the private sector merely reflects the rational investment decisions made by private individuals. Nigel Lawson, a former British chancellor, famously held this view; as a result it is often known as the "Lawson doctrine". But – as Mexico showed so spectacularly – large current-account deficits, even if the public finances are relatively healthy, can be a problem. Mexico's official budget deficit in 1994 was less than 1% of GDP, its current-account deficit almost 8%.

Contrary to the Lawson doctrine, there appear to be at least two good reasons for worrying about private borrowing. First of all, some private borrowers (particularly banks) may borrow more from abroad than is prudent, often because they think that governments will bail them out if they hit trouble.

Second, for all the talk of globalisation, capital markets are still not fully integrated, and the supply of funding from abroad is not limitless: again as Mexico showed, foreign funds can suddenly dry up if markets perceive a country to be too risky. At that point countries that have financed their current-account deficits with volatile portfolio capital, and especially with short-term debt, face problems.

For both these reasons, another test of whether a current-account deficit is healthy is the form and maturity of the financial flows into a country.

In sum, there are no simple rules to work out how much of a current-account deficit is safe. It depends on a country's stage of development, on how it is using the money, and on how markets perceive it to be using the money. What is certainly clear is that, contrary to what is often supposed, current-account deficits are not always bad.

The price of profligacy

How bad is America's borrowing binge?

"I JUST THINK IT'S A MEANINGLESS CONCEPT." That was the verdict of Paul O'Neill, George Bush's plain-spoken first Treasury secretary, on the current-account deficit. Mr O'Neill reckoned it was silly to worry about external imbalances in a global economy where capital flows freely. Foreigners, he argued, put their money into America because it offered the best risk-adjusted returns. A current-account deficit was merely the accounting consequence of these capital inflows.

Mr O'Neill was pushed out in December 2002 and Mr Bush's economic team may put things less bluntly, but many of them are equally relaxed about the current-account deficit. Some acknowledge that, over time, the deficit may need to shrink, but reckon that in large liquid global capital markets, any adjustment will be gradual and benign. None of them appears to lose sleep over the sustainability of America's external account.

Are they right to be so complacent? The current account is a tricky concept that reflects several different balances at the same time. From one angle, it is just the accounting counterpoint to capital inflows. Viewed from a different perspective, however, it is the sum of the trade deficit (showing how much more Americans import than they export), plus interest payments to foreigners on previous borrowing. In other words, it reflects how much Americans are borrowing to finance today's spending and to service yesterday's debt. If they are borrowing too much, the deficit becomes unsustainable.

Just as an individual cannot pile on credit-card debt forever, so a country cannot increase the burden of its foreign debt indefinitely. Eventually, interest on the accumulated debt would use all the economy's resources, leaving nothing for domestic spending. In practice, however, the current-account deficit would have to adjust much earlier. Just when depends on a variety of indicators: the size of the accumulated debt; the rate at which new debt is piling up (the current-account deficit); the speed of economic growth; and the interest rate paid on the borrowed funds.

America's rate of borrowing is high and rising. At just under 5% of GDP in 2003, the current-account deficit is the highest in the country's history. Even in the final decades of the 19th century, after the Civil War, America's deficit was generally below 3% of GDP (though Canada and Argentina ran deficits as high as 10% of GDP in that period). In the Reagan era, the current-account deficit peaked at 3.4% of GDP.

Some of the rise may be a statistical quirk. According to official numbers, the world as a whole runs a current-account deficit with itself, and one that has risen sharply since 1997. Since the world does not, as yet, trade with Mars, the numbers must be wrong, so some of America's current-account deficit may be more apparent than real. But not all of the rise, or even most of it, can be explained this way.

In fact, America's current-account deficit is becoming worryingly large. Several studies suggest that economies hit trouble when their current-account deficits reach 4–5% of GDP. Caroline Freund, an economist now at the IMF and before that at the Federal Reserve, looked at 25 episodes of current-account adjustments in rich countries between 1980 and 1997 and found that the current account typically begins to reverse after the deficit has grown for about four years and reached 5% of GDP.

Another study at the IMF found only 12 episodes since 1973 where industrial countries have run a deficit of over 4% of GDP for more than three years in a row. All of the countries involved were relatively small and open economies.

Does it matter that America's current-account deficit is already an outlier by conventional benchmarks? Optimists claim not, pointing out that America has seen a big rise in productivity growth. That not only explains the higher borrowing (to fund the investment boom), but also makes it easier to finance the debt. There is something in that. America's productivity growth did rise sharply in the late 1990s, pushing the economy's trend rate of growth from about 2.5% to 3–3.5%. But the current-account deficit has increased far more rapidly. Worse, it is still rising, even though the investment boom is over.

America is different

Second, argue the sanguine, America has unique characteristics that allow it to run a larger deficit. It can borrow in its own currency, which also happens to be the global reserve currency. And it has the world's largest and most liquid stock and bond markets. Certainly these advantages allow America to borrow more than others. They reduce the risk of balance-of-payments crises of the sort that befall emerging markets, such as Argentina or Mexico, where no one is willing to lend them money at almost any price. But they do not remove all limits.

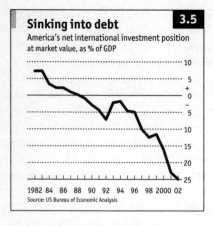

Sinking into debt `3.5`

America's net international investment position at market value, as % of GDP

10
5
+
0
–
5
10
15
20
25

1982 84 86 88 90 92 94 96 98 2000 02
Source: US Bureau of Economic Analysis

A better reason to take comfort is that the stock of debt is still relatively modest. America resembles a rich man who has discovered credit-card bingeing late in life. At the end of the 1970s, after decades of almost continuous current-account surpluses, the United States was a creditor country, with a net stock of foreign assets worth about 10% of GDP. Persistent current-account deficits turned the country into a net debtor in 1985, since when it has been getting deeper and deeper into the red. At the end of 2002, net external debt reached 25% of GDP (see Chart 3.5).

That is higher than the debt levels at which some Latin American countries hit financial disaster in the 1980s debt crisis, and on a par with the peak debt level America reached in the 19th century, but it is not especially high by the standards of other rich countries. Many industrial nations have net foreign debts worth 40–50% of GDP. Australia's debt stock, for example, reached 60% of GDP in the mid-1990s, and Ireland's peaked at over 70% in the early 1980s. The trouble is that on current trends, America's debt stock looks set to rise sharply. If the current-account deficit remains at 5% of GDP, and the economy grows by 5% in nominal terms (roughly its trend rate of real growth plus inflation of just under 2%), America's debt stock will reach 40% of GDP by 2007 and 60% in a decade (see Chart 3.6).

The bottom line

Can America afford this kind of indebtedness? That depends on the interest rate it must pay. So far, it has got away lightly. Until 2001, more income was generated by America's investments abroad than was paid out from the United States to foreign investors, even though the country became a net debtor in the mid-1980s. Even in 2002, America's net payments on foreign investments were less than $4 billion, a relative trifle.

No one is sure why America pays so little for its borrowing. One factor is the difference in returns on foreign direct investment. Americans have tended to earn higher returns on their FDI than foreigners have earned on direct investment in America. This may be

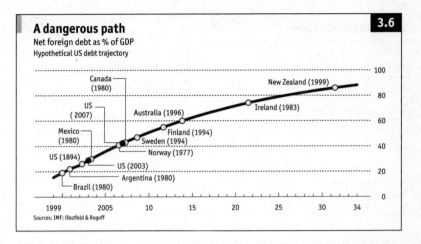

3.6

A dangerous path

Net foreign debt as % of GDP
Hypothetical US debt trajectory

Canada (1980)
New Zealand (1999)
US (2007)
Australia (1996)
Ireland (1983)
Mexico (1980)
Finland (1994)
Sweden (1994)
Norway (1977)
US (1894)
US (2003)
Argentina (1980)
Brazil (1980)

1999   2005   10   15   20   25   30   34

Sources: IMF; Obstfeld & Rogoff

due to different tax treatment, or to the age of the investment. American investments in foreign factories are usually older and generate a bigger stream of dividends than foreigners' more recent purchases in America. The difference in returns earned by foreigners and Americans on portfolio investment, in contrast, is much less marked.

More important, the returns – to both Americans and foreigners – have been falling. Wynne Godley, an economist at Britain's Cambridge university, in a paper published by the Levy Economics Institute of Bard College, in New York state, has calculated a crude "quasi-interest rate" earned on America's external financial assets and liabilities, by dividing the payments received [and made] in one year by the stock of assets [and liabilities] at the end of the previous year. For the past two decades, both rates of return have closely tracked the yields on Treasury bills (ie, fallen sharply). In 2002 this quasi-interest rate fell to just over 1%. Falling borrowing costs have, so far, masked the rising external debt.

That is unlikely to continue. In the years ahead, America faces a sharply rising debt stock and, quite probably, higher interest rates, so net interest payments to foreigners could become much more significant. If the average interest rate paid on external debt goes up to 3%, for instance, and the debt stock rises to 40% of GDP in 2007, as current trends suggest, Americans will be paying out close to $150 billion in interest, the equivalent of 1.2% of GDP. That would mark a huge increase from the current $4 billion, and could start to hurt.

Add all these factors together, and the trend in America's indebtedness will become unsustainable, but not for a while yet. More debt

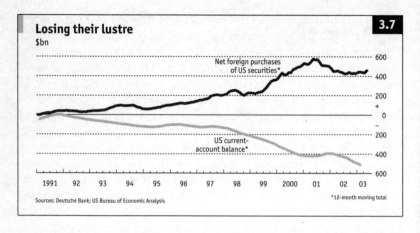

Losing their lustre

$bn

3.7

Net foreign purchases of US securities*

US current-account balance*

| 1991 | 92 | 93 | 94 | 95 | 96 | 97 | 98 | 99 | 2000 | 01 | 02 | 03 |

Sources: Deutsche Bank; US Bureau of Economic Analysis

*12-month moving total

could be built up through a few more years of large and rising current-account deficits before the costs of borrowing start to have a dramatic effect on the economy.

But long before that happens, foreigners may become less willing to hold yet more American assets. Foreign investors' decisions are affected by two, sometimes conflicting, factors: the risk-adjusted returns that American assets offer, and the desire for a diversified portfolio. If American assets offer high returns, then investors may be prepared to buy more of them. But at some point the desire for a diversified portfolio will impose a limit.

Got enough greenbacks, thanks

Investors' recent behaviour suggests that foreigners' appetite for American assets may already be beginning to flag. In 2001 and 2002, the composition of capital inflows changed significantly, and in a worrying direction. Private investors, who in the late 1990s were snapping up American shares, bonds and factories, more or less stopped buying anything but bonds in 2001. Foreign direct-investment flows, which reached a peak of 1.6% of GDP in 2000, turned negative. And as purchases of American securities by private foreign investors have fallen, the current-account deficit has risen (see Chart 3.7). According to Jim O'Neill, head of economic research at Goldman Sachs (and no relation to Paul), private portfolio flows and direct investment in the first three months of 2003 were worth only 1.4% of GDP. The remainder of the current-account deficit of 5.1% of GDP was funded by short-term speculative capital flows and official purchases of bonds by foreign central banks.

This lack of enthusiasm for American assets clearly shows up in the fall in the dollar since the beginning of 2002: to entice buyers, their relative price had to fall. Some of this drop may have been temporary, caused by low bond yields and a sluggish stockmarket. Indeed, as bond markets temporarily rallied in the second quarter of 2003, portfolio flows picked up. And as America's economic prospects brightened, part of the dollar drop was reversed. But there are also good reasons to believe that foreign investors have got enough dollar assets in their portfolios.

Every three months, *The Economist* asks a group of global portfolio investors about their asset allocation. In 2003 these showed that American stocks made up 53% of the typical investor's equity portfolio and American-issued dollar bonds around 44% of the typical bond portfolio. Those proportions are slightly lower than at their peak in 2001, with 54% and 50% respectively. In the mid-1990s, in contrast, global investors allocated only around 30% of their assets to American dollar assets. In the late 1990s, therefore, the typical investor hugely increased the average share of American assets in his portfolio. In order to raise the average so quickly, the marginal investment in American assets must have shot up.

Catherine Mann, an economist at the Institute for International Economics in Washington, DC, who has pioneered the portfolio-based analysis of current-account sustainability, calculates that in 1998–2001 the typical investor allocated an average of 80% of his increased wealth to American assets. The question is whether this can continue. Ms Mann calculates that if the current-account deficit is to remain sustainable, foreigners will have to go on allocating 80–90% of their marginal investments to American assets. That is not inconceivable, but it seems unlikely.

In sum, even if America could afford to take on more debt, foreign investors appear increasingly unwilling to hold it. True, foreign central banks, whose asset-allocation decisions are based on political as well as economic criteria, could continue to pick up an ever-increasing share of the burden. But central banks cannot underwrite America's current-account deficit indefinitely. The chances are that an adjustment is close. It will not be easy.

Shrink-proof

Why America's deficit is hard to turn around

IF FOREIGNERS LOSE ENTHUSIASM for American assets, they simply click on a mouse. Capital markets are the most liquid and efficient markets in the world; billions of dollars can shift at the touch of a button. The problem is that the other side of America's balance-of-payments ledger – the world of imports and exports – is much more sluggish.

According to economics textbooks, shrinking an external deficit should be straightforward enough. For the current-account deficit to shrink, the trade deficit must fall, which means that America must import less and export more. That, in turn, means raising foreigners' appetite for American goods and services relative to Americans' own demand for them.

There are two main routes. Either overall spending by foreigners rises relative to American spending as other economies perk up, or (more painfully) America's economy slows down. To help things along, Americans should shift their spending towards goods produced at home. A cheaper dollar will encourage them to do that while boosting American exports at the same time.

The most effective engine of adjustment would be an autonomous increase in demand abroad for American goods, perhaps through faster growth in customer countries. In practice, though, it tends not to happen that way. The typical current-account adjustment, according to the IMF study cited earlier, is associated both with a sizeable fall in the exchange rate and with a drop in output in the adjusting economy. Caroline Freund's study for the Federal Reserve reached the same conclusion, suggesting that a sustained export surge is the most important factor in turning round a deficit.

Although America finds it easier than most countries to fund its external deficit by sucking in foreign capital, its economy has a number of characteristics that make it much tougher than elsewhere to shrink that deficit. The first problem is the sheer size of it, and the huge gap between imports and exports (see Chart 3.8). At just under $1.4 trillion in 2002, America's imports are worth almost 50% more than its exports ($974 billion). Closing the gap means exports have to grow much faster than imports. If imports were to increase by, say, 4% (about half their average growth rate since the mid-1990s, and consistent with modest economic growth in America), exports would have to rise by 11%, more than 1.5 times the average of the booming late 1990s, to reduce the trade deficit to $300 billion over two years.

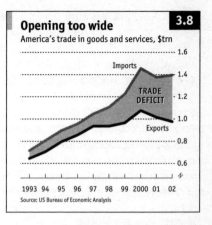

Opening too wide   3.8

America's trade in goods and services, $trn

Source: US Bureau of Economic Analysis

Moreover, Americans have a particular penchant for imports. Back in 1969, two economists, Hendrik Houthakker and Stephen Magee, noticed an odd phenomenon: for any given rate of economic growth, America's imports tended to grow faster than those of other countries (and faster than America's exports). So if all countries were growing at the same speed, and exchange rates remained stable, America's trade deficit would worsen inexorably. To stop the deterioration, the American economy would have to grow more slowly than others, or the dollar would have to fall.

This phenomenon has long perplexed economists. Why should America be more addicted to imports than other countries? For a long time, economists thought it must have something to do with trade barriers abroad that prevented American exports from flourishing. But trade barriers, at least in the rich world, have been lowered substantially since the 1960s.

Another theory, pioneered by Paul Krugman in the late 1980s, is that Americans' apparent love of imports reflects the growing array of products made by countries that export to America. For any given rise in income, America's import demand is not abnormally high, he argued. Rather, it is the supply of exports from fast-growing supplier regions, such as East Asia, that has been rising.

Another explanation points to the high levels of immigration into America. Immigrants, goes the argument, have a particular penchant for goods from their own country. Thus imports in a country with lots of immigrants will be relatively higher than elsewhere.

Lastly, there is the possibility that the relationship between growth and imports shifts as economies develop. Catherine Mann, from the Institute for International Economics, finds that the predilection for imports is much less pronounced in services than in goods. That suggests America's import bias will become less marked as the share of services in the global economy becomes ever larger.

For the moment, however, the import bias remains. In a detailed re-estimation of the statistics in 2000, three economists at the Federal Reserve, Peter Hooper (now at Deutsche Bank), Karen Johnson and Jaime Marquez, found that America's imports rose 1.8% for every 1% increase in overall spending. A 1% rise in foreign demand, in contrast, produced a less than proportional (0.8%) rise in American exports.

This lopsidedness, together with the sheer scale of America's current-account deficit, means that tackling it will be tricky. Unless other countries grow substantially faster, relative to America, than they do now, the bulk of any adjustment will depend on a depreciation of the dollar.

Down with the dollar

Back in the world of economics textbooks, a fall in the exchange rate improves the trade balance in two stages. First, the cheaper dollar increases the relative price of Japanese cars, French wines and Italian holidays. Cars from Detroit, chardonnay from California or trips to DisneyWorld, in contrast, become relatively less expensive. Second, this shift in relative prices encourages Americans to spend less on imports while boosting American exports.

In the real world, however, matters are more complicated. First, a drop in the exchange rate does not necessarily lead to an equivalent rise in the price of imported goods. This is partly because the final price of an imported good includes numerous costs, such as distribution and marketing, that are not affected by the exchange rate. Second, many countries that export to the United States (especially Asian ones) price their goods in dollars. Since these exporters are usually extremely keen to maintain their share in the world's biggest market, they often absorb the effect of a drop in the dollar by cutting their profits rather than raising the price.

Economists reckon that in the 1990s only about half of an exchange-rate change had worked its way through to manufacturing import prices after a year. Over a shorter period the effect can be even less. In the year to May 2003, says Michael Rosenberg, chief currency strategist at Deutsche Bank, import prices to America, excluding oil, rose only 0.9%, even though the trade-weighted dollar fell by 6%.

But even if prices do move, spending patterns may remain much the same for a while, because consumers tend to be slow to adjust their spending in response to price changes. It also takes firms time to change orders and production levels. And even in the long run, the impact on imports of a drop in the dollar is weaker than that of a drop in income. According to calculations by Ms Johnson and Messrs Hooper and Marquez, a 1% drop in the dollar reduces Americans' demand for imports by only 0.3% in the long term. A 1% drop in income, on the other hand, reduces imports by 1.8%. So if a drop in the dollar is to make much of a dent in the trade deficit, it will have to be really big.

But just how big? The exact estimates differ, depending on how economists construct their models, but virtually all the numbers are startling. In perhaps the most optimistic analysis, Fred Bergsten of the Institute for International Economics reckons that the dollar needs to fall by another 15–20% on a trade-weighted basis to bring America's current-account deficit down to 3% of GDP. His calculation assumes some increase in relative demand from abroad. Failing that, the necessary currency adjustment becomes much bigger. Ken Rogoff, who returned to Harvard University after a two-year stint as chief economist at the IMF, and Maurice Obstfeld, an economist at the University of California at Berkeley, reckon it will take a fall of closer to 35% to get the current account back into balance. Mr O'Neill from Goldman Sachs is even more pessimistic, estimating that a trade-weighted drop of 43% will be needed to reduce the current-account deficit by 2% of GDP by 2007. And Mr Rosenberg of Deutsche Bank thinks that if demand patterns stay as they are, a depreciation of 40–50% may be called for to get the current-account deficit down to 3.5% of GDP.

These are enormous shifts. If the burden were spread equally across America's trading partners, a 50% drop in the dollar would send the euro to well over $2 and the yen to less than 60 per dollar. With exchange-rate changes of this magnitude, the risk is that currencies may move too fast and perhaps even too far. Historically, exchange rates have tended to overshoot. In the 1980s the dollar soared, then plummeted. In Mexico in 1995, the peso plunged and then recovered. In the 1997–98 Asian crisis, Indonesia's rupiah dropped by over 75% before gradually creeping back.

Even big exchange-rate shifts can be absorbed if they occur slowly. But if they happen quickly, financial markets are roiled, and at worst financial institutions are unable to cope with the strain. LTCM, a hedge fund, collapsed when interest rates suddenly shifted after Russia's default in the summer of 1998. If the dollar suddenly plunged, similar problems could arise.

The risk of a dollar crash and a subsequent financial meltdown are not negligible. Discussing the coming fall in the dollar, Mr Rogoff commented: "The world is set to jump off the top of a waterfall without knowing how deep the water is below."

Nonsense, say the optimists; just look at history. In the early 1980s, America's current-account deficit rose sharply. Policymakers, economists and journalists fretted about the prospect of a dollar crash. A book published in 1985, *Deficits and the Dollar*, by Stephen Marris, epitomised the mood. "On present policies a hard landing has become inevitable for the dollar and the world economy," Mr Marris argued. "The dollar will, over time, go down too far and there will be an unpleasant world recession."

The dollar did indeed go down, just as he had predicted, but there was no nasty recession. Can history repeat that feat?

Endnote

The dollar fell by almost 16%, in trade-weighted terms, from February 2002 to December 2004, but regained some ground in 2005. America's current-account deficit was expected to top $800 billion in 2005, nearly 6.5% of GDP.

The material on pages 69–86 was first published in *The Economist* in September 2003.

4
CHINA'S RISE

In 1792 the Qianlong emperor of China granted an audience to Lord Macartney, an envoy from Britain's King George III. The envoy, eager to secure better terms of entry into China's market, hoped to impress the emperor with various examples of Britain's produce – the early fruits of the industrial revolution. Neither his gifts nor his requests met with much success. "I set no value on objects strange or ingenious, and have no use for your country's manufactures," the emperor sniffed.

In its pomp, China treated the outside world with disdain. Now, the rest of the world views China with disquiet. If its emperors once flaunted their lack of appetite for foreign commerce, China's current rulers display a vast determination to succeed in foreign markets.

This change of attitude has recast the world economy. China's multitudes were once shackled to the land or indentured to a central plan. Now they are migrating to coastal cities, better to serve international markets. It is as if hundreds of millions of people had suddenly been added to the world's workforce: a new frontier of labour akin to the vast tracts of land opened up by the pioneers of 19th century America.

Multinational companies have been keen to plot and settle this new frontier: more than a quarter of China's exports are the result of joint ventures with foreign companies. The rest of the world's workers are less pleased. In economics, value derives from scarcity. The new abundance of unskilled labour will drive down its price, relative to capital and to skills, just as the cultivation of America's hinterland drove down the price of land relative to the other ingredients of production.

Those with most to fear are the weavers and garmentmakers of Bangladesh and the assembly-line workers of the Mexican *maquiladoras*. But it is America's workers whose complaints ring most loudly. Some of their congressmen, like Chinese emperors past, even want to raise barriers against the cheap and ingenious objects that ordinary Americans seem happy to buy.

The economic rivalry between China and America obscures a deeper "co-dependency", as Catherine Mann of the Institute for International Economics puts it. America buys China's goods; China buys America's debt. Their fates are locked together by China's decision to peg its currency to the dollar. As the greenback fell from the spring of 2002 to the end of 2004, the yuan fell with it. Americans complained that the yuan was too cheap, giving China an unfair competitive edge.

But to maintain its peg, in early 2006 about eight yuan to the dollar, China's central bank must stand ready to buy as many dollars as people can sell at that price. This is not without its costs. The inflow of dollars from exporters and from speculators sneaking past China's capital controls collects in the central bank's vaults, earning a miserable return. China passes up the opportunity to invest its savings at home, or to spend the dollars it earns on American goods, rather than American paper.

In centuries past, trade disputes with China were resolved with gunboats. The current arguments fall well short of that. But both sides of the dispute are worryingly self-absorbed. China's rulers have their own preoccupations – exports must grow at a fast enough pace to employ the legions of peasants leaving the land – and America's politicians have their own electoral calculations. The benefits of America's relationship with China – cheap goods and cheap credit – are less apparent to the voters than the costs – the hollowing out of American manufacturing. It is not clear that the two de facto rulers of the world economy will always have its best interests at heart.

The dragon and the eagle

American consumers and Chinese producers have led a global boom. China is creating genuine wealth, but America's binge is based partly on an illusion

THE WORLD ECONOMY grew by over 5% in 2004, its fastest pace in two decades. Growth was powered by two high-octane fuels: America's exceptionally loose monetary policy, which has encouraged consumers to keep spending; and an unprecedented investment boom in China. America and China together accounted for almost half of global growth in 2004. If American consumers and Chinese producers were to retreat at the same time, global growth could slump.

Until the Federal Reserve started to lift interest rates in June 2004, money had been cheaper than ever before, and not just in America: average short-term interest rates in the world's big economies were at their lowest in recorded history. Average real interest rates are still at their lowest since the high-inflation 1970s. By slashing rates to 1% after the stockmarket bubble burst, the Federal Reserve saved America from a deeper recession and the risk of deflation.

But inflation is now rising, so monetary policy needs to be tightened. How will the American economy – indeed, the world economy – fare if interest rates return to more normal levels of perhaps 4–5%? Super-low rates have encouraged consumer behaviour that will look a lot less sensible as interest rates rise. And to make things trickier, crude-oil prices have surged to new heights at the very time that the Fed has started to raise rates. Dearer money and dearer oil have already caused consumers to cut back.

Only a few years ago, the term "the world economy" was used as shorthand for the economies of the developed world; China would at best rate a brief mention. But now it is too big to ignore (see Chart 4.1 on the next page). It was largely thanks to China's robust growth that the world as a whole escaped recession after America's stockmarket bubble burst in 2000–01. But its recent boom is also responsible for much of the surge in global energy demand that has pushed up oil prices. China's massive purchases of American Treasury bonds explain why the dollar has not fallen further or bond yields risen more sharply – even though America's huge current-account deficit continues to widen. Last but not

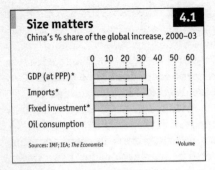

Size matters 4.1
China's % share of the global increase, 2000–03

GDP (at PPP)*
Imports*
Fixed investment*
Oil consumption

Sources: IMF; IEA; *The Economist* *Volume

least, many people blame the sickly state of America's jobs market on imports from China and on outsourcing.

China is home to one in five of the world's people, and has long been the most populous country on earth, but economically it has started to matter only recently. China's GDP already accounts for 13% of world output (at purchasing-power parity), second only to America's. By the end of 2004 China was the world's third-biggest exporter (after America and Germany). It is also the largest recipient of foreign direct investment as multinationals have moved operations to China to take advantage of its low labour costs and huge domestic market. It is the new workshop of the world, producing two-thirds of all photocopiers, microwave ovens, DVD players and shoes, over half of all digital cameras and around two-fifths of personal computers.

But China is not only a big new producer, it is also a big new market. Its imports grew by 40% in 2003, and from 2002 to 2004 it accounted for one-third of the total increase in world import volumes. China has become a locomotive for the rest of East Asia, accounting for half the total export growth of the other East Asian economies in 2003. Indeed, exports to China have played a big part in Japan's economic recovery. China's demand for commodities has also rocketed, driving up world prices.

If China sneezes

During 2004, China's policymakers tried to cool the economy, and there were signs that they were succeeding. Both investment and bank lending slowed quite sharply. But will the economy land gently or with a crash, as it did after the 1993–94 boom? A crash would dent growth in the rest of the world just when the Fed is raising interest rates.

Yet China's boom is itself partly the product of the Fed's super-lax monetary policy. With its currency pegged to the dollar, China has been forced to import America's easy monetary conditions. Its higher interest rates have attracted large inflows of capital that have inflated domestic liquidity, encouraging excessive investment and bank lending in some sectors which could lead to a bust. Fortunately the economy is not as overheated as it was in the early 1990s, when investment, credit and inflation were all growing much faster; and this time the authorities have acted sooner. But even if China can engineer a soft landing (which is generally defined as growth slowing to around 7%), growth in investment and imports of capital equipment and raw materials would slow much more severely, causing some global discomfort.

Some commentators liken China's boom to America's dotcom bubble in the late 1990s; but although investors have clearly got carried away, much of the exuberance about China is rational. The country's recent ups and downs are reminiscent of America's booms and busts during the period of industrialisation in the late 19th century. These did not prevent America becoming the world's economic giant, creating fast-growing markets for European goods. If China continues with its reforms, it will enjoy faster growth than America ever achieved. Within a decade it will probably be the world's largest exporter and importer, and one day it may overtake America as the world's largest economy.

That strikes fear in the heart of many businessmen and workers in rich countries. In America's presidential-election campaign, China has been widely blamed for America's "jobless recovery"; yet faster growth in China should mean faster rather than slower growth elsewhere too. China has a unique combination of a huge population and an economy that is unusually open to the rest of the world, as measured by trade or foreign direct investment. China's catch-up in income and its integration into the world economy could be the single biggest driver of global growth over coming decades. Indeed, China's boost to global growth could exceed the much-trumpeted gains from the IT revolution.

China's road to prosperity is not without risks and its economy may well stumble. But its future prospects remain excellent, built on genuine wealth creation as currently underemployed labour is put to productive use. In contrast, American consumers have been living in never-never land, financing their spending by borrowing against illusory gains in wealth.

Not as rich as you think

Economies can get truly richer only through increased productivity growth, either from technological advances or from more efficient production thanks to international trade. Thus China's integration into the world economy genuinely creates wealth. The same cannot be said of all the "wealth" produced by stockmarket or housing bubbles.

In recent years, many people around the world have found it easier to make money from rising asset prices than from working. Roger Bootle, the managing director of Capital Economics, a London consultancy, calls this "money for nothing". The surge in share prices in the late 1990s boosted the shareholdings of American households by $7 trillion over four years, equivalent to almost two years' income from employment – without requiring any effort. The value of those shares has since fallen, but the drop has been more than offset by soaring house prices. Since 2000 the value of homes in America has increased by more than $5 trillion, making many Americans feel richer and less inclined to save. But much of this new wealth is an illusion.

The first mistake, at the end of the 1990s, was to believe that shares were actually worth their quoted price. The second mistake, today, is to view higher house prices as increased wealth. A rise in share prices can, in theory, reflect expected future gains in profits. The stockmarket boom did reflect some genuine wealth creation in the shape of productivity gains, however exaggerated they may have been. But rising house prices do not represent an increase in wealth for a country as a whole. They merely redistribute wealth to home-owners from non-home-owners who may hope to buy in the future. Nevertheless the illusion of new-found wealth has caused households as a whole to save less and spend and borrow more.

Historically low interest rates have fuelled housing bubbles in America and many other countries around the globe. At some stage prices will fall, obliging consumers to save much more and spend less. The unwinding of America's vast economic imbalances could depress growth there for many years, whereas China's slowdown looks likely to be fairly brief.

Oddly enough, China may be partly to blame for this wealth illusion in rich economies, because central bankers have been slow to grasp the consequences of China's rapid integration into the world economy. By producing goods more cheaply and so helping to hold down inflation and interest rates in rich economies, China may have indirectly encouraged excessive credit creation and asset-price bubbles there. Inflation has remained low, but excess liquidity now flows into the prices of houses and shares rather than the prices of goods and services. And to keep its exchange rate pegged to the dollar, China has been buying vast amounts of American Treasury bonds, which has helped to depress bond yields and mortgage rates, fuelling America's property boom.

The integration of China's 1.3 billion people will be as momentous for the world economy as the Black Death was for 14th-century Europe, but to the opposite effect. The Black Death killed one-third of Europe's population, wages rose and the return on capital and land fell. By contrast, China's integration will bring down the wages of low-skilled workers and the prices of most consumer goods, and raise the global return on capital.

Some central banks, slow to grasp the effect of these structural changes on inflation and monetary policy, have been running overly loose policies that have fuelled unsustainable booms in America and some other economies. In the short term, therefore, China could make growth more volatile, but in the long term it will be a powerful engine of global growth. The Black Death is thought to have originated in China and spread to Europe through trade. This time China will export vitality to the world economy instead.

The real Great Leap Forward

If reforms continue, China's economy could sprint ahead for many more years

"LET CHINA SLEEP, for when she awakes she will shake the world," runs Napoleon's famous saying. He was ahead of his time, but now the dragon is certainly stirring. Since 1978, when Deng Xiaoping first set his country on a path of economic reform, its GDP has grown by an average of 9.5% a year, three times the rate in the United States, and faster than in any other economy. The official figures may slightly overstate the growth rate, but China is still likely one day to overtake America and become the world's number one economy.

In fact, China was the largest economy for much of recorded history. Until the 15th century, China had the highest income per head and was the technological leader. But then it suddenly turned its back on the world. Its rulers imposed strict limits on international trade and tightened their control on new technology. Measured by GDP per person it was overtaken by Europe by 1500, but it remained the world's biggest economy for long thereafter. In 1820 it still accounted for 30% of world GDP. However, by 1950, after a century of anarchy, warlordism, foreign suppression, civil war and conflict with Japan, its share of world output had fallen to less than 5% (measured in purchasing power, not at market exchange rates).

Now China is making up lost ground. Even if its economy slows sharply over the next few years, its long-term prospects remain bright. If rich economies want rapid economic growth they have to get it the hard way, by inventing new technology or adopting better management methods. But poor countries, at least in theory, should find it easier to grow fast because they start with low levels of income and capital per worker. With the right policies, they have huge scope to grow rapidly by importing capital, ideas and techniques from developed economies and using rich countries' markets as a springboard for growth. As a latecomer, China does not need to reinvent the wheel, but merely to open its economy to ideas from the rich world – which it has done with gusto.

Most of China's growth over the past quarter-century can be explained by high rates of investment and the movement of workers from subsistence farming, where their marginal productivity is close to zero, to more productive use in industry. But China's growth is not based simply on cheap labour: wages are lower in India and Vietnam. It also has the advantages of good infrastructure, an educated workforce, a high rate of saving available to finance investment and, most important of all, an extremely open economy. China's average tariffs have fallen from 41% in 1992 to 6% after it joined the WTO in December 2001, giving it the lowest tariff protection of any developing country.

Many non-tariff barriers have also been dismantled. Moreover, China has welcomed foreign direct investment, which has bolstered growth by increasing the stock of fixed capital and by providing new technology and management know-how. Joint ventures with foreign firms produce 27% of China's industrial output.

China faces many obstacles to growth: its fragile banking system, the lack of a transparent legal system, corruption, the risk of social and political unrest caused by widening income inequalities or the abuse of human rights, and severe environmental pollution. Yet if reforms continue, there are good reasons to believe that rapid growth can be sustained.

For example, there is still huge scope to increase productivity as workers move from rural occupations into industry. Over 60% of China's population still lives in the countryside, a much higher share than in Japan at the same stage of development. The steady shrinking of the state-owned sector will also boost productivity by ensuring a better use of resources. China's private sector, which now accounts for about half of its GDP, is growing twice as fast as the rest of the economy.

The main constraint on China's growth is its financial system's inability to allocate capital efficiently, with the associated risk of bad loans in the banking system. Some commentators fret that China's inefficient investment will soon drag down its growth rate, pointing out that China's incremental capital output ratio (ICOR – the increase in annual investment divided by the increase in GDP) has risen in recent years. This suggests that the country is having to plough in more money to generate the same amount of growth – ie, its return on investment has fallen. There certainly has been overinvestment in some sectors, such as cars, steel and property, and inevitably some projects will prove unprofitable. The financial system needs to be reformed to improve investment decisions. But as a measure of the return on investment in China, the ICOR is badly flawed.

First, Chinese government figures overstate investment; they include purchases of land rather than just showing value added, as GDP does.

Second, they are for gross investment, whereas a more meaningful measure would be net investment after depreciation and the writing off of poor-quality capital equipment in state-owned firms. On the basis of net investment, the ICOR has risen more modestly, in line with what happened in other Asian economies during industrialisation.

Lastly, a high level of investment is what you would expect, given China's rapid industrialisation and urbanisation, which requires massive infrastructure investment and residential construction. According to Hong Liang at Goldman Sachs, China's rising ICOR simply shows that the economy is at a stage of development where it needs to become more capital-intensive. In manufacturing, the ICOR has in fact fallen slightly.

The IMF reckons that, so long as structural reforms continue, notably in the banking sector and in state-owned enterprises, China should be able to sustain annual growth of 7–8% for at least another decade. At that pace, China's GDP, measured at PPP, would overtake America's before 2020, although its GDP per head would remain much lower. Measured at market exchange rates, it would take longer to top America's. A study by Goldman Sachs concluded that this might not happen until around 2040, although China could overtake Japan as early as 2016.

This forecast was based on realistic assumptions about the likely slowdown in capital accumulation and productivity growth as well as on demographic forecasts. It predicted a slowdown in China's annual real GDP growth rate to 5.5% for 2010–20, and only 4% after that. It also foresaw that over time China's real exchange rate would appreciate against the dollar in line with its faster productivity growth.

Goldman Sachs's forecast may be too cautious. A study by the IMF compares China's rapid integration into the world economy with similar developments in the past, for example when growth first took off in post-war Japan, and later in the East Asian newly industrialising economies, such as South Korea or Taiwan (see Chart 4.2). China has grown a little faster during the past 25 years than Japan or the East Asian newcomers during their first quarter-century of boom, but these economies then maintained rapid growth for a long time. Despite hiccups along the way, South Korea and Taiwan sustained average growth rates of almost 8% for four decades.

Growth rates inevitably slow as average income rises towards that of developed economies, but China's GDP per person is still well under a third of South Korea's and one-fifth of Japan's, so there is plenty of room

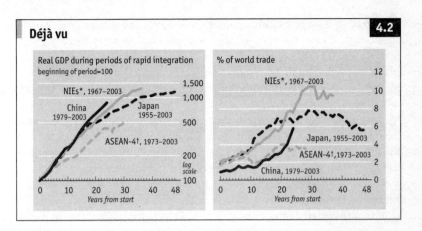

Déjà vu **4.2**

Real GDP during periods of rapid integration
beginning of period=100

NIEs*, 1967–2003

China 1979–2003

Japan 1955–2003

ASEAN-4†, 1973–2003

1,500
1,000
500
200
log scale
100

0   10   20   30   40   48
Years from start

% of world trade

12
10
8
6
4
2
0

NIEs*, 1967–2003

Japan, 1955–2003

ASEAN-4†,1973–2003

China, 1979–2003

0   10   20   30   40   48
Years from start

to catch up. China's share of world trade is also still lower than that of Japan or the combined trade of the East Asian tigers at a similar stage in their integration process, suggesting that China could continue to maintain rapid export growth for some years. For example, it currently accounts for 13% of all American imports, whereas Japan's share of the American market peaked at 22% in 1986.

Even if China's economic performance so far is not all that exceptional compared with that of its Asian forerunners, the country will almost certainly play a bigger future role in the world economy because of the sheer weight of its population. As China's income per head catches up, its economy will soon dwarf those of its Asian neighbours. How will the awakening dragon affect the rest of the world?

Endnote

China's economy grew by almost 10% in 2005, according to official estimates. It overtook France and possibly Britain to become the fourth biggest economy in the world in dollar terms.

A fair exchange?

China has helped to finance America's vast current-account deficit

UNTIL 2003 nobody seemed to care that the Chinese yuan was pegged to the dollar. But now China's exchange-rate regime has become one of the hottest topics in international finance – yet more evidence of China's growing influence on the world economy.

Many economists argue that China's fixed exchange rate distorts trade and investment flows. By refusing to allow its exchange rate to rise against the dollar, China, they say, is hindering the adjustment in global exchange rates needed to reduce America's current-account deficit, which stood at more than 5% of GDP in 2004. As a result of its pegged exchange rate and large capital inflows, China's foreign-exchange reserves have more than doubled since early 2002 to over $480 billion in 2004, most of it in American government securities. China is not alone: other Asian economies have also intervened heavily to prevent their currencies appreciating. But sooner or later, those economists say, China will lose its appetite for dollars, causing the greenback to tumble.

However, Michael Dooley, David Folkerts-Landau and Peter Garber at Deutsche Bank reject this view. In a series of papers, they argue that America's current-account deficit will be happily financed by China and other Asian countries for at least another decade. The present arrangements, they say, look rather like a revived Bretton Woods, the system of fixed exchange rates that prevailed for a quarter of a century after the second world war. Once again, America is at the centre of the system. The old periphery consisted of Europe and Japan, which used undervalued currencies, supported by capital controls and the purchase of dollar reserves, to rebuild their economies after the war. But the new periphery is made up of China and other Asian economies which, it is argued, also peg their currencies to the dollar at artificially low rates. These countries want to keep their exports competitive in order to create jobs for their vast pool of underemployed workers.

But will America accept the political costs of rising imports and job losses in manufacturing? The three Deutsche Bank economists argue that China compensates America in two ways. First, it allows foreign firms to invest in Chinese factories, using cheap labour to earn fat profits (which turns those firms into an effective American lobby to counter resistance to Chinese imports). Second, the Chinese government invests a large chunk of its export earnings in Treasury bonds, helping to finance America's current-account deficit. This keeps American interest rates low and so supports consumer spending. In essence, China is buying dollar assets to ensure that Americans can afford to keep buying its exports. The return on Treasury bonds is lower than the returns at home in China, but, according to Messrs Dooley, Folkerts-Landau and Garber, the Chinese government is prepared to pay that price to ensure export-led growth.

America and Europe used to enjoy a similar relationship. The main question mark was, and still is, over the willingness of the periphery to accumulate claims on America. As Jacques Rueff, a French economist, put it in 1965: "If I had an agreement with my tailor that whatever money I pay him returns to me the very same day as a loan, I would have no objection at all to ordering more suits from him."

A marriage of convenience

This view of Asia's relationship with America helps to explain why in recent years it has proved possible to finance America's large current-account deficit without a bigger rise in American bond yields or a bigger fall in the dollar. However, the authors' claim that this arrangement is in the mutual interest of both America and Asia is questionable, as is their conclusion that America can therefore continue to run a large current-account deficit for another decade.

For a start, it seems doubtful that a cheap yuan is part of China's long-term development strategy. Until 2002, China's trade-weighted exchange rate was being dragged up by the strong dollar. China even passed up an opportunity to devalue the yuan during the Asian crisis. A second problem with the theory is the assumption that China can control both its exchange rate and its inflation rate. If a country holds down its nominal exchange rate, its real exchange rate tends to rise through the effect of higher inflation, which blunts its international competitiveness in just the same way. Indeed, large capital inflows into China are currently creating excess liquidity and pushing up its inflation rate.

A third flaw is that in the original Bretton Woods system there was no real alternative to the dollar as a reserve currency. Today there is the euro, into which the Asians could diversify instead of holding dollars. And lastly, if China continues to run a large trade surplus with America and Europe while holding down its exchange rate, exporters may face mounting protectionism. The "revived Bretton Woods" may be a brief marriage

Value for money? `4.3`
Yuan, real trade-weighted exchange rate
2000=100

Source: J.P. Morgan Chase

of convenience, but there is a high risk of a messy divorce.

The marriage could prove particularly costly for America. In 2003 China and the rest of Asia financed over half of America's budget- and current-account deficits. This benefits America in the short term, but at the cost of allowing bigger imbalances to build up in the long term. The Asian central banks are masking market signals; America's current-account deficit reflects insufficient saving by households and an excessive budget deficit. Normally, investors would demand higher bond yields to compensate them for the increased risk, thereby giving the government a warning as well as an incentive to borrow less. But Asia's buying of Treasury bonds, with little regard for risk and return, is keeping yields artificially low, which makes pruning the budget seem less urgent. At the same time low interest rates prolong America's unhealthy consumer spending and borrowing binge.

James Carville, Bill Clinton's campaign manager, once said: "I used to think if there was reincarnation I wanted to come back as the president or the pope … but now I want to come back as the bond market. You can intimidate everybody." Thanks to the behaviour of Asian central banks, the bond market has lost its bark. It is subsidising rather than punishing American profligacy, allowing deficits to grow for longer. When the inevitable correction comes, it will be all the more painful.

True value

China's purchases of American bonds are clearly distorting financial markets, but how undervalued is the yuan? It is tricky to estimate the equilibrium exchange rate for a country that is undergoing massive structural change. The yuan was grossly overvalued in the 1980s and was then devalued several times. But between 1994 and 2001 its real trade-weighted index rose by 30% (see Chart 4.3). As the dollar declined from 2002, the yuan fell with it.

According to some observers, the rapid growth in China's exports proves that China's exchange rate is too low. In fact it proves no such thing: China's imports are growing equally fast. And although China has a big trade surplus with America, its overall trade surplus had virtually disappeared by the middle of 2004.

On the other hand, China's large surplus on its "basic balance" (the current-account surplus plus net inflows of foreign direct investment) and its rising foreign-exchange reserves suggest that in a free market the yuan would rise. But in the longer term, if China scrapped its capital controls, the yuan would probably fall as households diversified into foreign assets. Overall, therefore, the case for a big yuan revaluation is weaker than is commonly claimed.

American politicians shout the loudest for a yuan revaluation, but if it happened it would probably do little to reduce America's trade deficit. Few firms in America still make goods that compete directly with China. China's exports also have a high import content, so a rise in the yuan makes imported components cheaper, limiting the rise in export prices. According to a study by Lawrence Lau at Stanford University, only 20 cents in every dollar of Chinese exports to America reflect value added by domestic Chinese production, so even a 20% rise in the yuan against the dollar would increase the price of Chinese exports to America by only 4%.

Nevertheless, many economists think that the dollar does need to come down to help reduce America's current-account deficit, and China must play its part in that. Morris Goldstein, an economist at the Institute for International Economics in Washington, DC, reckons that the yuan is at least 15% undervalued. He feels that an appreciation on this scale would ensure both that China achieved an overall balance on its external payments (ie, it would run a current-account deficit sufficiently large to offset its underlying net inflow of capital) and that China bore its fair share of the adjustment in the dollar.

By itself a stronger yuan might make little difference, but it would encourage other Asian countries to revalue their currencies too. Asian currencies together account for 40% of the dollar's broad trade-weighted index. Unless they revalue, the euro will continue to bear the brunt of the adjustment in global current-account imbalances. Since mid-2001 the euro has risen by almost 50% against the greenback.

By far the strongest argument for a revaluation of the yuan is that it is in China's own economic interest. The dollar peg has, in effect, forced it to adopt America's super-lax monetary policy. Large capital inflows and rising foreign-exchange reserves have caused rapid growth in the money supply and bank lending as well as rising inflation. Excessive credit has fuelled over-investment and a property bubble, increasing the risk of yet more bad loans. The central bank cannot easily raise interest rates to cool down its economy, because that would attract more foreign money.

Moreover, an undervalued exchange rate, by subsidising exports, discourages investment in the non-tradable sector and cramps domestic consumption. A revaluation of the yuan would help to reduce China's reliance on exports as well as stemming the inflows of foreign money and allowing China to regain control of its monetary policy.

Easy does it

Until its shaky banking system has been stabilised, it would be foolish for China to open its capital account and let its currency float. That could risk massive capital flight and a banking crisis. Mr Goldstein instead suggests a two-stage currency reform. First, China would switch from pegging the yuan to the dollar to pegging it to a basket of several currencies, including the yen and the euro; its exchange rate would also be increased by 15% and its permitted trading band widened modestly to allow more flexibility. At a later stage, China could move on to liberalise capital flows and adopt a floating exchange rate.

Eswar Prasad, head of the IMF's Asia and Pacific department, disagrees. In a recent speech he argued that given the huge uncertainty about the correct level of the yuan, it made more sense to introduce greater exchange-rate flexibility for China as soon as possible rather than trying to settle on a particular exchange rate. A flexible exchange rate would help to buffer the economy against shocks. But greater flexibility should not be confused with fully opening up the capital account, which cannot safely be done yet. Indeed, says Mr Prasad, during the period of transition to a more flexible exchange rate, some capital controls might even need to be tightened to protect the banking system.

Whatever happens to China's exchange rate, it is clear that China is carrying increasing weight in international finance. Not only does America's monetary policy affect China, but increasingly China is affecting interest rates in America.

Endnote

China revalued the yuan in July 2005, but only by about 2%. Its trade surplus topped $100 billion in the 12 months to December 2005, and its foreign-exchange reserves stood at almost $820 billion by the year's end.

The material on pages 89–102 was first published in a survey in *The Economist* in October 2004.

5

THE UNDERACHIEVERS

Japan's economy, measured in dollars, is still much bigger than China's; and the 12 economies of the euro area, taken together, rival America's in size. But although they occupy space on the economic stage, the euro area and Japan offer relatively little to the plot. For years, both Germany, Europe's biggest economy, and Japan have stagnated. What growth they have enjoyed has trickled down from elsewhere. Neither are the engines of growth – the independent sources of demand – the world economy needs.

The third and fourth articles in this chapter explain how Japan's financial "crisis" became a way of life. What started out as an acute complaint – a sudden collapse of asset prices that hobbles firms and banks alike – became a chronic condition. The mistakes of the past were not written off, but repeated. Banks rolled over bad loans to ailing firms, starving healthy firms of credit. Firms hoarded workers, sparing their life-time employees from the rigours of unemployment, but also depriving new firms of a potential workforce.

For all its problems, Japan remains a wealthy country, enjoying admirable social calm. And after many years in the doldrums, the economy is now catching a fair wind. Its lost decade-and-a-half is best measured not by how bad things got, but by how much better they might have been. The third article calculates the billions of dollars of economic output that might have been produced had Japan resumed normal economic growth.

That waste is matched in the euro area, where 12m educated, able-bodied people lack work. Europe, though rich by world standards, is not so prosperous it can afford to squander over 8% of its labour force. The first article in this chapter condemns Europe's mass unemployment, but also cautions against a broader indictment of European capitalism. The contrast between a dynamic, boundlessly enterprising America and a hidebound, inefficient Europe is overdrawn, it says. The average American worker is not that much more productive than his European counterpart: output per hour is much the same. Americans are better off because more of them work, and they work longer hours.

The article speculates that American policymakers have a natural tendency to play up their economy's strengths, while Europeans dwell morbidly on their economies' flaws. Perhaps Europe's economic woes command more public attention because so many of them are laid at the state's door. In Europe, unskilled workers are wards of the state, subsisting on generous welfare benefits. In America, they are the silent working poor. In Europe, pensions are still overwhelmingly the state's responsibility: if the state fails to provide, Europeans take to the streets. Americans rely, to a much greater extent, on private pension schemes. If those funds disappoint, the pension-holder's disgruntlement is between him and the financial pages. You cannot take to the streets to protest against the Dow Jones Industrial Average.

The second article in this chapter describes one European attempt to lighten the burden the state must carry. Germany's "Agenda 2010" covered pensions, health-care and unemployment benefits among other things. It probably cost Gerhard Schröder the 2005 election. But Mr Schröder's replacement was a pro-business conservative, Angela Merkel. And even if Germany's political leaders cannot carry the cause of reform, Germany's companies are taking matters into their own hands. They have negotiated longer hours, for no extra pay, with their workforce. This wage restraint may have laid the foundations for a more optimistic future.

Japan and Germany, for so long bystanders of the world economy, both seem poised to become protagonists once again.

Mirror, mirror on the wall

America is widely admired as the beauty queen of the economic world. But the euro area's figures are more shapely than its reputation suggests

A S AMERICA'S ECONOMY has bounced back, the economies of the euro area still seem to be crawling along. This perception has reinforced pervasive gloom about continental Europe's economic future. A great deal has been written about America's superior performance relative to the euro area. But wait a minute: the widely held belief that the euro area economies have persistently lagged America's is simply not supported by the facts.

America's GDP surged by 5% in the year to the first quarter of 2004, while the euro area grew by only 1.3%. Europe's GDP growth has consistently fallen behind America's over the past decade: in the ten years to 2003 America's annual growth averaged 3.3%, compared with 2.1% in the euro area. Yet GDP figures exaggerate America's relative performance, because its population is growing much faster. GDP per person (the single best measure of economic performance) grew at an average annual rate of 2.1% in America, against 1.8% in the euro area – a far more modest gap.

Furthermore, all of that underperformance can be explained by a single country, Germany, whose economy has struggled since German reunification in 1990. Strip out Germany, and the euro area's annual growth in GDP per person rises to 2.1%, exactly the same as America's. Germany does represent around one-third of euro-area GDP, but still the fact is that economic statistics for the 11 countries that make up the other two-thirds look surprisingly like America's (see Chart 5.1 on the next page). (Were Britain part of the euro area, this effect would be even more striking.)

The most popular myth is that America's labour-productivity growth has outstripped that in the euro area by a wide margin. America's productivity has indeed quickened in recent years, but the difference between productivity growth in America and the euro area is exaggerated by misleading, incomparable figures. In America the most commonly used measure of productivity is output per hour in the non-farm business sector. This grew by an annual average of 2.6% over the ten

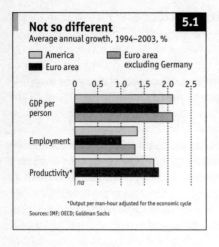

Not so different `5.1`

Average annual growth, 1994–2003, %

- America
- Euro area
- Euro area excluding Germany

GDP per person

Employment

Productivity*

*Output per man-hour adjusted for the economic cycle

Sources: IMF; OECD; Goldman Sachs

years to 2003. For the euro area, the European Central Bank publishes figures for GDP per worker for the whole economy. This shows a growth rate for the period of only 1.5%. But unlike the American numbers, this figure includes the public sector, where productivity growth is always slower, and it does not adjust for the decline in average hours worked.

Using instead GDP per hour worked across the whole economy, American productivity has risen by an annual average of 2.0% since 1994, a bit faster than the euro area's 1.7% growth rate. However, a study[1] by Kevin Daly, an economist at Goldman Sachs, finds that, after adjusting for differences in their economic cycles, trend productivity growth in the euro area has been slightly faster than that in America over the past ten years. Since 1996 productivity growth in the euro area has been slower than America's. But it seems fairer to take a full ten years.

But has not America combined rapid productivity growth with strong jobs growth, whereas continental Europe's productivity growth has been at the expense of jobs? This may have been true once, but no longer is. Over the past decade, total employment has expanded by 1.3% a year in America against 1% in the euro area. Again, excluding Germany, jobs in the rest of the euro area grew at exactly the same pace as in America. And since 1997 more jobs have been created in the euro area as a whole: total employment has risen by 8%, compared with 6% in America.

It is true that, during the past decade, productivity growth has accelerated in America, but slowed in the euro area. Alan Greenspan, chairman of America's Federal Reserve, blamed Europe's rigid labour and product markets. Structural barriers to laying off workers or to new methods of work may have prevented firms from making the best use of IT equipment.

However, there is another, less worrying reason why productivity growth has slowed in continental Europe. Reforms to make labour markets more flexible have deliberately made GDP growth more job-intensive. Firms now have more incentive to hire new workers, thanks to lower labour taxes for low-paid workers and a loosening of rules on hiring part-time and temporary workers, which allow firms to get around strict job-protection laws. The flipside is slower productivity growth for a period, as more unskilled and inexperienced workers enter the workforce. This is exactly what happened in America in the 1980s. In the longer term, more flexible labour markets should help to boost growth.

Another popular misconception is that the return on capital is much lower in the euro area than in America, because European business is inefficient and hobbled by high wage costs and red tape. This argument is often given in defence of America's large current-account deficit. America's higher return on capital, it is argued, attracts a net inflow of foreign money, so it has to run a current-account deficit. But according to calculations by Goldman Sachs, the return on capital in the euro area has actually been roughly the same as in America in recent years. The total return on equities over the past decade has also been broadly the same – which is what you would expect given their similar pace of productivity growth.

Nonsense in, nonsense out

So far we have established that, based on official statistics, productivity growth over the past decade has been virtually the same in the euro area as in America, and although GDP per person has grown a bit slower, the gap is modest. However, using official statistics can be like comparing apples with pears, because of differences in the way that GDP is measured in different countries. For example, American statisticians count firms' spending on computer software as investment, so it contributes to GDP. In Europe it is generally counted as a current expense and so is excluded from final output. As a result, the surge in software spending has inflated America's growth relative to Europe's.

A second important difference is the price deflator used to convert growth in nominal spending on information technology equipment into real terms. In America, if a computer costs the same as two years ago, but is twice as powerful, then this is counted as a 50% fall in price. Though logical, this is nevertheless a contentious issue among economists. Most euro area countries do not allow fully for improvements in computer "quality", so again official figures probably understate Europe's growth (in both GDP and productivity) relative to America. This reinforces the argument that the euro area has not been doing that badly.

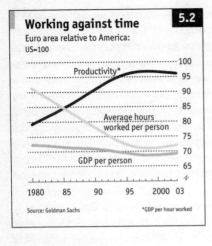

Working against time `5.2`

Euro area relative to America:
US=100

Productivity*

Average hours
worked per person

GDP per person

1980   85   90   95   2000   03

100
95
90
85
80
75
70
65

Source: Goldman Sachs   *GDP per hour worked

Despite such statistical quibbles, however, it is undeniable that the average person in the euro area is still about 30% poorer (in terms of GDP per person measured at purchasing-power parity) than the average American, and this gap has barely changed over the past 30 years. Thus even if income per person is growing at almost the same pace as in America, Europeans are still stuck with much lower living standards than Americans.

Olivier Blanchard, an economist at the Massachussetts Institute of Technology, offers a more optimistic view[2]. The main reason why the income gap has not narrowed, he argues, is that over time Europeans have used some of the increase in their productivity to expand their leisure rather than their incomes. Americans, by contrast, continue to toil long hours for more income. Who is really better off?

In fact, Europe's GDP per person is no longer lower than America's because its economies are much less productive. Average GDP per hour worked in the euro area is now only 5% below that in America; 30 years ago it was about 30% lower. GDP per hour in Germany and France now exceeds that in America. Income per person is higher in America largely because the average person there works more hours. In the euro area, fewer people work and those who do hold a job work shorter average hours. By one estimate the average American worker clocks up 40% more hours during his lifetime than the average person in Germany, France or Italy.

The narrowing of the productivity gap between America and the euro area over the past 30 years has not been reflected in a catch-up in the euro area's GDP per person because hours worked have fallen sharply. Compare France with America. Between 1970 and 2000 America's GDP per hour worked rose by 38% and average hours worked per person rose by 26%, so GDP per person increased by 64%. French GDP per hour rose by a more impressive 83%, but hours worked per person fell 23%, so GDP per person increased by only 60%. Chart 5.2 shows for the whole of the euro zone how its improvement in productivity relative to America has also been fully offset by a fall in hours worked.

If leisure is a normal good, then it is surely appropriate that demand for it increases in line with income. A broader analysis of living standards based on economic welfare rather than GDP should place some value on longer leisure time. The tricky question is whether the decrease in hours worked is due to employees' preference to take more leisure rather than more income, or due to distortions from maximum working hours, forced early retirement or high taxes.

Lovely leisure

Mr Blanchard's analysis finds that most of the fall in hours worked in Europe has been a result of a decline in average hours per worker (thanks to longer holidays or shorter working weeks), rather than a rise in unemployment or a fall in the proportion of the population seeking work. Furthermore, most of the reduction in average hours worked was because of full-time workers putting in shorter hours, not because of an increase in part-time workers who might not have been able to get full-time jobs. Mr Blanchard concludes that the fall in hours worked is mostly voluntary.

But that does not settle the matter. Perhaps Europeans choose to work fewer hours because of high taxes. Marginal tax rates have indeed risen by more in Europe than in America over the past 30 years. Taxes reduce the incentive to work an extra hour rather than go home, once a reasonable standard of living has been reached.

This is a hotly debated issue. A study[3] by Edward Prescott, an economist at the Federal Reserve Bank of Minneapolis, claims that virtually all of the fall in hours worked in the euro area can be blamed on higher taxes. But the flaw in this theory, says Mr Blanchard, is that within Europe there is little correlation between the fall in hours worked and the increase in taxes. Ireland has seen a 25% fall in average hours worked since 1970, despite an even smaller increase in tax rates than in America. Other studies have found that taxes have played a more modest role, accounting for about one-third of the fall in hours worked per person.

Mr Blanchard concludes that most, but not all, of the fall in hours worked over the past 30 years is due to a preference for more leisure as incomes have increased. Europeans simply enjoy leisure more. Americans seem more obsessed with keeping up with the Jones's in terms of their consumption of material goods. As a result, they may work too hard and consume too little leisure. Their GDP figures look good, but perhaps at a cost to their overall economic welfare.

Robert Gordon[4], an economist at Northwestern University, agrees that GDP comparisons overstate America's living standards, but he goes even further. America has to spend more than Europe, he says, on both heating and air conditioning because of its more extreme climate. This boosts GDP, but does not enhance welfare. America's higher crime rate means that more of its GDP is spent on home and business security. The cost of keeping 2m people in prison, a far bigger percentage of its population than in Europe, boosts America's GDP, but not its welfare. The convenience of Europe's public transport also does not show up in GDP figures. Taking account of all these factors and adding in the value of extra leisure time, Mr Gordon reckons that Europe's living standards are now less than 10% behind America's.

Flexing the macro-muscles

But even if the euro area has not lagged far behind America, does not its pathetic growth over the past few years bode ill for the future? Surely America's stronger rebound since the global economic downturn in 2001 is proof of greater flexibility in its economy? In fact, both suggestions are questionable. The main explanation for America's more rapid recovery is that it has enjoyed the biggest monetary and fiscal stimulus in its history. Since 2000 America's structural budget deficit (after adjusting for the impact of the economic cycle) has increased by almost six percentage points of GDP. Meanwhile, the euro area has had no net stimulus (see Chart 5.3).

American interest rates were also cut by much more than those in the euro area. Without this boost, America's growth would have been much slower. In other words, America's much faster growth of late may mainly be the result of looser (and unsustainable) fiscal and monetary policies, rather than greater flexibility.

While this might have been the right policy to support America's economy, it means that America's recent growth rate says little about its likely performance over the coming years. Indeed, the super-lax policies of the past few years have left behind large economic and financial imbalances that cast doubt on the sustainability of America's growth. From a position of surplus before 2000, the structural budget deficit (including state and local governments) stood at almost 5% of GDP in 2004, three times as big as that in the euro area. America had a current-account deficit of 5% of GDP, while the euro area had a small surplus.

American households saved little if any of their disposable income in 2004; the saving rate in the euro area stood at a comfortable 12%. Total household debt in America amounted to 84% of GDP, compared with only 50% in the euro zone.

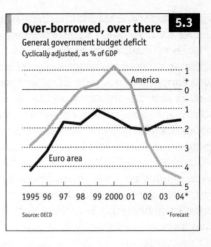

Over-borrowed, over there 5.3
General government budget deficit
Cyclically adjusted, as % of GDP

Source: OECD   *Forecast

America's recent rapid growth has been driven partly by a home-mortgage bubble. As interest rates fell and house prices rose, people took out bigger mortgages and spent the cash on a car or a new kitchen. House prices have also been lively in some euro-zone countries, with house prices rising at double-digit rates during 2004 in France, Italy, Spain and Ireland. But in general, households have not borrowed to the hilt against those capital gains. Some European policymakers hope that America's bubble will soon burst and that Europe could then sprint ahead. That may be wishful thinking: a sharp slowdown in American consumer spending is also likely to dent Europe's growth rate. It is true, however, that the eurozone's consumer finances are in much better shape.

So, America's superior economic performance over the past decade is much exaggerated. Productivity has grown just as fast in the euro area; GDP per person has grown a bit slower, but mainly because Europeans have chosen to take more leisure rather than more income; European employment in recent years has grown even faster than in America; and America has created some serious imbalances which could yet trip the economy up badly.

"Bullish on America"

Indeed, one might say that the economic performance of the euro zone and America has not been hugely different over the past decade, but that American optimism has disguised this. European policymakers are forever fretting aloud about structural rigidities, slow growth, excessive budget deficits and the looming pensions problem. In contrast, American policymakers love to boast about America's economic success while playing down the importance of its economic imbalances.

This does not mean that the euro area can be complacent. It still

111

needs to push ahead with structural reforms. Its average jobless rate of over 8% is too high. Contrary to the beliefs of many Americans, there has been labour- and product-market reform in continental Europe over the past decade, which is why employment has perked up. But unemployment remains a problem and, sadly, economic reforms now seem to have stalled in France and Germany.

The biggest snag, of course, is that because of its less favourable demographics, Europe has an older economy than America. With lower birth and immigration rates and an ageing population, Europe's labour force will soon start to shrink as a share of the population. That will make it harder for Europe to maintain its current pace of growth in GDP per person – and thus harder for governments to pay pension bills. Without faster growth, Europe will be unable to afford its welfare system.

If Europeans do not want to slip down the rankings of GDP per person in future, then they will need to work longer hours during their lifetimes. Alternatively, they may continue to attach more value to leisure and the quality of life, rather than hard cash. That is their choice. A truer picture of their economy might help them make it in an informed way.

Notes

1 "Euroland's secret success story", Goldman Sachs Global Economics Paper No. 102, January 2004.
2 "The economic future of Europe", NBER Working Paper No. 10310, March 2004.
3 "Why do Americans work so much more than Europeans?", Federal Reserve Bank of Minneapolis Research Staff Report 321, November 2003.
4 "Two centuries of economic growth: Europe chasing the American frontier", October 2002.

How to pep up Germany's economy

Germany needs to do much more than tinkering if it is to rescue its stalled economy

LIKE CHAIRMAN MAO, Gerhard Schröder has published a little red book. Nearly 6m copies of the German chancellor's colourful tract explain to the people how Agenda 2010, the economic reform process unveiled in March 2003, is supposed to be changing their lives. Health, education, labour, training, tax, social security, family welfare, unemployment benefit and pensions are distinct areas of reform. But they all form one glorious building site that should restore Germany to its rightful place as the most productive, most competitive country in Europe. "Germany", asserts the little book, "is on the move."

Well, no it isn't, says a frustrated business community from the Rhine to the Oder. From its position as the economic powerhouse of Europe, Germany has stumbled badly since reunification in 1990, and it is showing few signs of new momentum. Its GDP, once among the most dynamic in the European Union, has grown by a meagre annual average of 1.4% over the past decade, half the EU average and well below America's 3.3%. Only 4 of the EU's 15 members before enlargement on May 1st 2004 have a lower income per head. It says much about Germany's relative decline that it now relies on the much poorer accession countries to help lift it above the latest EU measure of average income.

One feature of Germany's stagnation is its poor record on jobs. Since 1993, the number of jobs in Germany has grown by only 0.2% annually, against a rate of 1.3% in the rest of the EU. Unemployment has been stubbornly high at around 4m. Many German businesses, especially those small and nimble enough to move elsewhere, are seriously considering relocation abroad. Even those bent on keeping their headquarters in Germany say they are likely to shift as much of their workforce abroad as they can.

In March 2004, Ludwig Georg Braun, the president of DIHK, the federation of chambers of commerce and industry, said firms should not wait for reforms to change things in Germany, but turn eastward to the accession countries joining the European Union on May 1st. Mr Schröder responded angrily, calling this exhortation an "unpatriotic act".

But why are businesses so urgently considering a move out of

Germany? Apart from the high level of taxation – the highest in Europe – the simple answer, and one not properly addressed by Mr Schröder or his Agenda 2010, is German labour law.

Germany will not truly be on the move until the rules on hiring and firing are radically altered. Yet Agenda 2010 does no more than tinker with them. Since the beginning of 2004, job protections have been loosened, but only by a little.

Software AG, a globally active firm based in Darmstadt, wanted to lay off around 200 staff at the end of 2003. The new rules certainly made it easier and the firm was quick to take advantage of them; but the lay-offs still took three painful months. In America the same exercise took two weeks, and in Britain four. "It is getting better," says Matthias Faust, Software AG's head of human resources. But when his company is back in hiring mode, where is it most likely to add staff? "Can I honestly advise the board to hire in Germany rather than in a country where it's easier to lay people off again?" he asks rhetorically. It is not just firing that is difficult: German labour relations are hedged about with troublesome rules.

At the core is the position of the workers' representative, the *Betriebsrat*. Co-determination between management and employees is a worthy principle which, in its 1960s heyday, helped to build strong German companies, maintaining harmony between workers and employers. But that was during Germany's *Wirtschaftswunder*, a period of high growth following the post-1945 reconstruction. Now the *Betriebsrat* has too much power, especially in smaller companies, including the right to determine how bonuses are distributed and to object to the relocation of an employee to Germany from abroad – including from EU member states.

Any company with five employees or more can be landed with a *Betriebsrat* if the workers decide they want one. "Can you imagine", says an employment expert, "the anxiety in a small law firm, with four staff and one part-time worker, about the implications of taking on another worker if one of them gets sick?"

A measure of its lack of radicalism, Agenda 2010 simply steers clear of the law that governs the *Betriebsrat*. On the first anniversary of its launch, business leaders were lukewarm about the achievements so far and said the reforms had not gone far enough. Heinrich von Pierer, chief executive of Siemens, said the direction was right, but "concrete steps" were needed to promote innovation and growth. Jürgen Hambrecht, head of BASF, a chemical firm, praised the direction too, but not the speed.

Corporate tax reform has been a stop-start process, leaving companies uncertain about future tax bills and benefits. The level of basic corporate tax is still the highest in western Europe, at 38.7%, compared with 35.4% in France, 34% in Austria (falling to 25% in 2005) and 12.5% in Ireland. There are many ways for companies to reduce this burden, but they tend to favour the larger firms. Cynics say that is because the architect of tax reform, Heribert Zitzelsberger, was previously head of the tax department at Bayer, a chemical giant.

For big companies Germany is a kind of tax haven, according to Lorenz Jarass, an economics professor at Wiesbaden University. In aggregate, the top 30 listed companies tend to get more credits back from the government than they pay in tax. For example, in 2002, Daimler-Chrysler reclaimed a net €1.2 billion ($1.5 billion), while the tax payments of Thyssen Krupp and Lufthansa netted out at zero. That sort of thing irks the smaller, *Mittelstand* companies, which insist they are the backbone of the German economy, employing 70% of the workforce, accounting for 46% of investment and creating 70% of all new jobs. There are fewer ways open for them to reduce their tax bills. The option of offsetting the previous year's losses against the current year's tax, for example, has been greatly curtailed since the start of 2004.

Every third German company now wants to locate at least part of its production in central Europe, says Heiko Stiepelmann, spokesman of the Building Industry Federation. His industry has been particularly hard hit. It has long been heavily supported by subsidies, such as those for building private homes. But since 1995 employment in the building industry has fallen from 1.4m to 814,000. Building firms are finding financing a problem for several reasons. Banks are reluctant to lend or give guarantees because of their own tougher capital regulations, while fierce competition means firms cannot raise prices, as they normally have done, to build capital coming out of a recession.

The pressure on them to cut costs and wage packets is immense. There is hardly a mid-size builder that does not employ foreign workers, says Mr Stiepelmann. Lower wage levels in the neighbouring eastern countries are a gathering threat. For the next few years firms from the ten accession countries may not set up shop in Germany, but this respite should not make German builders complacent. "Building firms must invest in the east as well," says Mr Stiepelmann. He argues that they cannot hope to compete on labour costs, but should play to their skills as "project and facility managers".

Tough talking

IG Bau, the building workers' union, is one of the few to understand the gravity of the situation. It did not even attempt a round of wage negotiations in 2004. Unions in other industries have been less co-operative. IG Metall, Germany's biggest blue-collar union, had a showdown in 2003 in eastern Germany. Although it was forced to back down, Jürgen Peters, its leader, retained enough credibility to be elected to another term. Mr Peters then negotiated modest wage increases throughout Germany, showing that unions remain a force to be reckoned with, at least among firms that are still unionised. In eastern Germany, union membership is declining.

The unions just do not understand economics, complains one German economist. They believe there is a finite number of jobs to go round and do not see that reducing a workforce or even locating operations abroad can make a company more competitive and thus able to create new jobs at home. Professional economists in general are frustrated by the government's handling of the reforms. This may partly be sour grapes: the Hartz Commission, established to reform the labour market and create new jobs, has sociologists on board but not a single economist.

If they had been included, economists might have offered a few useful observations, such as disabusing the unions' belief that wage hikes invariably stimulate demand. Baron Münchhausen, the legendary German braggard, once boasted that he rescued himself from a swamp by grabbing his own forelock and pulling himself out, followed by the horse he was sitting on. Michael Burda, an economics professor at Berlin's Humboldt University, uses this image to illustrate why Germany must shake off its illusions and reduce its labour costs. Workers in Germany earn an average of $26 an hour, compared with $21 in America and $17 in France and Britain. In neighbouring eastern Europe, where the German unions' stiffest competition lies, the average is around $4 an hour.

Unfortunately, Germany suffers from another economic affliction, claims Mr Burda. He cites William Baumol, an American economist, who pointed out in 1967 that productivity in services lags productivity in manufacturing, because most services, such as health care and teaching, are difficult to automate. So developed economies are spending an ever-increasing proportion of their wealth on services. In Germany, observes Mr Burda, productivity gains in services have been particularly sluggish.

One of the Hartz Commission's most dubious achievements was to revamp the Federal Agency for Jobs into a commercial-style operation that spent millions on publicity and flashy new premises. Its original boss, Florian Gerster, was fired in January 2004 for overspending on consultants. His high salary and flamboyant lifestyle did not sit well with the agency's poor record for getting people back to work, especially the long-term unemployed of whom Germany has proportionally more than rival big economies.

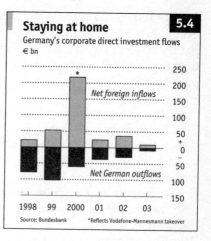

Staying at home 5.4
Germany's corporate direct investment flows
€ bn

Net foreign inflows
Net German outflows

1998 99 2000 01 02 03

Source: Bundesbank   *Reflects Vodafone-Mannesmann takeover

Ersatz employment

One much-trumpeted government measure has been the introduction of "mini-jobs", casual jobs that pay between €400 and €800 a month. These have attracted around 1m people. But Viktor Steiner of DIW, the German Institute for Economic Research in Berlin, has argued that these jobs are cannibalistic. They have tempted the young and the old out of full-time employment rather than attracting the long-term unemployed. Options to take early retirement or quit the labour market have been too cushy. From 2005, unemployment benefits will no longer last indefinitely, but will stop after a year – a long overdue change – and those who consistently refuse job offers will be penalised.

These areas of reform – unemployment benefit, mini-jobs, reallocating benefits and spending more on education and training – do not delight hard-nosed entrepreneurs. The last thing a cost-cutting company wants is to have to spend more on training and other welfare contributions that do not directly help its business. Yet the government has been dithering about whether or not to levy fines on companies that have not filled their training quota.

This vacillation, combined with sudden U-turns and a cacophony of conflicting proposals, characterises the government's approach to the reforms. For example Manfred Stolpe, minister for construction and transport, and the only east German in the cabinet, called for fresh efforts to enliven the labour market in the former East Germany with new wage subsidies. There was an immediate protest: surely the wage subsidies should be applied in the west as well? So Mr Stolpe extended the plan to cover the entire country, a hugely backward step. The last thing Germany needs are new, expensive wage subsidies which will have to be paid for by those already in employment.

Despite years of public discussion about labour-market reforms, the truth is that the debate has sadly lost sight of the basic obstacles to economic recovery:

- European economic and monetary union in January 1999, although enthusiastically endorsed by Germany, has robbed it of the means to adjust interest rates and exchange rates to optimise its own economic recovery.
- Reunification with East Germany has been colossally expensive, costing €1.25 trillion since 1990, and still consuming 4% of GDP in transfers, with the added burden of 20% unemployment in the region.
- The country's federal power structure, spread over 16 independent *Länder*, was deliberately designed after the second world war to weaken the ability of a central government to impose radical reform, and it is proving all too effective.
- The country's cumbersome and expensive labour laws are a crippling anachronism in a globalised, service-driven and high-tech world economy.

Money in, jobs out?

There are a few mildly optimistic voices to be heard. German businessmen, like farmers, tend to talk doom and gloom, says David Marsh, managing director at Droege, the consultancy. He argues that they never expected much from Mr Schröder's reforms and have been pleasantly surprised even by what little has been achieved. Investment flows in and out of Germany paint a less than gloomy picture, he says. The net capital flow is positive, which means more corporate and portfolio investment is coming in than going out (see Chart 5.4 on the previous page). However, the sums are modest compared with the flows in and out until 2002 – especially after discounting the €180 billion purchase of Mannesmann by Vodafone in 2000. Nevertheless, non-German private-equity firms continue to buy and restructure German companies, seeing value in them despite their location. Indeed, Mr Marsh believes that many German companies today are undervalued.

A few companies are defying Germany's reputation and are quietly investing in a German-based future. AMD, an American chip manufacturer, is building a second plant in Dresden at a cost of about €2 billion.

While AMD has laid off 2,000 people worldwide, it managed to keep up its numbers in Dresden, though it put some workers on short-term contracts. "The Saxons are a highly flexible people," says Hans Deppe, head of AMD's Dresden operation. That includes local authorities, which have been quick to approve and support investment plans. BMW, a successful carmaker, is building a new €1.3 billion plant in Saxony.

But these are exceptions. Most business people simply long for the government to get on with it, as Margaret Thatcher did in Britain in the 1980s. However, that would be very un-German. Modern Germans, it seems, are prepared to put up with a great deal before endorsing an abrupt change of direction. The post-war consensus model remains robust, even if the German economy no longer is.

Endnote

Gerhard Schröder's Social Democrats narrowly lost the September 2005 election to Angela Merkel's Christian Democrats (and its sister party, the Christian Social Union). Both sides formed a "grand-coalition" government under Ms Merkel, which turned its attention to Germany's public finances, not its labour laws.

Kill or cure?

Japan's comatose economy may be about to revive

ALTHOUGH JAPAN'S ECONOMY is still the world's second-biggest, outsiders pay little attention to it, since the country contributes so little to global growth. Between 1997 and 2002 – after half a decade of stagnation had already passed, and long after the stock- and property-market bubble had collapsed – Japan's economy actually shrank in nominal terms, from ¥523 trillion ($4.3 trillion) of annual output to ¥500 trillion. Even if it had grown an exceptionally modest 2% a year in nominal terms during that period, it would be 16% bigger now. Cumulatively, it would have generated roughly ¥78 trillion, or more than $650 billion, of additional output.

That staggering sum is several times the estimated cost of rebuilding Iraq, and more than all the rich countries between them spend on defence. Japan's lost $650 billion or so, moreover, is far more wasteful than money that has merely been spent for one bad purpose (rice subsidies) rather than a better one (alleviating poverty). It is potential output that was never produced, which means that nobody, rich or poor, will ever spend it on anything.

Many pundits assume that growth can no longer be revived, or not for several more years. They are wrong. To see why, start with a quick look at recent indicators. GDP has perked up a bit. From April to June 2003 it actually grew at a 3.9% annual rate, after adjusting for falling prices; even nominal GDP grew during the quarter, at a 1.2% annual rate. Cost-cutting by Japanese companies, combined with low profit margins to begin with, has allowed small increases in sales to generate big jumps in earnings. Operating profits at large firms rose by 17.3% in the fiscal year that ended in March 2003, and have continued to look strong since. Japanese companies have, in turn, been investing some of those higher profits in new machinery and other equipment, giving a fillip to domestic demand.

Pundits either read these signs as evidence that this is a great time to jump into shares (the stockmarket, driven partly by global factors, has risen 38% since April; see Chart 5.5); or they dismiss it as yet another false dawn for Japan's economy, the latest in a series. Yet this debate obscures a simpler observation: that some market forces are still at work in Japan. Price opportunities still lead to bouts of capital spending, and price expectations affect demand. The latest blips on Japan's monitor may be confusing and weak, therefore, but they serve as a reminder that the patient is still alive – and might, with the right treatment, walk again on its own two feet.

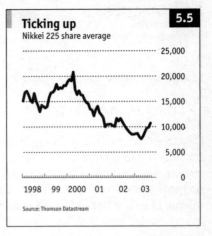

Ticking up 5.5
Nikkei 225 share average

Source: Thomson Datastream

First, diagnose

So what exactly ails Japan? Clearly not just the usual sort of business downturn, which can be cured, though painfully, with lay-offs and closures and sometimes with a government shot in the arm. Nor can its chronic weakness be attributed solely to a burst bubble and falling asset prices, though that is clearly part of the problem. Many other countries have been similarly stricken, and have managed to recover. In Japan, the misery has lasted for 14 years.

The Economist would like to suggest its own label for Japan's illness. It is "dysflation": a form of deflation in which dysfunctional economic-policy institutions counteract what would otherwise be good medicine for falling prices. The policies, especially with regard to banks, combine in ways that do more harm than good. More important, policymakers themselves are more inclined to avoid problems than address them; would rather win bureaucratic feuds than co-operate; and base most of their decisions on emotion (such as fear of shame) rather than reason.

It helps to keep all these aspects of dysflation in mind when assessing Japan's problems. Consider, for example, the Bank of Japan. Ordinarily, the best response to deflation – that is, falling prices throughout the economy, and not merely for a few products such as Chinese manufactures – would be lower interest rates and feverish printing of money. Japan has had zero interest rates since 1999, however, and has been boosting the money supply at a rapid clip since early 2001 – and prices have continued to fall. According to the most respectable measure, the GDP deflator, they fell by over 7% from 1997 to 2003, and are still dropping fast. Eventually, all the money that the bank has been printing will be sucked through the financial system and expelled into the economy

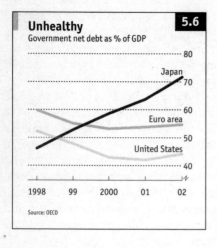

Unhealthy `5.6`
Government net debt as % of GDP

80

Japan
70

60
Euro area

50
United States

40

1998   99   2000   01   02

Source: OECD

in the form of higher prices and rising nominal interest rates. But it is taking a perplexingly long time to happen.

The bank's explanation is that Japan's deflation is a very rare strain indeed. It points to the large quantity of non-performing loans that have piled up in the banking system. Never in the history of human endeavour have so many owed so much for so long. And as the bank's officials like to point out, new bad loans, at least until recently, continued to accumulate faster than the banks were writing off old ones, and the Financial Services Agency (FSA), which regulates banks, has done nothing to stop this. Banks are lending mainly to their worst borrowers; and with the credit channel not operating properly, the usual monetary-transmission mechanism cannot work either.

There is probably some truth in this argument. What it ignores, however, is the overarching role that expectations – of firms, workers, consumers and investors – play in transmitting the central bank's policies into rising or falling prices, and the need for the central bank to manage those forecasts. The Bank of Japan has not only failed utterly in this role, but has refused to take responsibility for trying.

Under the previous governor, Masaru Hayami, whose term began in 1998, every constructive policy that the bank undertook was undermined by a statement that the bank did not really expect its policy to get prices rising again, at least not quickly. This had a sort of reverse placebo effect. Even as the central bank was administering potent medicine, Mr Hayami said that it was only doling out sugar cubes. A new governor, Toshihiko Fukui, took over in March 2003, and has been an improvement. Conceivably he will do a better job than Mr Hayami of convincing people that all that loose money will not be vacuumed up again at some point by the bank.

More government spending?

Since the Bank of Japan is independent, there is not much Mr Koizumi can do about this. Having appointed Mr Fukui, monetary policy is now out of his hands, and the best he can do is co-ordinate more effectively with the central bank. Most of Mr Koizumi's efforts should probably be devoted towards the most harmfully dysfunctional bits of economic policy: ie, those that are preventing the bank's loose money from generating the inflation that Japan so badly needs.

This may shed some light on arguments over fiscal policy. The case against spending more money seems simple. Japan's public debts have risen sharply over the past decade, and its gross debts, as measured by the IMF, reached 158% of GDP at the end of 2002. The main international rating agencies have downgraded Japanese government debt several times over the past few years. The most visible aspect of Japanese fiscal spending, moreover, is the LDP's addiction to public-works projects, which benefit the party's friends in the construction industry and deliver largesse to small rural districts. Such projects – dams, bridges and roads to nowhere – have continued to get media attention.

Mr Koizumi and his supporters have drawn two conclusions from this. First, they argue, fiscal spending has been tried and has not worked. Second, they say, Japan's debt has now risen to the point where more fiscal spending will merely aggravate the problem by raising the future debt burden, perhaps even harming confidence now. When Mr Koizumi took over as prime minister in April 2001, he pledged to limit new public debt issues to ¥30 trillion a year. Even though he broke that pledge – government bonds increased by over ¥35 billion in 2003 – he is still against more public-works spending. He pledged to privatise Japan's four public-highway corporations, and arranged public hearings on their profligacy and influence-peddling.

On further inspection, however, Mr Koizumi's arguments are not as compelling as they appear. For one, Japan's high debt ratios, taken in isolation, do not shed much light on whether more borrowing is a good idea. The gross government-debt ratio ignores many of the offsetting assets of the social security system, as well as many liabilities held by other public-sector outfits. The IMF reckons that net public debt came to around 72% of GDP at the end of 2002, less than half the gross figure. That is still a high number, of course. And high debt levels should especially worry Japan: since its population is projected to be the world's oldest by 2025, it will soon have to face a massive deficit in its pension system.

Indeed, Japan's problem is not so much its current debt as its future expected liabilities, many of which are being exacerbated by a looming demographic crunch and poor growth. Low growth is the main reason that Japan's debt ratios have deteriorated so badly over the past few years. In 2000–02, for example, tax revenues fell from ¥50.7 trillion a year to ¥43.8 trillion, mainly because of weak demand. The best way to look at Japan's budget, therefore, is to ask whether it is promoting or helping growth. On this question, Mr Koizumi is on weak ground.

It is an exaggeration to say that Japan has exhausted the possibility of using fiscal stimulus to solve its problems. It may have borrowed a lot of money, but much of that borrowing goes towards debt-service payments and social-security transfers, which do not stimulate the economy. Studies by Adam Posen, of the International Institute for Economics in Washington, DC, and several others suggest that when Japan has tried a little stimulus over the past decade it has had an effect. And the fiscal contraction caused by a rise in the consumption tax in 1997 was one of the main reasons why a previous budding recovery ended in a bust.

Dealing with the zombies

The question that Japan should be asking, therefore, is not so much whether to spend money, but where. Public-works projects probably help the economy somewhat more than Mr Koizumi and his supporters claim. However, the best use of money would be to tackle the most dysfunctional aspects of dysflation head on. That means doing something about bad loans.

Mr Koizumi is right to focus attention on this problem. So is his main economic-policy minister, Heizo Takenaka, who in 2002 was given a second cabinet-level post overseeing the FSA. Mr Takenaka's headline policy, of requiring banks to dispose of their non-performing loans much more quickly, made him the chief target of Mr Koizumi's opponents.

Bad loans are not just a result of Japan's slump, but a mechanism that is helping to prolong it. Anil Kashyap, an economist at the University of Chicago's business school, reckons that by keeping so-called "zombie" companies alive, rather than letting them die a natural death, the banks and their regulators are allowing too great a burden to fall on more productive companies. Otherwise healthy firms face higher real wages, lower prices and other distortions as a result of this warped competition.

Many of Mr Takenaka's critics complain that writing off more bad loans will lead to more bankruptcies and unemployment. If Mr Kashyap, and many others, are correct about the effects of the zombies, however, then writing off their loans will actually foster the creation of new companies and more productive jobs, as well as boosting output. Since new firms are more likely to hire young workers, there would also be long-run productivity gains. More youngsters would be working in interesting jobs and developing their skills, rather than doing nothing, as too many are now (see Chart 5.7).

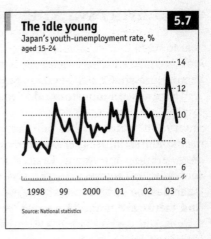

The idle young
Japan's youth-unemployment rate, %
aged 15-24

Source: National statistics

So if generating growth is more important than shrinking the budget deficit, and if the mountain of bad loans is hampering growth, why doesn't Mr Koizumi use government money to help the banks write off bad loans faster? That, alas, is not something he has been willing to countenance. In May 2003, the government used some money to rescue a big regional bank, Resona, which suddenly found itself with too little capital on its books. Mr Takenaka's main approach to the banks, however, has been to encourage them to write off loans faster, while presenting them with inconsistent incentives that do not really encourage them to rush.

The best way to cure the patient would be to spend the money now and do the job properly. More money for a social safety net, as the Democrats advocate, might also help to ease the transition as bankruptcies and lay-offs increase and raise unemployment. Haruo Shimada, an academic economist and informal adviser to Mr Koizumi, has summed it up nicely: "If you want to do radical surgery, you need to set aside a big enough supply of blood."

Endnote

Japan grew by 2.9% in the year to the third quarter of 2005 and deflation abated: "core" consumer prices, which exclude fresh food, even rose by 0.1% in the year to December 2005.

Dead firms walking

Japan's unproductive service industries are holding back its improving economy from achieving even better performance

FOR A COUNTRY THAT BOASTS some of the best manufacturers in the world, Japan's service sector remains strikingly poor. In recent years precious little has been done to improve things – businesses and individual consumers must struggle with outdated and inefficient services. Yet the sector represents a huge opportunity for Japan. Reformed and galvanised, it could take up the slack of future economic slowdowns and lessen the burden on export-led manufacturing. Why are service industries so backward and what might be done to improve them?

For more than a decade after a financial crisis in 1989 plunged once-booming Japan into a long period of slow growth, weak companies and wobbly banks clung to each other in mutual defiance of reality. Troubled borrowers needed the banks to overlook their problems and keep open the flow of money; the banks, too short of capital to admit that their loans had soured, obliged. Over time, this led to the emergence of so-called "zombies" – companies that are competitively dead, but, sustained by their banks, continue to walk the Earth and give healthier firms nightmares. And zombies are most prevalent in the service sectors of the economy, especially construction, property and wholesale and retail distribution.

The unholy alliance between zombies and banks has proved one of the most durable, distorting and debilitating compacts in modern economic history. It has set Japan apart from other countries stricken with financial crises and greatly prolonged its economic suffering. Lately, however, there are signs that things are changing.

Consider, for example, the story of a dysfunctional duo that has been hogging Japan's headlines: UFJ Holdings and Daiei. UFJ is a troubled megabank that has gone to great lengths to avoid facing its problems. It received a dose of reality in 2004, when regulators discovered a brazen attempt by UFJ managers to mislead them about the state of its loans. In order to put its books in better order, UFJ agreed to merge with Mitsubishi Tokyo Financial Group (MTFG) – Japan's best-capitalised megabank. But it has also done something almost unprecedented: it has threatened to call time on its worst debtors, including Daiei, Japan's third-biggest retailer and UFJ's biggest bad debtor. The parties have now turned against each other. And that marks a welcome, and potentially decisive, change in Japan's traditional way of doing things.

Although Japan's economy is enjoying an impressive cyclical rebound, such a change is sorely needed. Since the bubble burst in 1989, Japan's previous upturns have followed a familiar and frustrating pattern. While exports and overseas manufacturing earnings, led by strong global firms such as Toyota and Canon, gave a temporary fillip to growth, much of the service sector remained bogged down by debt, depressed confidence and widespread inefficiency.

That could still happen again. Overall growth has already begun to slow. And even if exports continue to stimulate manufacturing growth, manufacturers – which now account for less than half of Japan's output – can no longer carry an inefficient ¥500 trillion ($4.5 trillion) annual economy on their back. If Japan's service firms are to contribute to a lasting recovery, they must boost their efficiency, improve convenience for Japanese consumers and seek out higher profit margins.

It is hard to think of a single non-manufacturing sector in which Japan excels. High domestic transport costs hinder distribution, travel and tourism. A lack of competition in energy and telecoms keeps business costs high. Professional services, such as law and accountancy, remain hidebound. Health care, a crucial sector for a country that is ageing rapidly, has shamefully low levels of productivity by international standards. Consumers of many basic services, from finance to fitness, routinely encounter inefficiency and inconvenience. Above all, says Richard Jerram of Macquarie Securities, Japan conspicuously lacks "that American feeling that if you don't want to do it yourself, you can pay somebody to do it for you".

The most abysmal service sectors over the past decade have been those at the core of the banks' bad-debt woes: construction, property and distribution. To some extent, this is natural. Sectors that get hit hard by an economic shock will end up littered with firms that cannot repay debts. In Japan, however, the problem has gone far beyond that. During financial crises elsewhere bankers typically stop lending to unviable borrowers. Japan allowed the zombies to emerge.

Daiei of reckoning

The archetypal zombie is Daiei. Throughout the miserable 1990s the company simply avoided its problems. Its inefficient retail operations range from supermarkets to clothing and household goods, and many of its giant stores lease space to dozens of its smaller, unprofitable subsidiaries. Daiei conspicuously lacks focus: it keeps chains of restaurants and hotels in its stable, along with a baseball team.

Daiei was bailed out in 2001 and 2002. Yet both times its lenders seemed more interested in relabelling Daiei as a healthy borrower than in pressuring it to fix its problems. They allowed it to leave its ill-fitting array of businesses intact. Two years later, Daiei was still carrying ¥1 trillion of debt, ¥400 billion of which it owed to UFJ.

Compare Daiei's behaviour with that of Aeon, Japan's biggest retailer. Motoya Okada, Aeon's president, says that his company and its rivals can no longer hide behind the regulations and maddening business practices that used to frustrate big foreign rivals. Since zoning restrictions were relaxed in the 1990s, a few global retailers, such as America's Wal-Mart, Britain's Tesco and France's Carrefour, have taken their first tentative steps in the Japanese market. Mr Okada's biggest challenge over the next few years, he says, will be managing the tension "between how much time we will need to become competitive, and how much time global retailers will need to understand Japanese consumers and the market."

A few years ago, therefore, Aeon began to cut off inefficient wholesalers and streamline its logistical system. In some cases, it has done this by taking shipments directly from manufacturers, just as Wal-Mart does. Aeon started with a handful of suppliers: unsurprisingly, two of the first to co-operate were Japanese subsidiaries of western consumer-goods companies, Procter & Gamble of America and Unilever of the Netherlands. By 2004, Aeon had similar arrangements with over 40 companies. Although Aeon continues to use wholesalers rather than direct delivery for many of its products, it is trying to boost its wholesale suppliers' efficiency by working with fewer of them on a bigger scale.

Aeon's next-biggest rival, Ito-Yokado, is also in a hurry to raise its game. It is copying the global giants by learning more about consumers' buying patterns, designing new foods that grab their tastes and delivering them to its supermarkets and convenience stores when and where they are needed. If Japanese retailing is to have any hope of becoming a healthy and profitable sector, firms like Aeon and Ito-Yokado will have to build on these initial efforts and drive their suppliers and competitors to adapt along with them or exit the business. It is hard for that to happen, however, when companies such as Daiei continue to exist only thanks to over-generous banks.

In retailing, property, construction and other zombie-laden sectors, it is the losers that have held the upper hand, forcing the winners to follow their lead. Research by Alan Ahearne of America's Federal Reserve and Naoki Shinada of the Development Bank of Japan found that productivity growth in the 1990s was exceptionally low in sectors that had lots of

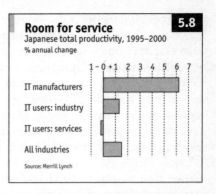

Room for service 5.8
Japanese total productivity, 1995–2000
% annual change

IT manufacturers	
IT users: industry	
IT users: services	
All industries	

Source: Merrill Lynch

firms with non-performing loans. Even more damagingly, resources consistently flowed in the wrong direction within those sectors, with the least efficient firms gaining market share at the expense of healthier ones.

Research by Anil Kashyap of the University of Chicago's business school and others suggests that misdirected investment is the main culprit. In one poor-performing sector after another, the firms with the most bad loans increased their investments at the expense of healthier competitors. The zombies' twisted relationship with Japan's broken banks is clearly at the centre of this problem. Mr Kashyap shrewdly likens competing with zombies to trying to make money in a sector dominated by state-run firms. The zombies have been propped up by banks that were in turn given unjustified leeway by accommodating regulators. The bill will one day land on taxpayers' doorsteps.

Such distorted competition has hurt Japan's service sectors in countless ways. Perhaps most important, the tendency to prop up weak firms has held back investments in information technology, one of the best ways in which service firms can boost productivity (see Chart 5.8). Some of the most successful retailers in Japan over the past few years have been convenience-store operators such as Seven-Eleven Japan (owned by Ito-Yokado) and Lawsons, which make far better use of IT than the country's supermarkets and department stores. In 2003 Wal-Mart took a stake in Seiyu, another troubled retailer, since when it has invested heavily in IT. Many of Seiyu's stores now have advanced inventory and point-of-sale tracking systems. Employees no longer have to run to the back room to print out lists of goods that are in stock.

Back from the dead?

Dealing with Daiei and the other zombies is crucial to reviving retailing and other long-depressed sectors. But there have been encouraging signs. Japan's financial regulators have begun to force the biggest banks to assess their loan books more honestly and tackle more of their bad loans. Three of Japan's four remaining megabanks – Mizuho, MTFG and SMFG – issued sizeable chunks of equity in early 2003 and have used their stronger capital bases to make far greater strides than UFJ in cleaning up their bad loans. A profit-driven economic recovery has also allowed many marginal borrowers to regain solvency. Moody's Investors Service, an international rating agency, upgraded the credit ratings of 38 Japanese firms in the first nine months of 2004, while downgrading only three.

In the equity markets, too, there has been a gradual improvement. As their cross-shareholding ties have wound down, Japanese companies are under more pressure from independent shareholders to boost returns. This has led many of them to jettison business partners that are not helping their bottom line. David Marra, a consultant at A.T. Kearney in Tokyo, reckons that competitive forces are even stirring up the sleepy world of distribution. He points out that five of the world's ten-biggest retailing mergers in 2003 took place in Japan.

In a range of other service sectors, too, more competition, faster asset restructuring and slightly more openness to foreign direct investment are driving the adoption of commonsense business practices. In telecoms, Softbank, an information-technology firm that includes a broadband internet service and the Yahoo! Japan web portal, has declared a price war against NTT, the former telecoms monopoly. In May 2004, Masayoshi Son, Softbank's founder, bought the fixed-line assets of Japan Telecom from Ripplewood, an American private-equity fund that had acquired the assets in 2003 in a ¥260 billion leveraged buy-out, Japan's biggest ever. Mr Son announced that he would begin offering new discounted fixed-line rates, in a direct attack on the former monopoly's highly priced service.

Even in financial services, the banks are waking up to the need to seek out better business lines and boost profits. The big banks have been teaming up with consumer-finance outfits, for example, which offer better prospects than their moribund corporate-lending businesses. Still, Japan's banks remain woefully unprofitable. It is no coincidence that two of the most successful have been Shinsei Bank and Aozora Bank, both bought and turned around by foreign private-equity firms.

Aiming to serve

Japan's decision-makers also face a huge challenge among regional banks, many of which remain fused to their zombie borrowers. Here, the government has barely begun to employ the same combination of tough bank regulation and recapitalisation that has worked so well at the big banks. Regional banks tend to have bad loans from a range of small companies on their books. Although profits at small companies have begun to rise (see

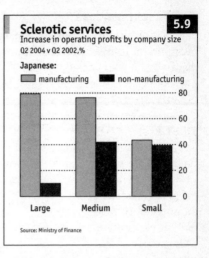

Sclerotic services 5.9
Increase in operating profits by company size
Q2 2004 v Q2 2002,%

Japanese:
manufacturing   non-manufacturing

Source: Ministry of Finance

Chart 5.9), buoyed by the latest recovery, the process of gradually weeding out the weakest firms and forcing them to merge or shut down altogether could be lengthy.

Given Japan's ageing and wealthy population, the provision of better services could be a huge growth industry. Japan could conceivably at last contemplate the kind of virtuous cycle that would help it achieve long-run growth. As its service sectors expand and adopt better practices, they can begin delivering the sorts of convenient services that allow people to live – and work – more flexibly. Some of those people, including many retirees and homemakers, might then be freed up to join the labour force or work more hours, giving a further boost to the service sector. What holds for labour is equally true for capital, which can be redirected from inefficient domestic sectors to creative entrepreneurs who figure out how to offer a better deal to consumers.

In the end, those sorts of mutually reinforcing ties will prove to be far healthier and sustainable than the dysfunctional relations that have bound banks and zombies together. The bust-up at UFJ and Daiei? It is an early skirmish in the battle for Japan's economic future.

Endnote

UFJ and MTFG completed their merger in 2004, becoming the world's biggest lender by assets. Daiei received yet another dollop of financial aid, closed scores of stores and cut staff. It even turned a profit in the year to February 2006. In September 2005, Junichiro Koizumi, Japan's prime minister, fought and won an election on the single issue of privatising (eventually) Japan's postal system, which doubles as a financial institution and must count as one of the biggest service companies of them all.

The material in this chapter was first published in *The Economist* in June 2004 (pages 105–12), May 2004 (pages 113–19), September 2003 (pages 120–5) and September 2004 (pages 126–32).

PART 3

THE ARTERIES OF CAPITALISM

6

FINANCE

Wall Street in New York and "the City" of London are two of the most recognised landmarks in the geography of capitalism. But precisely what goes on there remains a little mysterious to non-natives. Fortunes are secured and squandered within a few city blocks, but what is it exactly that these world financial centres produce or provide? What do they do that justifies the rich rewards they earn? Not much, in the view of many people. The suspicion lingers that financiers are little more than parasites, living off the earnest endeavours of industrialists and the honest toil of working men.

The mystery clears a little once you understand that the assets on which our prosperity depends lead a double life. On the one hand, there are "real" assets, as economists call them, and on the other, their financial doppelgangers. Real assets can be tangible and physical, like machinery and land, or intangible, like know-how or brand recognition. Financial assets, however, are simply the paper claims to these real, productive assets and the goods and services they generate. At the end of 2004, according to the McKinsey Global Institute, financial assets amounted to 334% of world GDP. In other words, about 40 months' worth of global output is already pledged to someone, somewhere.

The financial system creates a bewildering variety of such claims – from plain-vanilla bonds to exotic derivatives. It also reshuffles and reschedules them, in large volume and at great speed. But while this frenetic activity continuously allocates and reallocates wealth, it does not add to it in aggregate – at least not directly. Every financial asset is someone else's liability; every entitlement someone else's obligation.

But that does not mean that the financial system contributes nothing to the economy. Stripped to its essentials, it is the economy's way of handling the two elements of time and chance. It matches savers, who have money now but want to squirrel it away for the future, with entrepreneurs, who need money now in order to make money later. It also matches those exposed to risks with those best placed to bear them.

Of course, most of the activity on financial markets is "churn", the sale and resale of existing securities that may have changed hands many times already. But even these vast and hectic aftermarkets serve a useful purpose. They make it possible for lenders, should they want their money back right away, to pass their claims on to someone else. This reconciles a lender's demand for liquidity with a firm's desire for steady financing.

The following articles spell out the functions that banks, insurance companies, stockmarkets and derivatives perform. The chapter dispels much of the fog that surrounds the financial system and most of the opprobrium heaped upon it. It is wrong to think of the great financial centres as leeches, however engorged some of their denizens become. Indeed, for some economists, such as John Hardman Moore of the London School of Economics, an opposite analogy would be more apt. "The flow of money and private securities through the economy is like the flow of blood," he says, dispatching resources where they are most needed. The economy would be listless and anaemic without it.

Finance: trick or treat?

During recent decades, financial transactions have grown much faster than global output. What role does the financial system play in a modern economy?

THEODORE ROOSEVELT, an American president, once claimed that there was no moral difference between gambling on cards or horses and gambling on the stockmarket. Jacques Chirac, the president of France, has denounced currency speculators as "the AIDS of the world economy". Bankers are widely condemned either as greedy usurers or as incompetent fools. At best, the financial system is seen as a wasteful sideshow that relies on churning money earned in "real" businesses and adds no economic value. At worst, it is portrayed as an irrational casino, in which 22-year-old traders are able to bankrupt economies. Might we be better off without all the financiers?

A stockmarket crash or a run of bank failures can clearly do serious economic harm. The worst recessions in history, including the Great Depression in the 1930s and, more recently, Japan's stagnation during the 1990s and East Asia's slump in 1997–98, all followed financial crises. Yet, for all its failings, the financial system provides services that are vital for long-term economic growth.

Finance has existed in some form since the dawn of recorded history. Credit was used in agriculture in Mesopotamia in 3000BC. Banks existed in Egypt in 200BC. Even derivatives are not new: futures contracts were traded on the Amsterdam exchange in the 17th century. There is nothing inherently new about borrowing, lending and investing.

Even so, in *Hamlet*, Polonius advised his son "neither a borrower nor a lender be". If everybody followed that advice the financial system would not exist. Most people, however, need to borrow or save at some time in their life – from taking out a student loan or home mortgage to paying into a savings account or a pension fund. Even share ownership is no longer the preserve of a rich few. America entered the 21st century with half of all households owning shares directly or through mutual funds, compared with 25% in the mid-1980s and only 5% in the 1950s.

In the 1980s and 1990s there was, indeed, something of a financial revolution. Advances in computing and telecoms, financial innovation and liberalisation of capital controls combined to reduce the costs of

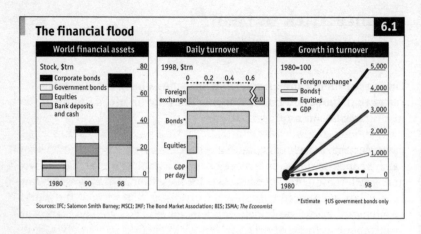

The financial flood | 6.1

World financial assets

Stock, $trn

- Corporate bonds
- Government bonds
- Equities
- Bank deposits and cash

80 / 60 / 40 / 20 / 0

1980 90 98

Daily turnover

1998, $trn

0   0.2   0.4   0.6

Foreign exchange 2.0

Bonds*

Equities

GDP per day

Growth in turnover

1980=100

- Foreign exchange*
- Bonds†
- Equities
- GDP

5,000 / 4,000 / 3,000 / 2,000 / 1,000 / 0

1980 98

Sources: IFC; Salomon Smith Barney; MSCI; IMF; The Bond Market Association; BIS; ISMA; *The Economist*

*Estimate †US government bonds only

financial transactions. There was a corresponding explosion in the volume of transactions. The global stock of financial assets (shares, bonds, bank deposits and cash) increased more than twice as fast as the GDP of rich economies, from $12 trillion in 1980 to almost $80 trillion in 1999. The volume of trading in financial securities increased even faster (see Chart 6.1). Note that the markets for bonds and foreign exchange have far higher turnover (ie, are more "liquid") than does the equity market.

The go-betweens

Financial firms come in many shapes and sizes, but they all serve the same purpose: to channel funds from those who wish to save to those who need to borrow. In many ways, finance is like any other market, matching demand and supply – in this case of loanable or investable funds. However, financial markets are special in one crucial way: they link the present and the future, allowing savers to convert current income into future spending, and borrowers to do the reverse. By acting as a channel through which savings can finance investment, the financial system helps to spur growth.

In doing this, financial institutions can be divided into two broad types. First, savers provide money indirectly to borrowers through intermediaries, such as banks, savings-and-loan associations (building societies), mutual funds and pension funds. Banks, for instance, take deposits from savers, which they use to make loans to borrowers. Mutual funds sell "units" to the public and invest the proceeds in different securities.

The second type of institution is one where savers provide money to firms or governments directly through financial markets. These include the stock-market, the bond market (government and corporate) and the money market for short-term securities, such as commercial paper. Alongside these markets stand other markets such as those for foreign exchange; and for various instruments derived from standard securities, such as futures, swaps and options (collectively

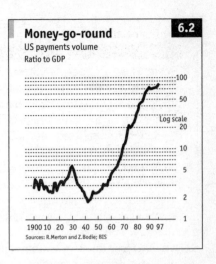

Money-go-round   6.2
US payments volume
Ratio to GDP

Sources: R.Merton and Z.Bodie; BIS

known as "derivatives"), all meant to help the primary markets to work more efficiently.

In a classic analysis of the financial system,[1] Robert Merton and Zvi Bodie, two American economists, identify several important functions that financial intermediaries and markets perform:

- ◪ **Clearing and settling payments.** Cheque accounts, credit cards and wire transfers provide means of payment for the exchange of goods and services, and financial assets. The total value of financial payments in America jumped from around five times GDP in the mid-1960s to around 80 times in 1997 (see Chart 6.2). Wire-transfer systems such as FedWire and CHIPs (the Clearing House Interbank Payments System) account for about 85% of all payments by value; cheques and credit cards account for only 13%. But by volume, however, cheques and credit cards account for 98% of transactions.
- ◪ **Pooling of savings.** If the owner of a factory had to rely entirely on his own savings, he would be unable to make large capital investments. Big firms such as GM or IBM could not exist. Instead, the financial system gives entrepreneurs access to the savings of millions of households. The pooling of savings makes financial assets much more liquid. If you invest all your savings in a neighbour's factory, it is difficult to get your money back quickly if you need it. Financial markets and intermediaries allow people

139

to hold assets in more liquid form, such as shares or bank deposits. By pooling the funds of small savers, mutual funds also reduce transaction costs (eg, brokers' fees) through economies of scale. There has been an increasing concentration of assets in the hands of mutual funds, pension funds and insurance companies. Institutional investors now manage more than two-fifths of American households' financial assets, twice as much as in 1980.

Savers do not like to relinquish control of their savings for long periods, so increased liquidity makes it easier for firms to finance long-term investment. Sir John Hicks, a British economist, argued that the increased liquidity of capital markets and not technological innovation was the critical new ingredient that ignited growth in 18th-century England. Most of the early manufactured products had been invented earlier, but large-scale capital investment was impossible without liquid capital markets. Without a financial revolution, the industrial revolution might never have taken place.

- **Transfers across time and space.** Financial intermediaries and markets allow individuals to reallocate consumption over their lifetimes. For instance, the young may borrow to buy a house, and the middle-aged may save for their retirement. Likewise a newly emerging economy often requires large amounts of capital to support growth, but more mature economies will tend to have surplus income. An efficient financial system ensures that savings can flow to the most productive industry or economy.

- **Pooling of risk.** It is risky for an individual to invest all his savings in a single firm, because it could go bust. Financial intermediaries such as mutual funds allow individuals to reduce their risks by diversifying their investment portfolios. By pooling the risks of millions, insurance companies are able to sell protection against future loss – whether through fire, burglary or death. Derivatives can also help firms to manage their risks. For example, a risk-averse firm might use derivatives to hedge against a possible rise in interest rates by shifting the risk to an investor more willing to take it.

- **Reduce information costs.** The financial system communicates information about borrowers' creditworthiness. Prices of securities provide signals that assist managers in making investment decisions and households in making savings decisions, helping to ensure that funds are efficiently allocated.

Banks and capital markets help to reduce "information asymmetries" caused because a borrower tends to know more about his prospects than a lender. An individual finds it costly to obtain information on a borrower's creditworthiness. If a financial intermediary does it on behalf of thousands of such small savers, search costs are reduced. This is not to say that markets are perfect at processing information. They can often be subject to herd behaviour that drives asset prices out of line with fundamentals.

Follow the money

Several empirical studies have confirmed that there is a strong link between financial development and economic growth. Countries with well-developed banking systems and capital markets tend to enjoy faster growth than those without. A study[2] by two economists, Ross Levine and Sara Zervos, examines 47 economies over the period from 1976 to 1993. They find that stockmarket liquidity (the value of shares traded relative to stockmarket capitalisation) and the size of the banking sector (measured by lending to the private sector as a percentage of GDP) are good predictors of future rates of growth – even after controlling for other factors such as the initial level of income, education and political stability.

In rich economies the assets of financial intermediaries and the size of stock and bond markets all tend to be bigger in relation to GDP than in poor ones. In emerging economies, the banking system is often quick to develop, but capital markets take longer because they need a financial infrastructure that provides, among other things, adequate accounting standards, a legal system that enforces contracts and protects property rights, and bankruptcy provisions.

Alan Greenspan, chairman of America's Federal Reserve, stressed the importance of a diversified financial system, which, he argued, helps to cush-

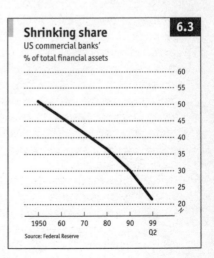

Shrinking share 6.3
US commercial banks'
% of total financial assets

Source: Federal Reserve

ion an economy in times of stress. For example, when America's banks got into trouble in 1990 as a result of the property bust, capital markets provided an alternative source of finance. And in autumn 1998, when capital-market liquidity dried up, America's banks took up some of the slack.

In contrast, Japan, more heavily dependent on bank lending and with poorly developed corporate-debt markets, has suffered a prolonged credit crunch. East Asia is another example of how countries with narrow capital markets and few alternatives to banks can suffer deep recessions. During the boom times, nobody worried about Asia's dependence on bank lending. "The lack of a spare tyre", said Mr Greenspan, "is no concern if you do not get a flat." Japan and, later, East Asia, found out they were missing one too late.

Notes

1 "A Conceptual Framework for Analysing the Financial Environment", in *The Global Financial System: a Functional Perspective*, Harvard Business School Press, 1995.
2 "Stockmarket, Banks and Economic Growth", *American Economic Review*, June 1998.

The business of banking

Banks have been at the heart of economic activity for eight centuries. Why did banks evolve, how do they function, what do they do, and what challenges do they face?

W HEN ASKED why he had robbed a bank, Willie Sutton, a 19th-century American outlaw, replied: "Because that's where the money is." His reasoning is hard to fault: since modern banking emerged in 12th-century Genoa, banks and money have gone hand in hand.

Banks are still pre-eminent in the financial system, although other financial intermediaries are growing in importance. First, they are vital to economic activity, because they reallocate money, or credit, from savers, who have a temporary surplus of it, to borrowers, who can make better use of it.

Second, banks are at the heart of the clearing system. By collaborating to clear payments, they help individuals and firms fulfil transactions. Payments can take the form of money orders, cheques or regular transfers, such as standing orders and direct-debit mandates.

Banks take in money as deposits, on which they sometimes pay interest, and then lend it to borrowers, who use it to finance investment or consumption. They also borrow money in other ways, generally from other banks in what is called the interbank market. They make profits on the difference, called the margin or the spread, between interest paid and received. As this spread has been driven down by better information and the increasing sophistication of capital markets, banks have tried to boost their profits with fee businesses, such as selling mutual funds.

Deposits are banks' liabilities. They come in two forms: current accounts (in America, checking accounts), on which cheques can be drawn and on which funds are payable immediately on demand; and deposit or savings accounts. Some deposit accounts have notice periods before money can be withdrawn: these are known as time deposits or notice accounts. The interest rate paid on such accounts is generally higher than on demand deposits, from which money can be immediately withdrawn.

Banks' assets also range between short-term credit, such as overdrafts or credit lines, which can be called in by the bank at little notice, and

143

longer-term loans, for example to buy a house, or capital equipment, which may be repaid over tens of years. Most of a bank's liabilities have a shorter maturity than its assets.

There is, therefore, a mismatch between the two. This leads to problems if depositors become so worried about the quality of a bank's lending book that they demand their savings back. Although some overdrafts or credit lines can easily be called in, longer-term loans are much less liquid. This "maturity transformation" can cause a bank to fail.

A more common danger is credit risk: the possibility that borrowers will be unable to repay their loans. This risk tends to mount in periods of prosperity, when banks relax their lending criteria, only to become apparent when recession strikes. In the late 1980s, for example, Japanese banks, seduced by the country's apparent economic invincibility, lent masses of money to high-risk firms, many of which later went bust. Some banks followed them into bankruptcy; the rest are still hobbled.

A third threat to banks is interest-rate risk. This is the possibility that a bank will pay more interest on deposits than it is able to charge for loans. It exists because interest on loans is often set at a fixed rate, whereas rates on deposits are generally variable. This disparity destroyed much of America's savings-and-loan (thrifts) industry. When interest rates rose sharply in 1979 the S&Ls found themselves paying depositors more than they were earning on their loans. The government eventually had to bail out or close much of the industry.

One way around this is to lend at variable or floating rates, so as to match floating-rate deposits. However, borrowers often prefer fixed-rate debt, as it makes their own interest payments predictable. More recently, banks and borrowers have been able to "swap" fixed-rate assets for floating ones in the interest-rate swap market.

Minding the bank

Because banks provide credit and operate the payments system, their failure can have a more damaging effect on the economy than the collapse of other businesses. Hence governments pay particular attention to the regulation of banks. Individual banks have reserve requirements; that is, they must hold a proportion of their deposits at the central bank, where they are safe and immediately accessible. The central bank typically pays little or, in America, no interest on these reserves. However it can charge interest on its loans, which is one way in which the banking system pays for its own regulation.

As a second cushion against a liquidity crisis, the central bank acts as lender of last resort. That is, when it worries that solvent banks might struggle to raise money, it will step in and provide finance itself. America's Federal Reserve did this after the 1987 stockmarket crash. Ten years later the Bank of Japan did the same because it thought that the difficulties the country's banks had in raising money were only temporary.

Another way in which regulators have tried to keep banks' heads above water is to force them to match a proportion of their risky assets (ie, loans) with capital, in the form of equity or retained earnings. In 1988 bank regulators from the richest countries agreed that the capital of internationally active banks should, with a few variations, amount to at least 8% of the value of their risky assets. This agreement, called the Basel Accord, is being revised, largely because the original makes only crude distinctions between loans' different levels of risk.

It is not just the failure of individual banks that gives regulators sleepless nights. The collapse of one bank can spread trouble throughout the financial system as depositors from other, healthy, banks suddenly fear for their money. Regulators step in because they want to prevent a collapse of the entire system.

Governments try to minimise the risk of such failure in several ways. One is to impose harsher regulation on banks than on other sorts of companies; often, the regulator is the central bank. Another tack is to try to prevent runs on banks in the first place. Following the collapse of a third of all American banks in 1930–33, the government set up an insurance scheme under which it guaranteed to repay depositors, up to a certain limit, in the event of bank failure.

Following America's lead, other countries have also introduced deposit-guarantee schemes. Even where they have not, depositors often assume that there is an implicit guarantee, because the government will step in rather than risk a collapse of the whole system. In the 1990s, the Japanese government went to the extreme of guaranteeing all lenders (not just depositors) to the country's biggest banks until the end of the century.

Some argue that these guarantees make bank failures more likely, because they encourage depositors to be indifferent to the riskiness of banks' lending. Moreover, as banks get bigger, they are also likely to conclude that they are "too big to fail", which is an incentive to take more risk. Both are a form of moral hazard.

To combat moral hazard, regulators try to be ambiguous about how big is too big, and to restrict the amount of insurance they provide. In

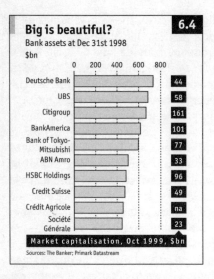

Big is beautiful? 6.4

Bank assets at Dec 31st 1998
$bn

Deutsche Bank	44
UBS	58
Citigroup	161
BankAmerica	101
Bank of Tokyo-Mitsubishi	77
ABN Amro	33
HSBC Holdings	96
Credit Suisse	49
Crédit Agricole	na
Société Générale	23

Market capitalisation, Oct 1999, $bn

Sources: The Banker; Primark Datastream

recent years, none of these measures has prevented ill-advised lending by banks around the world. Failures include the excessive loans of American banks to Latin America in the 1980s; and banking crises in Japan, Scandinavia and East Asia.

In many countries, governments have responded to emergencies by nationalising the worst banks, often pledging to inject capital, take on their dud loans, and reprivatise them. This is fine in theory, but in practice it often distorts the market for the remaining privately owned banks by keeping too many banks in business and by allowing nationalised banks with the benefit of a government guarantee to borrow more cheaply.

A mixed bank

Another difficulty increasingly faced by both regulators and banks is the plethora of institutions that conduct banking business. In Germany, for example, less than a third of deposits by value are held within the privately owned banking sector. Retail banks – those that do business mainly with individuals – often compete with mutual or state-owned institutions. Often, such institutions were founded to provide mortgage financing. Spain has its *cajas* – savings banks owned by regional governments; France, the Netherlands and Japan all have agricultural co-operative banks that were created to finance farmers.

Active mutual and state-owned banks can lower the profitability of privately owned banks, since they tend to care less about profits. In France and Germany, banks' returns are far below those in Britain or America. As a result, banks' assets – the traditional measure of size – are often unrelated to the value of the banks on the stockmarket (see Chart 6.4).

Increased competition in lending has meant that over the past couple of decades banks have expanded their lines of business. In Europe, in particular, a new type of banking, called *bancassurance* (*Allfinanz* in

Germany) has grown up. This is a fusion of banking and other financial services and involves banks selling life assurance and long-term savings products, such as pensions, as well as taking traditional bank deposits.

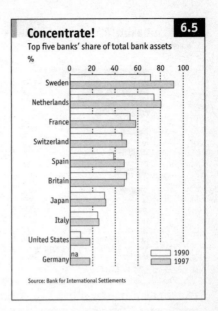

Concentrate! 6.5

Top five banks' share of total bank assets
%

Source: Bank for International Settlements

Banks that combine all of these elements are known as universal banks. Germany's big three Frankfurt-based banks, Deutsche, Dresdner and Commerzbank, are all universal banks, as is HSBC, the Anglo-Chinese giant.

Banking is a lot messier than it was. In Britain, two big supermarket chains, Tesco and J. Sainsbury, now take deposits. Many non-banking firms, such as General Motors, also now provide credit, although regulators are less worried about institutions lending money than about those collecting it. American credit-card operators, such as Capital One and MBNA, have entered the market, using the techniques of database marketing to identify the most lucrative customers. This has caused established lenders to trim their rates.

Worse still for traditional banks, many companies in America raise money by selling bonds rather than by borrowing from banks, a process called disintermediation. In America, the share of business finance that comes from banks shrank from 59% in 1970 to 46% in 1999. With the single market and the euro, European firms are increasingly following suit. This has benefited investment banks.

Investment banks, as distinct from ordinary "commercial" banks, help firms raise money in the capital markets, and advise them whether to finance themselves with debt or equity. They underwrite such issues by agreeing, often with other banks in a syndicate, to buy any unsold securities, and are paid a commission for this service. They provide a liquid market in securities, and (now less than in the past) invest their own capital, an activity known as proprietary trading. In addition to advising clients on raising finance, they also advise on mergers and acquisitions, usually their most lucrative work.

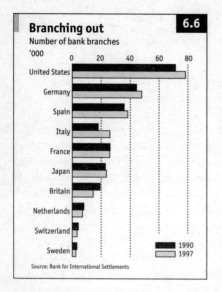

Branching out 6.6

Number of bank branches '000

Source: Bank for International Settlements

■ 1990
□ 1997

In America the Glass-Steagall Act prevented commercial banks from acting as investment banks and also from underwriting insurance. But the act was repealed in 1999. Commercial banks have been able to underwrite some securities. Investment banks have offered services that look exactly like current accounts. Some now even offer credit cards.

Endnote

Since this article was written in 1999, banking has become messier still. Even Wal-Mart, a huge retailer, has applied for a bank licence. The repeal of the Glass-Steagall Act and the collapse of Enron have also revived worries about the conflicts of interest that might arise when a bank lends to a client, advises it on mergers and acquisitions, and also ventures its own money on the markets.

Moneyed men in institutions

The institutions that dominate securities markets are pension funds, mutual funds and insurance companies

A T THEIR MOST BASIC, they are simply vast pools of money. Pension funds, mutual funds and insurance companies – collectively known as "institutional investors" – control a huge chunk of most rich countries' retirement savings and other wealth. They are like trustees of the world's capital. By allocating it – shifting into and out of shares and bonds, countries and currencies – they move markets, hold governments to account, sire new companies and dispatch moribund ones. Understanding how they do this is essential to grasping the capitalist system.

Institutional investors worldwide controlled over $26 trillion in 1996, of which America accounted for over $13 trillion, Europe over $7 trillion and Japan close to $4 trillion. To put this into perspective, institutional investors in America held securities worth almost twice their country's GDP, and more than three times the assets in the banking system. Pension and mutual funds, in particular, have been growing in importance at the expense of banks (see Chart 6.7 on the next page).

Because institutional investors, as well as banks, are subject to local culture and regulation, however, regional differences are huge. In Germany and France, for instance, the largest share of financial assets is still in the hands of so-called "universal banks"; and insurers are the largest institutional investors, because private pension funds barely exist. Elsewhere pension funds are easily the largest category: in the Netherlands they control 56% of all institutional assets (see Chart 6.8 on page 151).

The growth of institutional investors at the expense of banks is likely to spread from America to other countries. As the biggest owners of stocks and bonds they will exert a growing influence in corporate finance and, hence, corporate governance. Already, institutional investors in America have huge power over company management.

Yet for now the differences – national and institutional – are more striking. Not only do some markets (English-speaking countries, mainly) have "equity cultures", whereas others (continental Europe, say) are more risk-averse and stick to bonds; but each type of institution works within its own set of regulatory and economic restraints. The pension fund of a British company with a young workforce, for instance, would

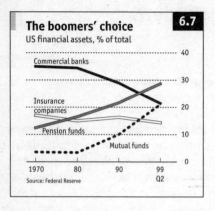

The boomers' choice 6.7
US financial assets, % of total

Commercial banks

Insurance companies

Pension funds

Mutual funds

1970 80 90 99
Source: Federal Reserve Q2

have most of its assets in the stockmarket. An earthquake insurer that may suddenly need a lot of cash will prefer safer government bonds.

But except for pure property or casualty insurers, all three types of institution are similar to banks in one respect: they are intermediaries between savers and users of capital. Banks take "deposits", make "loans", charge borrowers "interest" and share it with depositors; life insurers or pension funds receive "premiums" or "contributions", invest them in securities and share the investment returns with "policyholders" or "plan members" in the form of "annuities" or "endowments".

Collectivist individualism

This intermediary function is most obvious in the case of mutual funds – or unit trusts, as they are called in Britain. These are vehicles for pooled investment: they give retail investors – those with only a few thousand dollars to invest – the same access to capital markets as that enjoyed by wholesale investors, with millions or billions at their disposal. So compelling are their advantages that in America, every other household now has some mutual funds (see Chart 6.9 on page 152).

Mutual funds are so appealing because small-time savers who invest their nest-eggs directly in the stockmarket discover that stockbroking commissions quickly become prohibitive, that diversifying their portfolios efficiently is hard, and that the search for good investments takes up a lot of time. Yet by buying shares in a mutual fund – ie, joining with thousands of other investors – they get wholesale rates, instant portfolio diversification, and professional investment advice.

Legally, these vehicles are either companies or trusts, overseen, respectively, by a board of directors or by trustees. Either way, mutual funds have no physical assets and no employees. So they outsource all of their activities – paying a custodian for record-keeping and securities handling, an "investment adviser" to manage the assets, and so forth.

Funds can be either "open-ended" or "close-ended". An open-ended fund issues new shares or units every time an investor puts money in, and retires them every time he takes money out. So the value of the shares is simply whatever the fund's investments are worth on a given day, divided by the number of shares. But a close-ended fund – sometimes called an investment trust – has a fixed number of shares, just as any other company does, and these are traded on a stock exchange, where their price reflects supply and demand. So shares in close-ended funds may trade above or (more often) below net asset value.

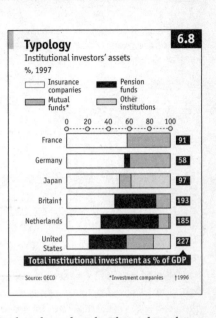

Typology 6.8
Institutional investors' assets
%, 1997

☐ Insurance companies ■ Pension funds
▨ Mutual funds* ☐ Other institutions

	0	20	40	60	80	100	
France							91
Germany							58
Japan							97
Britain†							193
Netherlands							185
United States							227

Total institutional investment as % of GDP

Source: OECD   *Investment companies   †1996

What investors care most about is a fund's mandate. In the past, most funds invested in stocks, bonds and cash. These days, however, funds increasingly specialise in one asset class – international equities, say – and investors do their own mixing. In this, preferences vary a lot. Equity funds are the most popular kind in English-speaking countries. Continental Europeans still prefer the relative safety of bond funds.

Funds also distinguish themselves by style. "Value" managers look for shares that seem cheap in relation to the firm's current profits. "Growth" managers hope to spot shares that have "momentum" or may be the next Microsoft.

However, growing numbers of investors have become disenchanted with both approaches. Having lost faith in active managers, they are giving ever more money to "passive" managers. These do not try to outperform the stockmarket, but instead track a broad market index, saving costs and charging lower management fees. Many pension funds, too, are moving in this direction.

There is one special category of fund that tries explicitly to make money whether markets are going up or down. So-called "hedge funds" follow complex strategies that combine positions in different securities. A fund might, for instance, bet that the spread between Danish and German government bonds will narrow and buy Danish paper, at the same time selling German bonds.

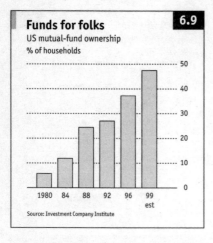

Funds for folks `6.9`

US mutual-fund ownership
% of households

Source: Investment Company Institute

Far from being "hedged" however, such strategies can quickly go belly up. This happened notoriously in 1998, when Long-Term Capital Management ran into trouble and had to be bailed out by its bankers. Because they are risky, hedge funds are mostly private partnerships instead of public companies, and most regulators allow only the rich (and supposedly savvy) to invest in them.

The company you keep

Whereas mutual funds serve retail investors, and hedge funds the very rich, occupational pension schemes are designed for employees of companies or governments. The degree to which employers are involved in pension provision varies. In America and Britain, the state plays a relatively small role, so most of the burden of retirement planning falls on employers and individuals. Elsewhere, as in France or Italy, the state is more generous, and employers play hardly any role at all.

The most common form of company pension plan is the trust fund. The employer establishes a trust, overseen by trustees for the benefit of plan members. Plan assets are separate from the sponsoring employer and do not appear on its balance sheet. But even this does not make pension funds totally secure. In the 1980s, Robert Maxwell, a British media tycoon, managed to steal a fortune from his companies' pension funds.

In a traditional pension plan, the employer guarantees a fixed pension in old age – for instance, two-thirds of final salary. The company and the employee both pay monthly contributions into a pension fund, where the money is invested. It is the trustees' responsibility to make sure that a fund's assets cover its liabilities, but to do this they hire actuaries who estimate the life expectancy of the workforce and future investment returns. Trustees may also hire outsiders to invest their plan assets.

Winning these mandates to manage the money of pension funds is a hugely competitive business. Often, "investment consultants" stage so-called "beauty parades", where a select group of fund managers woo trustees and show off their performance figures. Managers that underperform tend not to last long.

The performance of these managers matters not only to trustees, whose job is to make sure that pensions are paid, but also to sponsoring employers, as they bear the residual risk of funding the plan. Say the stock-market crashes and the pension assets no longer cover the liabilities. The employer now has to raise contributions, which depresses profits.

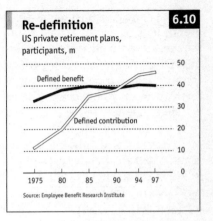

Re-definition 6.10
US private retirement plans, participants, m

Defined benefit

Defined contribution

1975 80   85   90   94 97

Source: Employee Benefit Research Institute

This risk is one reason why many employers have, in the past few decades, been opting for a different type of pension plan (see Chart 6.10). Traditional plans define the benefits of workers according to their final salaries (hence their name: "defined benefit" or "final salary"). Many new schemes, by contrast, define only the employer's contributions, and the ultimate pension depends on what the pot of money is worth at retirement (hence: "defined contribution" or "money purchase"). If the investments do well, the worker retires rich; if not, he may end his days poor.

Besides saddling their employees with investment risk, sponsors of defined-contribution plans are giving them more say over their investments. In America, many companies have set up so-called 401(k) plans. Here, plan members typically choose from a menu of mutual funds. The trend towards 401(k) and other defined-contribution plans is blurring the distinction between retail (mutual) and wholesale (pension) funds.

Life and non-life

Many of the trends that affect mutual and pension funds also affect the oldest types of institutional investor: insurance companies. The first proper life insurers were formed centuries ago in Swiss mountain valleys and sold policies (called "term life") designed purely to protect families against the risk that their breadwinner might die. Today, however, life insurance is as much about saving as about protection. "Endowment" policies, for instance, pay out at a fixed date and so have a cash value. Other policies explicitly link the ultimate payout to investment performance. Life insurers, therefore, are increasingly competing with banks and mutual funds for people's savings.

Rich-country demographics are increasing this overlap. In the past, life insurers protected people against the risk of dying too soon. Now they are increasingly insuring against the risk of not dying soon enough (ie, of outliving one's savings). So policyholders do a trade with life insurers: they hand over their piggy banks, and the insurers guarantee them an annuity until death. The risk that an individual turns out to be a Methuselah now lies with the insurer.

As for the investment risk, life insurers are increasingly passing this on to customers. Mainly, this is because savers want the upside of stockmarkets and are willing to take more risk for more return. Such policies, whose value fluctuates with the stockmarket, are called "variable annuities" in America and "unit-linked" policies in Britain. In essence, they are mutual-fund or 401(k) accounts by another name.

Property or casualty (P&C) insurers, by contrast, are genuinely different from other institutional investors. Their function is not to increase their customers' saved wealth, but to protect it from financial loss following, say, a car crash, a fire or a lawsuit. Whereas the time horizons of pension funds, life insurers and mutual funds stretch over decades, P&C insurers generally look ahead one year at a time.

This makes some types of P&C business comparatively straight-forward. Car insurers, for instance, have a reasonably good idea at the end of each year what their losses have been. Other types of insurance, however, can turn into nightmares. Remember Lloyd's of London? This 300-year-old insurance market nearly went under in the 1990s because of claims on policies it had written decades earlier. The policyholders were companies that accidentally exposed their workers in the 1950s and 1960s to asbestos. But it took years for them to develop cancer and sue. So, besides classifying P&C insurers into personal and commercial lines, it helps to distinguish between those with short and long "tails" – ie, those that know quite soon what claims they have to pay, and those that may not know for a long time.

Lawyers of large numbers

Despite these differences, however, all institutional investors share a basic principle. Whether they are life insurers protecting Swiss villagers, or P&C insurers indemnifying people for their flooded houses, they have to manage a lot of small risks. The key is a piece of magic called the "law of large numbers". It says that an unfortunate fact of life – risk – can be managed by pooling individual exposures in large portfolios – the larger, the more manageable.

Individuals cannot do this. For them, risk is all-or-nothing, and often life-or-death. This is why they buy insurance, which is a way of substituting a small certain cost (the premium) for a loss that is uncertain but potentially devastating. Thanks to insurance, as the British Insurance Act of 1601 put it, "there followethe not the undoinge of any Man, but the losse lightethe rather easilie upon many, than heavilie upon fewe".

Say, for instance, a company insures 1,000 houses. Thanks to the law of large numbers, it can calculate that an average of one house will burn down in any one year. If each house costs $1,000, the insurer must collect $1 each (not counting expenses and investment income) in premiums from policyholders, who thereby agree to share the risk.

But there are two catches. One is that the law works only if risks are not "correlated". In 1666, the thatched eaves of London's houses touched over its narrow medieval alleys: one spark was enough to burn them all. The other risk is that losses in any one year may differ hugely from the long-run trend. The average incidence of fire may be one out of 1,000, but what if that includes ten in some years and none in others?

This means that financiers can manage risk, but never dispose of it completely. This holds as much for banks estimating loan-default rates as for life insurers poring over mortality tables or P&C insurers calculating the risk of a fire. As dry and callous as the men of numbers may seem, they fulfil a useful social function.

Stocks in trade

Stock and bond markets are the trading places for capital. How do they guide capital around the world economy?

N OT SO LONG AGO, stockmarkets were derided by critics from communist countries as emblems of capitalism's greed and instability. Since the Berlin Wall came down it is now hard to find a country without its own bourse. In Poland, the Warsaw Stock Exchange even occupies the former headquarters of the Communist Party. Despite China's commitment to state control of its economy, it has two stock exchanges, even without counting a third that it inherited from Hong Kong. The number of developing countries with stockmarkets doubled during the 1990s. Why is everyone betting on the markets?

Part of the answer is that capital markets have proved remarkably efficient at bringing savers and borrowers together. Capital is just another word for stored wealth and resources, which can take many forms. And markets, as basic economics shows, are the least bad way to set prices and to allocate scarce resources.

The key difference between capital markets and financial intermediaries, such as banks or life insurers, is that capital markets cut out middlemen. Where banks and institutions stand between savers and investors, directing the flow of resources, capital markets bring the two parties face to face.

The two main types of capital markets are equity markets, for trading company shares (or equities), and bond markets, for trading the debt of companies and governments. Both perform two crucial functions in the economy. They move resources across space and time, from where they are in surplus to where they are needed most. And they produce valuable information, through the prices they set, that firms, households, and governments use to manage resources better.

Exchange and mart

Today's financial markets have come a long way from their humble origins. Securities that looked much like modern shares were issued as early as the late Middle Ages in Italian city states. Government bonds with publicly quoted prices date at least as far back as long-term Venetian loans called *prestiti*, in the 13th century. The New York Stock

Exchange started under a buttonwood tree in 1792 with just two equities and three government bonds. By 1998, the NYSE's average daily turnover – the value of traded shares – had reached $29 billion. In many rich countries, stockmarket capitalisation, the market value of all listed companies, now rivals or exceeds the size of the domestic economy (see Chart 6.11).

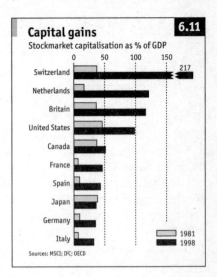

Capital gains — 6.11
Stockmarket capitalisation as % of GDP

Switzerland 217
Netherlands
Britain
United States
Canada
France
Spain
Japan
Germany
Italy

1981
1998

Sources: MSCI; IFC; OECD

Bond markets, too, play an essential role in raising finance for companies and governments. In 1997, the market for dollar-denominated bonds was worth $11 trillion, measured by publicly traded debt outstanding, almost twice as much as in 1989. Most of this (and also most equities) was traded by large institutions.

Most capital-market trading takes place between one investor and another. This is known as the secondary market, since it does not directly involve the company or government that issued the security. New shares and bonds, however, are born in what is called the primary market, where the money raised flows directly into the coffers of the issuers. The primary market includes initial public offerings (IPOs) of shares in the stockmarket as well as new debt issues in the bond market.

Capital styles

These shares and bonds are in essence only the receipts that savers get for lending money to, or investing in, a firm or a government. A bond, for example, is a loan that can be traded between investors. A government might issue a bond because it spends more than it receives in tax revenues, and needs to borrow the difference. Bonds are often called fixed-income securities because they give the investor a regular stream of interest payments, called coupons.

A bond is an agreement to repay an amount of principal at a future date, along with a schedule of interest payments over a period of time, usually several years. American Treasury bonds are a well-known example. An investor today who buys a newly issued $10,000 face-

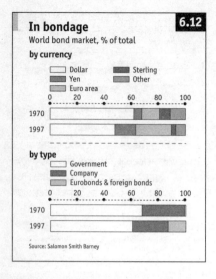

In bondage `6.12`

World bond market, % of total

by currency

Legend: Dollar, Sterling, Yen, Other, Euro area

0 20 40 60 80 100

1970

1997

by type

Legend: Government, Company, Eurobonds & foreign bonds

0 20 40 60 80 100

1970

1997

Source: Salomon Smith Barney

value, 30-year Treasury bond with a 6% coupon will receive 6% interest per year (or $600) until 2029, when he will also get back his $10,000 principal.

Bonds come in countless flavours. Government debt includes municipal bonds, central or federal government bonds, and the bonds of related agencies. Corporate issues include the relatively safe debt of a large company such as AT&T, as well as high-yielding "junk" bonds of riskier firms. Bonds are denominated in many currencies, but most often these days in dollars and euros (see Chart 6.12). Restrictive regulations in America in the 1960s spurred Europeans to issue dollar-denominated debt. These Eurobonds were an innovation that helped ensure London's continued prominence as a financial centre. The Eurobond market grew from $64 billion in 1980 to over $1 trillion in 1997.

The market price of a bond will vary over time in response to several factors: expected inflation, interest rates on competing investments and the creditworthiness of the borrower. The less worried investors are that inflation will erode the value of both interest and principal, the more they will pay for a bond. Bond prices are thus a good reflection of investors' expectations of future inflation. When interest rates offered on new investments rise, the fixed payments of older bonds become less attractive; so investors will bid the prices of these bonds down.

One way of summarising a bond's value is its yield. This is a measure of the return a bondholder receives on his investment, stated as a percentage of the bond's market price. As a bond's price falls, investors can purchase its stream of interest payments for less. Likewise, when that bond's price rises, investors pay more dearly for its cashflow. This gives rise to one apparent paradox about bonds: the cheaper they are, the more they "yield".

Fair shares

In contrast to bonds, shares are little slices of ownership in private firms.

As owners, shareholders elect a board of directors and vote on company business. They are also entitled to the firm's profits – the income that remains after payments for wages, materials, and any interest on the company's debt. This is one way to see that shares generally carry more risk than bonds: bondholders have a higher legal claim, or seniority, on the cashflows of a business than do shareholders. If a firm's business declines, bondholders will be paid first, and shareholders last, if at all. But if business booms, shareholders will do better.

For share valuation, one commonly cited measure is the price to earnings, or p/e ratio. The p/e ratio is the market price of shares divided by the firm's profits. P/e ratios are to shares what yields are to bonds; in fact, the inverse of the p/e ratio measures a firm's profits as a percentage of the market price of its shares, or earnings yield.

From the savers' perspective, bonds appear safer than shares. From the issuers' perspective, things look rather different. For a company issuing securities to fund its growth, shares are the least risky choice. Shareholders, unlike bondholders, receive no legal promise to be repaid in cash at a certain time. Shareholders can exchange their shares in the stockmarket at the market price, but the firm promises them no particular return.

For firms, as for people, taking on debt can be risky. If they are unable to meet interest payments, bankruptcy may ensue. So, in general, the more financially sound a company is, the more investors will be willing to pay for its debt. But it is costly and time-consuming for individuals to gather such credit information. Ratings agencies, such as Moody's and Standard & Poor's, reduce this cost by assessing companies' financial condition and publishing their conclusions. Debtor companies also face bond covenants restricting their activities to ensure that they can continue to service their debts.

For years, businessmen believed that having the right mix of debt and equity could make their company more valuable. But in 1958 Franco Modigliani and Merton Miller, two American economists, showed that the value of a firm should be unaffected by whether it is financed using all debt, all equity, or a mix of the two. What really matters is the value of the underlying business, not the details of its financing. But this theory, for which they were later awarded the Nobel prize in economics, relies on the crucial assumption that capital markets operate "perfectly": i.e., it ignores such real-world snags as tax, and differing costs of borrowing for firms and individuals.

Future perfect

The world of derivatives may seem arcane, but they are important to financial markets

IF YOU BELIEVE what you read in newspapers, derivatives (options, swaps and so on) are new, complex, risky and nasty – and of value only to those who make money selling them. In the mid-1990s, indeed, rapid growth in derivatives markets (not to mention some spectacular losses by those that used them) prompted concerns among regulators that derivatives might pose a threat to the global financial system.

These worries have abated, however, as regulators have become better acquainted with such instruments. Perhaps they should have learnt about them earlier. For although some (though far from all) of the mathematics used to calculate derivatives' prices is fiendishly difficult, even the most complex can be broken down into two easily understood blocks: forward contracts, in which one party agrees to buy something from another at a specified future date for a specified price; and option contracts, in which one party agrees to provide the right – but not the obligation – to another to buy or sell something in the future.

Neither is exactly new. Aristotle mentions options in "Politics"; and there was an active market in tulip options in Amsterdam in the 17th century. In the same century an organised market for future delivery of rice was developed in Osaka. Even before that, traders at medieval fairs used arrangements that were recognisably forward contracts. Much of the arcane language merely reflects the fact that these two blocks are being applied and combined in different ways.

Forward markets are the simplest. In the markets for perishable commodities, their forward price is determined by expectations about future demand and supply. For financial assets, the price is determined by the cost of holding the asset. In foreign-exchange markets, for example, the forward rate is arrived at by looking at the difference between two currencies' interest rates. Since no payments are made until the contract expires, the forward rate simply reflects the fact that one currency is paying higher interest. If it did not, somebody could buy the currency and sell it back at the same price, earning greater interest over the life of the contract. In other words, forward prices are not a market's prediction about the direction a financial asset is likely to take.

Although a recent innovation (the first currency swap was between the World Bank and IBM in 1981), swaps markets are, in essence, like forward markets. The difference is that, in this market, the principal is paid back at the prevailing rate when the contract was signed (the spot rate); the two parties exchange interest payments, again so that one cannot make a riskless profit. In a typical interest-rate swap, for example, one party pays a floating rate for the duration of the contract, and the other a fixed rate. Swaps are, in effect, a string of forward rates – that is forwards that begin when the previous one finishes.

Calling the options

Options are different. They are a form of insurance. They enable a purchaser to buy or sell an asset at a certain price on a given date, but allow him to walk away if he wishes. The right to buy is generally dubbed a "call", and to sell a "put". There is also a difference between European-style options, which can be exercised (cashed in) only when they expire, and American-style ones, which can be exercised at any time during the option's life. So, for example, if a person buys a European-style six-month call option on Citigroup, he would buy an option that has a six-month life, and can be exercised at the end of six months. If Citigroup's share price falls in the meantime, he will not exercise the option.

Derivatives are traded in two types of market. The first is on exchanges, such as Euronext.liffe (formerly the London International Financial Futures and Options Exchange – LIFFE), or the Chicago Board of Trade (CBOT). The second is the over-the-counter (OTC) market – that is, people and firms trading directly with one another.

Exchange-traded derivatives differ in two main respects from OTC ones. The first is that exchange-traded contracts are almost always standardised: they try to make trading more liquid (and thus cheaper) by getting everybody to trade the same contract. For many, such liquidity outweighs some disadvantages, such as the fact that the instrument on which the contract is based might not be their preferred choice.

The second difference is that contracts are (usually) with the exchange's clearing house, not with another bank, say. By guaranteeing that the contract will be honoured, the exchange removes so-called credit risk – highly pertinent for derivatives, because these are contracts to buy and sell things in the future and there is a risk, in the OTC market, of one of the contractors going bust or refusing to pay.

Clearing houses strip out this risk by asking users to stump up a deposit upfront (known as initial margin). They then ask for money

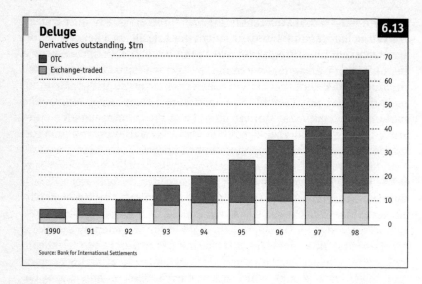

Deluge   `6.13`
Derivatives outstanding, $trn
■ OTC
▢ Exchange-traded

Source: Bank for International Settlements

from those that are losing on the contract and give it to those that are profiting. This is called variation margin. This mechanism, in essence, substitutes for credit risk, the risk that losers might have to fork out should their trades turn sour. In late 1993, an inability to find this margin nearly pushed Metallgesellschaft, a big German mining conglomerate, to the brink. The same fate befell Ashanti Goldfields, an African gold-mining firm, in 1999.

Most derivatives are variations of forwards and options, traded in different ways. A futures contract is really only a forward traded on an exchange. A swaption is an option on a swap. A futures option is an option based on a futures contract. A cap is the short-term interest-rate version of a call. Straddles are a strategy whereby somebody simultaneously sells a put and a call.

A hedge by any other name

Many things contributed to the 12-fold increase between 1990 and 1998 in the use of derivatives (see Chart 6.13). Originally, the main demand came from farmers and those to whom they sold. Farmers knew their costs; to prosper (even to survive), they needed to know at what price they could sell their produce. The CBOT was set up as an agricultural exchange in 1848.

In recent decades, demand has come mainly from those who wish to hedge financial exposures. Financial markets became more volatile in the 1970s and 1980s. After the breakdown of the Bretton Woods system of fixed exchange rates in the early 1970s, exchange rates became much more volatile. This was exacerbated by the two oil shocks in that decade and by higher inflation – which also led to more volatile interest rates. Demand for instruments to guard against these risks surged.

The first currency futures were launched by the Chicago Mercantile Exchange's International Monetary Market in 1972; and the first interest-rate futures by the CBOT in 1975. Since then, derivatives exchanges have sprung up in all developed economies and in many developing ones.

Demand comes from many quarters. Banks have used interest-rate derivatives to manage potential mismatches between their assets (loans and so forth) and their liabilities (checking accounts, for instance). Banks often have assets with a fixed rate of interest but pay a floating rate on their liabilities. To try to match these they could use interest-rate swaps, or they could purchase options that, for example, "cap" what they might be forced to pay out, or put a "floor" on the rate they would receive. Fund managers often use futures to protect against a decline in the value of their equity and bond portfolios. They might, for example, sell stock-index futures if they were worried that the stockmarket would fall: if it did, the gains from their futures would, with luck, offset the losses on their shares.

Companies also use derivatives to manage the risk that movements in the price of currencies and commodities might make their business uneconomic. Take the example of a British company exporting to America. If sterling rises too much against the dollar, its products might become too expensive. So it might try to protect itself by locking in an exchange rate using forward currency contracts, perhaps.

Derivatives are also commonly used by both financial and non-financial firms when they raise capital. A Japanese firm might want to borrow yen at a floating rate. However, there might be more demand for its debt from dollar-based investors who want to be paid a fixed rate. In that case it might be cheaper to issue fixed-rate dollar debt and use a currency swap (from dollars into yen) and an interest-rate swap (from fixed to floating interest rates) to achieve the desired result.

I have seen the future

At the same time, financial firms have been able to satisfy (and often to create) demand because they have become better able to put a price on derivatives and to develop almost limitless variants, some of them highly complex.

Probably the most fundamental advance in financial economics this century occurred in 1973, when two financial economists, Fischer Black and Myron Scholes (with help from a third, Robert Merton), published a paper with the snappy title "The pricing of options and corporate liabilities". This paper solved a riddle that many economists had failed to answer: what is an option worth? Take the example of a call option on a share. If the seller of the call buys the same amount of shares as he has granted the option buyer the right to buy, he runs the risk that the market will fall and the call buyer will not exercise his option. That would mean that the seller would be stuck with a loss-making holding. Calculating the worth of that option was little more than guesswork.

Messrs Black and Scholes provided an algorithm that worked out how to calculate an option's worth. There are a number of inputs into their model: the current price of the underlying asset; the option's strike price (the price at which the purchaser can buy or sell something); the level of interest rates; the time to maturity; and the volatility of the asset.

The last is the most important. The model does not try to predict in what direction the asset will move, but to calculate the risk of the option being exercised. This is best captured by seeing how volatile the asset is likely to be over the life of the option: the more volatile, the more likely it is that the option will be exercised – and the more expensive the option. Crucially, the model tells the seller how much of an asset a seller must buy or sell so as to cover his risks. This is called the hedge ratio or, more commonly, the option's delta.

Two other things have helped the development of the options market – and, indeed, other derivatives. The first has been immense advances in computer power and a relentless decline in its price. The first pocket calculator, from Texas Instruments, also came on to the market in 1972. And, second, new exchanges have sprung up. The Chicago Board Options Exchange opened its doors in 1973; LIFFE began trading in 1982; Matif in Paris in 1986. The rivalry among these exchanges is intense (see Chart 6.14). For instance, the floor-based LIFFE lost European business to the screen-based Eurex and was taken over by Euronext in 2002.

Risky galore

Do derivatives make the world riskier? Certainly, some companies that have used them have lost lots of money. Think, for example, of Procter & Gamble, which lost heavily in 1994 (as did several other firms) by using complex interest-rate swaps; or of Barings, a British bank that was

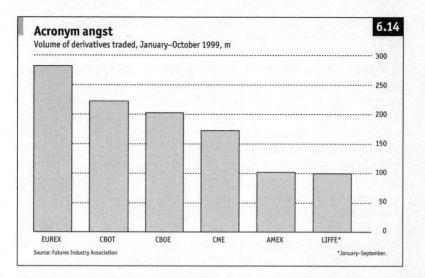

Acronym angst `6.14`
Volume of derivatives traded, January–October 1999, m

Source: Futures Industry Association *January–September.

EUREX CBOT CBOE CME AMEX LIFFE*

felled in 1995 by the activities of an employee, Nick Leeson, in Japanese stockmarket futures and options markets.

Yet in such cases derivatives were not, of themselves, the main culprits. Either or both of two other problems were generally to blame. Many companies that lost money using derivatives treated their treasury departments, which deal with the cash coming into and out of a company and organise its borrowing, as a profit centre. This gave them an incentive to take risk. The second common fault has been bad risk management. In some cases – Barings is an example – this has opened the way for fraud.

Others argue that derivatives increasingly affect the instruments on which they are based – the tail wagging the dog. This argument, too, is wrong-headed. Derivatives are simply another, more efficient way of dealing in the underlying instrument (and swaps have no underlying instrument anyway); there is no tail and no dog, since it is all one market.

A more sophisticated argument is that derivatives encourage risk-taking because they have natural leverage; somebody can gain control of an exposure to, say, a bond in the futures market for a small fraction of the amount that it would cost if he were to buy the bond itself. But leverage is not a property unique to derivatives markets. Companies can and do gain just as much leverage by buying an asset and using it as collateral for a loan. California's Orange County managed to bankrupt itself successfully by such means.

Might modelling be inherently risky? Or, to put it another way, do the models by which derivatives are priced have any bearing on what is actually happening in the real world? If they do not – and remember that derivatives are often long-term contracts – problems might build up unspotted. In fact, there is a market for bog-standard derivatives; to that extent it is easy to determine their correct price. The problem arises only for the small number of complex ones. Even then, it is unclear that it is worse than any other risk-management problem – putting your bad trades in the bottom drawer, for instance.

There is, however, one area in which derivatives might increase volatility. An option seller can hedge himself by buying another option or by buying or selling shares, say, in the market. In some cases, when everyone is trying to sell something at the same time, the market might be driven down and the model would then force investors to sell even more. This effect was widely blamed for the severity of the stockmarket crash in 1987. Under so-called portfolio insurance, by which investors had attempted to replicate the Black-Scholes hedge ratio for themselves (and thus cut costs), they were forced to sell increasing amounts of shares as the market fell.

Yet such effects aside, most of the academic studies that have looked at the question have found that derivatives do not make financial markets more volatile; many, indeed, have found that the opposite is true. Perhaps this should come as no surprise. Derivatives are really only an efficient way of transferring risk from those that do not want it to those that do. If risk is in safer hands, the net effect ought to be to reduce volatility. That's not so nasty, is it?

Shared values

How should shares and stockmarkets be valued by investors?

WHAT IS THE VALUE of a share of a company? This innocent-seeming question is a source of endless difficulty and controversy. One answer is clear, of course: the value of a share is the price it commands in the stockmarket. That is true enough, but not very satisfying. Share prices move around erratically, often for no apparent reason. Fundamental value, one supposes, should be more stable. And prices are not in fact entirely random: they seem anchored, albeit elastically, to some underlying notion of worth. That is why, amid all the chaotic fluctuations, unexpectedly good news about company profits moves prices up, not down. Fundamental forces are at work – but how are they to be assessed? How are investors to measure the underlying value of a share?

Economic principles (and common sense) suggest that there must be two basic components. First, the flow of income that the owner of the share can expect to receive over time. (A share that will generate no income in any form at any time is fundamentally worthless.) Second, the rate at which this flow of income received in the future should be "discounted", so that it can be compared in "present value" terms with income received today. All of the many different methods used by market professionals to value equities can be understood as attempts to gauge these two elements.

Shares would be much easier to value if investors received all their income from them in the form of dividends, and if they knew what those dividends would be year by year from now until the end of time. They would add up this infinitely long series of flows, discount it (let us suppose, for now) using the interest rate available on some alternative riskless asset, and thus calculate the present value of the income stream. This value would in turn be the share's underlying worth.

But the world is more complicated than this. The first and biggest problem is immediately apparent: nobody knows what the flow of future income from any share will be. So the first component of valuation calls for a forecast – and the scope for error and disagreement is already vast.

You would expect firms that do well to pay bigger dividends in future, and firms that do badly to pay smaller ones, or maybe to go out of business. Looking at the present level of dividends and supposing that it will persist indefinitely is therefore not a sound basis for valuation. Moreover, a growing number of firms do not pay dividends at all. So a more plausible guide is earnings (that is, profits). If a firm is profitable now, it has the means both to pay its owners a dividend and to retain some resources for investment. Retained earnings allow the company to grow, and provide the wherewithal for higher earnings and dividends in future. Earnings, in other words, provide the means to pay income to shareholders not just now but next year and the year after. Unlike dividends, they have a forward-looking character.

Highly valued

That is why the most popular traditional measure of valuation looks at earnings in relation to the share's price in the market. This can be done in two ways. First is the price/earnings ratio, probably the most quoted measure of valuation: the higher the p/e ratio, the more expensive a share is in relation to the firm's earnings. Wall Street's aggregate p/e ratio is currently more than 30 – astonishingly expensive by historical standards (see Chart 6.15).

The other way of looking at it is to turn the ratio upside down, and to consider earnings divided by price. This is called the earnings yield. As a valuation measure, this is very natural and appealing. In effect, it shows current profit as a rate of return. Not all earnings will be paid out as dividends immediately, but to the extent they are not, the value of the firm can be expected to grow thanks to investment from retained earnings. This growth, in turn, will be reflected in a rising share price. So you can think of earnings yield as the engine that drives both dividends and capital gains, the two forms in which shareholders receive most of their income from their shares.

Because the earnings yield is a rate of return, it can be directly compared with other rates of return. Wall Street's aggregate earnings yield was about 3% in 1999. Note that this was a real (after inflation) return. The rate of return on American index-linked government securities (also a real return) was roughly 4%. On this measure, then, American shares in the aggregate were paying a lower rate of return than a perfectly safe alternative investment. Given that shares are a riskier investment than index-linked liabilities of the American government, this was an extremely surprising state of affairs (and one that was the converse, of course, of the extraordinarily high p/e ratio mentioned a moment ago).

The earnings measures are not without their drawbacks. Although they are somewhat forward-looking (because they allow for investment and growth), and although their historical record in predicting total returns on shares is excellent, they may nonetheless lead investors astray. If companies grow faster in future than in the past, for reasons over and above the investment of retained earnings, then actual earnings will grow faster as well, and the earnings yield will prove to have been too gloomy an indicator.

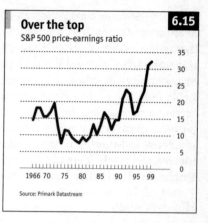

Over the top 6.15
S&P 500 price-earnings ratio

Source: Primark Datastream

This is not to say that there is no limit on what that growth might be. Logic and accounting identities set some ceilings – a fact that some market optimists tend to forget. (Obviously, for instance, earnings cannot grow faster than the economy as a whole for ever, for the simple reason that earnings cannot account for more than 100% of the economy.) Nonetheless, if the world were to undergo a new industrial revolution, it is possible that earnings would surge above their historical norms.

The forecasting problem is ultimately insoluble. However, some analysts have other reasons for preferring alternative measures of shareholder income to measures based on earnings. For instance, earnings is an accountant's concept: a clever finance man, it is said, can make a company's earnings come out at whatever he likes. Some analysts prefer measures less prone to manipulation, such as sales, or "cashflow" (which comes in various shapes and sizes). Still others prefer to look at the value of a firm's physical assets (such as buildings and equipment). None of these measures is perfect. The best course may be to weigh all of them. When all is said and done, however, the amateur investor is well advised to look hard, and think hard, about earnings yield.

Risks and returns

But now comes another problem. Suppose the earnings yield accurately predicts the return to be expected on equities. What is the appropriate rate to compare it with? And in making the comparison, how much of a premium (if any) should the investor expect to receive in return for bearing the extra risk (if any) of holding equities? Thinking back to the two components of valuation, income and the discount rate, this new question boils down to asking whether the discount rate should include an allowance for risk.

Many recent arguments about the level of Wall Street are really arguments about risk and the appropriate size of the risk premium. A crucial idea here is diversification. It makes sense for investors to diversify their holdings of shares, for two reasons. First, some firms are hit by random occurrences that affect only themselves (eg, the founder dies or a clever employee invents post-it notes). Second, even apart from such specific shocks, different firms thrive in different circumstances, in ways that are often predictable (eg, falling oil prices hurt Shell but help Singapore Airlines). As a result of these tendencies, a big portfolio is less risky than a single stock.

Cap in hand

This means not only that all investors should diversify, but that the risk premium on individual stocks should take account of this widespread practice. So when determining an individual equity's risk premium, the overall riskiness of its cash payouts is not important: what matters is how those payouts relate to the rest of the portfolio. In other words, the premium on an individual firm's shares should be based in some way on their contribution to portfolio risk.

The famous Capital Asset Pricing Model (CAPM, pronounced cap-m) is built on this idea. It relates the risk of shares to the risk of the market as a whole, rather than to the shares' specific risks. In this way the principles of diversification refine the way investors judge the risk of individual stocks. Using volatility as a proxy, they recognise that the risks of two stocks that bounce around a lot, but always do so in the opposite direction, net out to nil if they are mixed in one portfolio. So the volatility that matters to investors is only the residual riskiness that a stock brings to a portfolio (called "beta", in the jargon). And it is this aspect of volatility that determines what the expected returns should be. Shares that offer higher expected returns for the risk that investors bear are deemed cheap.

The CAPM is not uncontroversial. Debate rages over whether it, or some other model, best captures the link between risk and return. The main problem is in how to measure volatility. Invariably, any estimates must be based on past returns. And by using those data, economists tacitly assume the future is going to resemble the past. Forecasts again.

Consider the view that shares are a great buy for long-term investors, because the short-term "risks" of holding them balance out over time. But this ignores the possibility that the volatility of the stockmarket as a whole might change. More importantly, it helps to remember that volatility is just a variable that economists have chosen to measure risk. For short-term investors, who buy and sell frequently, it is an excellent measure. But for long-term investors, what matters more is whether they will enjoy high returns over the next 30 years or so. And that depends on other risks, such as the prospects for productivity growth, wars, disease and demographic and technological trends.

To realise the benefits of diversification, portfolios should contain shares that, on average, do not move in lock-step. But putting faith in historical correlations to estimate this can pose problems. The long-term investor might want to consider rather different things, such as the outlook for democracy in Asia, the future of Russia or the effect of the internet on established brands. American and European stockmarkets, for example, tend to move together now. But their value ten years from now could be very different, for reasons that have nothing to do with today's price gyrations.

Better be quick

Despite drawbacks with historical data, and some of the practical problems of measuring risk, the studies that economists have done paint an impressive picture of the way stockmarkets work. They suggest that most stockmarkets, especially in advanced economies, are extremely efficient at incorporating new information into share prices. This claim may seem fanciful to the average investor, who sees everyone around him trying to beat the market.

But economists do not define market efficiency in absolute terms. From its inception, the concept has been defined in terms of information. A market is efficient with respect to quarterly profit announcements, for example, if the implications of those announcements are immediately incorporated into share prices. If the effects of the announcements seeped into the price over a number of weeks, or even years, the market would not be efficient. Economists measure these effects through event studies, which capture the impact of such new information on the price of shares.

Over the past 25 years economists have published hundreds of such studies, examining the effects of mergers, R&D announcements, new product launches, changes in the boardroom, and just about everything else that investment gurus mention when hawking the latest hot stock. And overwhelmingly these studies tell the same story: you cannot beat the market, and you will make only your stockbroker rich by trying.

The material in this chapter was first published in *The Economist* in October 1999 (pages 137–48), November 1999 (pages 149–66) and December 1999 (pages 167–72).

7
CENTRAL BANKS

The best way to destroy the capitalist system is to debauch the currency. Whether Lenin actually made this remark, first attributed to him by John Maynard Keynes, is unknown. But many governments over the years have tested the proposition. They have "practised, from necessity or incompetence, what a Bolshevist might have done from design," Keynes complained.

The best way to debauch a currency is to supply too much of it. In 1989 Argentina's national mint churned out pesos at such a rate its printing presses broke down. When too much money chases too few goods, prices rise, and money loses its value. Those foolish enough to hold large amounts of cash – or any other financial asset that is not hedged against inflation – lose out. But the damage to the economy goes deeper.

High and unstable inflation makes it impossible to achieve the feats of co-ordination that underlie a successful economy. If you cannot know the purchasing power of money a year or two hence, you cannot make plans and contracts over such spans of time. During America's spell of moderately high inflation in the 1970s, the market for 30-year Treasury bonds broke down. No one wanted to buy a promise redeemable three decades in the future when it was impossible to say what those future dollars would be worth.

Keynes, with more dramatic monetary disruptions in mind, put it more forcefully:

> As the inflation proceeds and the real value of the currency
> fluctuates wildly from month to month, all permanent
> relations between debtors and creditors, which form the
> ultimate foundation of capitalism, become so utterly
> disordered as to be almost meaningless; and the process of
> wealth-getting degenerates into a gamble and a lottery.

In the advanced economies, such dramas are largely a thing of the past. Governments have come to recognise that the currency is safer out of their hands. Central banks, which once existed for their convenience, now stand aloof from the political fray. Charged with preserving price stability, not bankrolling improvident sovereigns, central bankers enjoy great freedom to restrict and regulate the supply of money as they see fit.

The monetary authorities no longer bow to politicians. But, according to the articles in this chapter, they still pay too much deference to financial markets. If firms mark up their prices, or workers hike their pay claims, central bankers are quick to step in to curb the inflationary pressure. But if asset markets get carried away, multiplying the price of shares or houses, the modern central banker steps back, telling himself that "the markets know best". Such forbearance allowed a stockmarket bubble to inflate in America in the 1990s. It is also partly responsible for house-price booms since then.

Why should we care about the price of goods and services, but not the price of assets? This is a question Irving Fisher posed in 1906, and that a number of economists are posing once again. An asset is a claim on future goods and services. A house, for example, will provide a roof over your head for as long as it stands. Central bankers worry about the price of shelter today – they watch rents very closely. But they care much less about the price of buying shelter for the future – they ignore house prices almost entirely. As a consequence, if you want to rent a room, your money has held its value. But if you want to buy a house, it has not.

Keynes bemoaned the arbitrary rearrangement of riches when inflation breaks out. Those with savings in the bank are pauperised; those who owe money escape their debts. But asset-price inflation can be equally arbitrary in its effects. During the stockmarket bubble of the 1990s, resources were raised, workers hired and office-space rented on the back of share prices that bore little connection to economic reality. More recently, the vast run-up in house prices has impoverished would-be homebuyers, even as it has enriched homeowners. Central bankers bask in their success at stabilising the price index of goods and services. But the price index of wealth is as unstable as ever.

Navigators in troubled waters

Central banks are now more powerful than ever before. They should enjoy their moment of glory: it will not last

The 1979 annual meeting of central bankers, which took place in Belgrade at a time of double-digit inflation and a sliding dollar, was memorable not for any policy decisions it took, but because Paul Volcker, then newly installed as chairman of America's Federal Reserve, suddenly decided to return home before the formal business had even begun. On October 6th 1979, following a secret meeting of the Federal Open Market Committee, the Fed's policymaking body, Mr Volcker announced his "Saturday Night Special": a package of measures designed to squeeze out inflation by radically changing the way the Fed controlled the money supply. This was a defining moment in the battle against inflation, and signalled the start of a new assertiveness among central banks.

Mr Volcker succeeded in crushing inflation, but at the cost of America's worst recession since the second world war. Nevertheless, the Fed's boldness encouraged other central banks to take up the fight. Today, central banks not only agree more or less unanimously that price stability should be the main goal of monetary policy, but most of them have in fact achieved it.

The power of central banks steadily increased during the 1980s and 1990s. Until the late 1980s, only the Fed, the German Bundesbank and the Swiss National Bank enjoyed legal independence. Most central banks remained firmly under the thumb of finance ministries. But the surge in global inflation in the 1970s and 1980s convinced many people that politicians were not always to be trusted with the monetary levers, so central bankers were allowed to take control. The Reserve Bank of New Zealand in 1989 became the first to be given independence and a clear mandate to fight inflation. During the 1990s more and more central banks, from the Bank of England to the Bank of Mexico, were set free.

In the mid-1980s the idea that European governments would hand over a large part of economic policy to unelected officials would have been laughed at; yet today the European Central Bank (ECB) is the most independent central bank in the world, even more insulated from political pressures than the Bundesbank. Even the Bank of Japan, blamed by many for the Japanese economy's painful progress from boom to bust, has been made independent. Never before in history have central banks wielded so much power.

And not only that: many of them also enjoy increased respect. This reflects their general success in defeating inflation, but more particularly, in America it also reflects the success of Alan Greenspan, who succeeded Mr Volcker as the Fed's chairman, in safely steering the economy through a long period of low-inflation growth. Mr Greenspan is probably the most revered central banker of all time. Contrast that with the early 1980s, when many small businesses saw Mr Volcker as public enemy number one and construction workers formed picket lines outside the Fed.

All at sea

Over the years, central bankers have popularly been referred to as captains, admirals, pilots and lifeboatmen. Implicit in all these nautical titles is the assumption that central bankers know exactly where they are heading, how their craft (ie, the economy) works, and how their actions will affect its course. Yet in reality central bankers have more in common with the early navigators. They operate in a world of huge uncertainty, with no reliable maps or compasses. Because of lags in the publication of statistics, they do not know precisely where the economy has got to even today, let alone where it is going. And some of the policy dilemmas they face are the equivalent of not knowing whether the earth is round or flat. So for all their increased power and independence, central banks still find that their ability to steer economies with precision is limited.

In some respects things have been getting more difficult for them. They have always had to live with uncertainty, but since the 1980s that uncertainty has been hugely compounded by financial deregulation and innovation. The role of central banks has traditionally been defined in terms of banks, money and inflation. Thus, at the very pinnacle of their power, it is disconcerting that they still have to ask three questions. What is a bank? What is money? And what is inflation?

As the boundaries between different sorts of financial institutions have become blurred, central banks have found banks increasingly hard to define, let alone police. The financial revolution has also distorted the traditional measures of the money supply, as people shift their savings from standard bank deposits to new financial instruments. But perhaps most worrying of all, a lively debate has recently got under way about how to measure inflation, and which prices central banks need to concern themselves with. Specifically, should they try to stabilise the prices of assets, such as property and shares, as well as the prices of goods and services?

Some central bankers brought up on the idea that their sole job was to kill inflation have not yet woken up to the fact that their new enemies are asset-price inflation and deflation. This does not mean that central banks should abandon the pursuit of price stability, which remains a proper long-term objective. However, they should remember that price stability is not an end in itself, but only a means to the real aim of sustaining economic growth. Price stability by itself will not prevent booms and busts, so central banks need to widen their vision to include other signs of economic imbalance. They must try to prevent both severe asset-price bubbles that can burst painfully, and deflationary conditions that depress growth.

Monetary metamorphosis

Central banks have broken out of their political cocoons

"THERE HAVE BEEN THREE GREAT INVENTIONS since the beginning of time: fire, the wheel and central banking," quipped Will Rogers, an American humorist. Yet central banking as we know it today is an invention of the 20th century. The first recorded reference in English to a "central bank" was in 1873 by Walter Bagehot, then editor of *The Economist*, who used it to refer to a bank with a monopoly on the issue of bank notes, and its headquarters in a nation's capital. But it is only in the past 50 years or so that the term has become widely used. At the start of the 20th century the world had only 18 central banks; today there are more than 170.

Central banks' original task was not to conduct monetary policy or support the banking system, but to finance government spending. The world's oldest central bank, the Bank of Sweden, was established in 1668 largely as a vehicle to finance military spending. The Bank of England was created in 1694 to fund a war with France. Even as recently as the late 1940s, a Labour chancellor of the exchequer, Stafford Cripps, took great pleasure in describing the Bank of England as "his bank". Today most central banks are banned from financing government deficits.

The United States managed without a central bank until early in the 20th century. Private banks used to issue their own notes and coins, and banking crises were fairly frequent. But following a series of particularly severe crises, the Federal Reserve was set up in 1913, mainly to supervise banks and act as a lender of last resort. Today the Fed is one of the few major central banks that is still responsible for bank supervision; most countries have handed this job to a separate agency.

The modern era of central banking, with its emphasis on monetary policy, began in the early 1970s, when the old link between money and gold was finally severed and the Bretton Woods system of fixed exchange rates broke down. When countries were on the gold standard or exchange rates were fixed, monetary policy was constrained by the need to maintain the peg. Only since exchange rates have been allowed to float has each country been able to have its own monetary policy.

At first, governments in most countries kept a tight grip on the mone-

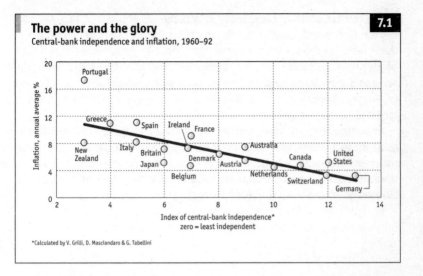

The power and the glory `7.1`

Central-bank independence and inflation, 1960–92

Index of central-bank independence*
zero = least independent

*Calculated by V. Grilli, D. Masciandaro & G. Tabellini

tary reins, telling central banks when to change interest rates. But when inflation soared, governments saw the advantage of granting central banks independence in matters of monetary policy. Short-sighted politicians might try to engineer a boom before an election, hoping that inflation would not rise until after the votes had been counted, but an independent central bank insulated from political pressures would give higher priority to price stability. If, as a result of independence, policy is more credible, workers and firms are likely to adjust their wages and prices more quickly in response to a tightening of policy, and so, the argument runs, inflation can be reduced with a smaller loss of output and jobs. Thus, like Ulysses, who asked to be roped to the mast so he would not succumb to the sirens' song, politicians have removed themselves from monetary temptation.

Several studies in the early 1990s confirmed that countries with independent central banks did indeed tend to have lower inflation rates (see Chart 7.1). And better still, low inflation did not appear to come at the cost of slower growth. Correlation, of course, does not prove causation. Some economists, such as Adam Posen at the Institute for International Economics in Washington, have argued that Germany's low post-war inflation rate and central-bank independence were both determined by a third factor: namely, Germans' dark memories of hyperinflation. Countries that dislike inflation develop institutions that will help ward it off.

No central bank is completely independent. Before the ECB was set up, the German Bundesbank was the most independent central bank in the world, yet the German government chose to ignore its advice on the appropriate exchange rate for unification, and thereby stoked inflationary pressures. Some central banks, such as the Bank of England, have full independence in the setting of monetary policy, but their inflation target is set by the government.

Independent central banks are more likely to achieve low inflation than finance ministers because they have a longer time horizon. But independence is no panacea: central banks can still make mistakes. Note that Germany's Reichsbank was statutorily independent when the country suffered hyperinflation in 1923.

Monopoly power over money

Central banks have a huge influence over the financial system. How do they conduct monetary policy?

D URING THE COLD WAR, Russian leaders' every word was scruti-nised by an army of Kremlinologists. Now, that honour is accorded to the world's central bankers, whose pronouncements are pored over by throngs of well-paid financial analysts.

For all central banks' importance, they remain tiny participants in huge financial markets. So how do they affect prices, ie, interest rates, in those markets? Consider America. Its fixed-income market (government and private) was worth some $13.6 trillion in 1999. Every day hundreds of billions of dollars of these securities change hands, and it is not unusual for a single private firm to buy or sell more than $1 billion in one go. The Fed itself buys or sells only between $1 billion and $5 billion of these securities each year: a mere drop in the ocean of a $14 trillion market. Yet somehow it affects the level and structure of prices and yields.

The reason the Fed can set interest rates is that it has a monopoly on supplying bank reserves. Banks are required to hold a fraction of the money deposited with them in a reserve account at the Fed (see Chart 7.2). They usually hold more, for precautionary reasons. The interest rate at which banks' demand for reserves matches the Fed's supply is known as the federal funds rate; this is also the rate at which banks lend reserves to each other overnight. The Fed controls it by changing the supply of reserves through sales and purchases of government securities, known as open-market operations.

When the Fed wants to raise the federal funds rate, it sells government securities. It receives payment by reducing the account of the buyer's bank, which reduces the volume of

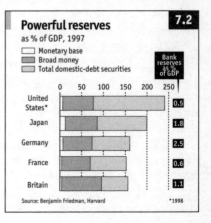

Powerful reserves

7.2

as % of GDP, 1997

☐ Monetary base
▦ Broad money
☐ Total domestic-debt securities

Bank reserves as % of GDP

	0	50	100	150	200	250	
United States*							0.5
Japan							1.8
Germany							2.5
France							0.6
Britain							1.1

Source: Benjamin Friedman, Harvard   *1998

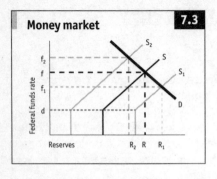

Money market `7.3`

reserves in the banking system. This is illustrated in Chart 7.3 by a shift in the supply curve for reserves from S to S2. Because banks' demand for reserves exceeds supply, the federal funds rate is bid up (from f to f2) until excess demand is eliminated. And when the Fed wants to lower the rate, it buys securities, which increases banks' reserves and bids down interest rates. The supply curve shifts from S to S1, and the rate falls from f to f1.

The Fed can also influence the federal funds rate indirectly, by changing the discount rate (d in Chart 7.3), the rate at which it will lend reserves to banks, or altering banks' reserve requirements, the fraction of their deposits that they are required to hold as reserves. Raising the discount rate makes it less attractive for banks to borrow reserves. This reduces the volume of reserves, which pushes up the federal funds rate. Increasing reserve requirements boosts banks' demand for reserves, which also bids up the federal funds rate. But the Fed usually prefers to control the rate through open-market operations, which have a more stable and predictable impact on the money market.

The long and short of it

Changes in the federal funds rate ripple through financial markets and the economy. They have knock-on effects on the interest rates at which banks lend to households and firms, and hence the amount of credit in the economy. And they influence long-term market interest rates too.

Take the yield on a five-year government bond. It is simply the weighted average of expected short-term interest rates over the next five years, plus a risk and a liquidity premium. A rise in short-term interest rates typically has two effects on long-term rates. It raises the five-year weighted average slightly. And it also affects expectations of future short-term interest rates.

If, for example, investors believe the Fed is raising rates pre-emptively to prevent inflation rising, then expected future interest rates may fall, and so would five-year yields. However, if the rate increase is seen as a belated recognition by the Fed that inflation is likely to rise, five-year rates may rise in anticipation of further rate increases to come.

The graphical relationship between interest rates on securities of different maturities is known as the yield curve. Yield curves typically slope upwards, as Germany's does in Chart 7.4, because investors demand a risk premium on bonds of longer maturities to compensate for the extra uncertainty associated with lending for a longer period. But when monetary policy is tightened and short-term interest

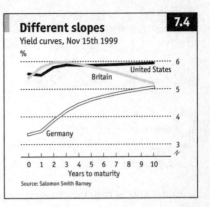

Different slopes 7.4
Yield curves, Nov 15th 1999
%

United States
Britain
Germany

Years to maturity
Source: Salomon Smith Barney

rates are increased, it is possible sometimes for the yield curve to become inverted, as Britain's is in the chart, sloping downwards for all but the shortest maturities.

A new economy for the New World?

Inflation may not be as dead as it seems

ONCE UPON A TIME sailors went to sea in the belief that the earth was flat, putting them at risk of dropping off the edge. Fortunately the discovery that it was round solved that problem. Economic thinking about monetary policy and inflation has undergone a similar about-turn.

In the 1960s, the conventional economic wisdom was that monetary policy could reduce unemployment. The theoretical underpinning for this was the Phillips curve, named after Bill Phillips, an economist from New Zealand based at the London School of Economics. Mr Phillips, also a trained engineer, constructed a machine to demonstrate the workings of the economy, using water to represent liquidity. In 1958 he published a study showing that between 1861 and 1957 some kind of trade-off between wage inflation and unemployment seemed to have been operating in Britain: when unemployment was high, inflation was low, and vice versa. This seemed to suggest that central banks could permanently reduce unemployment by tolerating a bit more inflation.

A decade later, however, two American economists, Milton Friedman and Edmund Phelps, challenged this theory. The trade-off between inflation and unemployment, they argued, was only short-term, because once people came to expect higher inflation, they would demand higher wages, and unemployment would rise back to its "natural rate", which depended on the efficiency of the labour market. There was no long-term trade-off between inflation and unemployment: in the long run, monetary policy could influence only inflation. If policymakers tried to hold unemployment below its natural rate (also known by an acronym, NAIRU, the non-accelerating inflation rate of unemployment), inflation would be pushed ever higher.

Just as Friedman and Phelps had predicted, the level of inflation associated with a given level of unemployment rose through the 1970s, and policymakers had to abandon the Phillips curve. Today there is a broad consensus that monetary policy should focus on holding down inflation. But this does not mean, as is often claimed, that central banks are "inflation nutters", cruelly indifferent towards unemployment.

If there is no long-term trade-off, low inflation does not permanently choke growth. Moreover, by keeping inflation low and stable, a central bank, in effect, stabilises output and jobs. Don Brash, governor of the Reserve Bank of New Zealand, explains how this happens, using Chart 7.5. The straight line represents the growth in output that the economy can sustain over the long run; the wavy line repre-

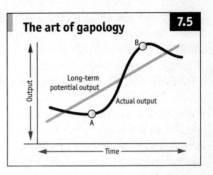

The art of gapology 7.5

Long-term potential output

Actual output

sents actual output. When the economy is producing below potential (ie, unemployment is above the NAIRU), at point A, inflation will fall until the "output gap" is eliminated. When output is above potential, at point B, inflation will rise for as long as demand is above capacity. If inflation is falling (point A), then a central bank will cut interest rates, helping to boost growth in output and jobs; when inflation is rising (point B), it will raise interest rates, dampening down growth. Thus if monetary policy focuses on keeping inflation low and stable, it will automatically help to stabilise employment and growth.

The Fed clearly understands this relationship between inflation and the output gap, but initial signs suggest that the ECB may underestimate the extent to which it can safely hold interest rates low in the short run to boost output and jobs. It has repeatedly said that lower interest rates cannot reduce unemployment. That is undoubtedly true in the long run, but if an economy is operating below potential and the jobless rate is above the NAIRU, then interest rates can safely be cut, and hence output boosted, without pushing up inflation.

Is a bit of inflation good for you?

When inflation was in double digits, central banks had a simple rule: bring it down. But now that the rate in almost all rich economies is 3.5% or less, they are being forced to ask: how low? This is hotly debated, because some economists believe that inflation has economic benefits as well as costs.

Consider, first, the costs. When inflation is high, people find it difficult to distinguish between changes in average prices and changes in relative prices. For example, a firm cannot tell if a rise in the price of copper reflects general inflation or a scarcity of the metal. This distorts important price signals, leading to a misallocation of resources. Inflation also creates uncertainty about the future, which reduces investment. And lastly, because of the way inflation interacts with tax systems, which are never fully indexed for inflation, it reduces the real return on saving and hence reduces future growth.

Inflation in double digits clearly does considerable harm, but what about lower rates? And does 5% inflation do more damage than 2%, or zero? Yes, answers Martin Feldstein, president of the National Bureau of Economic Research.[1] He believes that even modest inflation can do significant damage through its effect on saving. Tax is levied on nominal interest income, so as inflation rises, the real after-tax return on savings comes down and people save less, which depresses future growth rates. Mr Feldstein estimates that in America a cut in inflation from 2% to zero would permanently increase the level of GDP by 1%. To reduce inflation by two percentage points would involve a one-off loss in output of 5% of GDP, but the discounted present value of the future annual gains, of around 35% of GDP, would far outweigh the loss. Zero inflation, he concludes, is a worthy goal.

Yet there is little empirical evidence that lower inflation rates do noticeably improve growth performance once inflation is below 5%, say. A scatter plot of inflation against growth for a range of countries shows no clear trend (see Chart 7.6). A study by Robert Barro, an economist at Harvard University, found that a reduction in inflation of one percentage point increases the annual growth rate by a paltry 0.02 of a percentage point.

Some economists go further, arguing that modest inflation, of perhaps 3–4%, is good for growth and employment. Nominal wages, they say, tend to be rigid downwards. Workers may be prepared to put up with flat wages when the inflation rate is 3%, which amounts to a decline in real income, but they are reluctant to accept a pay cut in money terms. So if the inflation rate is zero, real wages cannot be adjusted downwards in declining industries or regions, which means that unemployment will rise. Inflation, the argument runs, greases the wheels of the labour market, allowing real wages to adjust more smoothly.

A widely cited study by the Brookings Institution,[2] which examined pay in America since 1959, confirmed that very few people take nominal wage cuts in any year. However, the problem of wage "stickiness" may be overstated. There have been few periods in the past when inflation has been less than 3% for an extended period, so it is not surprising that falling wages are rare. If inflation were to remain low, resistance to

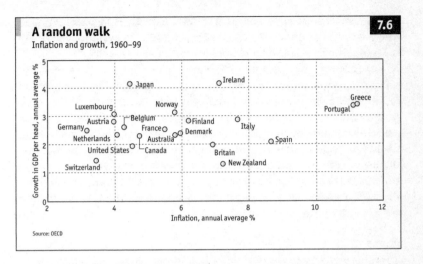

A random walk

7.6

Inflation and growth, 1960–99

Growth in GDP per head, annual average %

Inflation, annual average %

Source: OECD

wage cuts might fade. Indeed, in Japan wages fell during 1997 and 1998. And as long as productivity is rising, allowing unit labour costs to fall, there may be no need for nominal pay cuts anyway.

A second common worry about zero inflation is that interest rates cannot fall below zero, so there is no way of allowing real interest rates to become negative to help the economy out of a recession. But the need for negative real interest rates may be exaggerated. Mervyn King, governor of the Bank of England, argues that negative real interest rates have been rare in America during the past half-century.[3] During most recessions, low real interest rates have been enough to boost demand. The only time when there might be a problem is if the economy suffers a shock when the output gap is already large and inflation below target because policymakers have failed to react to a previous slump in demand. A pre-emptive policy which aims to prevent inflation going below target as well as above, argues Mr King, minimises the need for negative real interest rates.

The final and most serious concern is that if central banks aim for zero inflation, prices are more likely to fall for brief periods, and the experiences of the 1930s and Japan today show that deflation can be more dangerous than modest inflation. But falling prices are not necessarily a problem. Before the first world war, a decline in the average price level was quite common during periods of rapid technological change, such as the late 19th century; yet these were also periods of strong growth. This is quite different from the harmful sort of deflation seen during the Great Depression. Moreover, the odd year of falling prices does not matter so long as it does not feed expectations that they will continue to fall, causing households to delay spending.

On balance, the benefits of retaining some inflation are probably overstated. Price stability reduces uncertainty and so offers the best economic environment for firms and households. So why do central banks not invariably aim for zero inflation? The answer is that official consumer-price indices tend to overstate the true rate of inflation in all countries, because they do not adjust fully for improvements over time in the quality of goods and services. Estimates suggest that in most countries the official consumer-price index overstates inflation by around 0.5–2.0% a year. This is the best reason why central banks should aim for a slightly positive inflation rate.

Notes

1 Martin Feldstein, "The Costs and Benefits of Going from Low Inflation to Price Stability", NBER working paper No. 5469, 1997.
2 George Akerlof, William Dickens and George Perry, "The Macroeconomics of Low Inflation", Brookings Papers on Economic Activity 1, 1996.
3 Mervyn King, "Challenges for Monetary Policy: New and Old", Federal Reserve Bank of Kansas City symposium, August 1999.

Hubble, bubble, asset-price trouble

Central banks should pay more attention to rising share and property prices

ANY CENTRAL BANKER WORTH HIS SALT knows that his job is to aim for price stability. But stability of which prices? Should central banks worry only about consumer-price inflation, or also about the prices of assets, such as equities and property? Alan Greenspan asked this question in December 1996 when he made his famous speech about "irrational exuberance" in the stockmarket. Since then Wall Street has climbed another 70%. How to deal with asset prices is now one of the most serious dilemmas of monetary policy.

Consumer-price inflation may currently be modest, but another sort of inflation, in share prices, is rampant. Many central bankers are privately worried about the lofty heights share prices have reached, but they do not believe there is much they can or should do about it. Such diffidence could prove damaging. Price stability, remember, is only a means to the end of maximum sustainable growth. And asset-price inflation can be even more harmful to growth than ordinary inflation.

Policymakers often claim that by pursuing price stability they will reduce the risk of boom and bust. But history suggests that, although price stability does deliver big benefits, it does not guarantee economic and financial stability. Indeed, there is reason to believe that financial bubbles may be more likely to develop during periods of low CPI inflation. The two biggest bubbles this century – America's in the 1920s and Japan's in the 1980s – both developed when inflation was modest.

One explanation is that when inflation is subdued, interest rates look low, thanks to "money illusion": people fail to notice that in real terms rates are just as high as in more inflationary times. This encourages a borrowing binge and prompts investors to chase higher and hence riskier returns. When interest rates are low, people are also able to borrow a much bigger multiple of their incomes to finance speculative investment. At the same time, price stability can sometimes encourage economic euphoria. With seemingly no reason for central banks to raise interest rates, people start to expect that the expansion will continue indefinitely. This false sense of security encourages investors to take bigger risks, and lenders to relax their standards.

Flemming Larsen, a former deputy director of research at the IMF, pointed out that there was much evidence that an economy can overheat even at a time of price stability as conventionally defined. Excess demand shows up instead in balance sheets and asset prices. Traditional indicators of inflation may mislead monetary policymakers. Central banks, he argued, should pay more attention to asset markets and to unsustainable balance-sheet trends, and may need to raise interest rates even if inflation remains low.

William McChesney Martin, governor of the Fed in 1951–70, memorably described the Fed's job as being "to take away the punch bowl just when the party is getting going" – ie, before the economy overheats and pushes up inflation. But there is more than one sort of party. The Fed has failed to remove the punch bowl from Wall Street's speculative binge.

There are four reasons why it (and other central banks) should worry about asset-price inflation:

- It can be a leading indicator of CPI inflation, if rising asset prices spill over into excess demand. The increase in wealth encourages consumers to splurge. At the same time rising share prices reduce the cost of capital, so firms invest more.
- The consumer-price index is a flawed measure of inflation. Ideally, an effective measure should include not only the prices of goods and services consumed today, but also of those to be consumed tomorrow, since they, too, affect the value of money. Assets are claims on future services, so asset prices are a proxy for the prices of future consumption. For instance, a rise in house prices today will increase the cost of future housing services. A classic paper written in 1973 by two American economists, Armen Alchian and Benjamin Klein,[1] argued that central banks should try to stabilise a broad price index that includes asset prices.
- Just as high consumer-price inflation tends to blur relative price changes, surges in asset prices also distort price signals and cause a misallocation of resources. For instance, if the cost of capital is artificially low, firms may be tempted to overinvest in risky projects. American business investment jumped from 13% to 18% of GDP between 1993 and 1999, similar to the surge in Japan in the late 1980s. As the quantity of investment surges during a bubble, its quality typically deteriorates.
- When a bubble bursts, it can cause severe economic and financial harm. Rising asset prices encourage excessive borrowing by firms

and individuals, leaving them heavily exposed to a fall in asset prices and a recession. The longer the party continues, the worse the eventual hangover, because imbalances, such as the level of debt, will be even bigger.

Given these costs, there is a strong case for central banks to pay more attention to rising asset prices, and to raise interest rates to deflate a bubble in its early stages. This does not mean that central banks should try to target share prices, or change interest rates in response to every twitch in the Dow. But if a sharp rise in share prices is accompanied by rapid growth in domestic demand and a steep increase in borrowing, alarm bells should start ringing.

However, most central bankers, particularly those at the Fed, are hostile to the idea of trying to puncture bubbles. Monetary policy, they argue, should concentrate on stability in the prices of goods and services, and central banks should respond to asset prices only if they spill over into general inflation. Central bankers offer three reasons why they should not attempt to prick bubbles. First, they say, it is impossible to be sure that a rise in asset prices represents a speculative bubble, rather than an upturn justified by improved economic fundamentals. Intervening to prick a bubble, says Mr Greenspan, presumes that central banks know more than the market. But the market is not disinterested. It is to investors' and securities firms' advantage to keep a bubble going. Central banks, on the other hand, are able to take a more balanced view. True, it is impossible to estimate the "correct" value of equities, but monetary policy is always dealing with uncertainty. Central banks do not give up on trying to target consumer-price inflation just because they are unsure about the pace of productivity growth or the size of the output gap.

A second problem with pricking bubbles is that central banks have no laser-guided weapons for the purpose. The one they can deploy, interest rates, acts more like a nuclear bomb, affecting the whole economy. The link between interest rates and asset prices is also uncertain, so it is hard to know by how much to raise rates. Experience suggests that stockmarkets shrug off timid rate increases, but bold increases can have dangerous results.

Last, and most important, central banks do not have a political mandate to halt asset-price inflation. The awkward truth is that bubbles are popular. Whereas everybody accepts that inflation in goods and services is a bad thing, almost everybody regards rising equity and property prices as a good thing. If, by raising interest rates, the Fed were to reduce the wealth of the 50% of American households who own shares, it would not be long before Congress acted to curb the Fed's power.

How not to do it

There are two examples of central banks deliberately trying to burst a bubble: America in 1928–29 and Japan in 1989–90. Both attempts did indeed end in tears. But that was largely because both central banks left it very late before they acted, and then pursued over-tight policies after asset prices had crashed. The lesson may be not that central banks should keep clear of bubbles, but that they should intervene as early as possible to prevent them.

In Japan, share prices and property prices increased more than four-fold between 1981 and 1989. Geoffrey Miller, the director of the Center for the Study of Central Banks at New York University, who has studied Japan's bubble,[2] reckons that with hindsight it is clear that monetary policy was too lax. The Bank of Japan started to fret about rising property and share prices and rampant bank lending in 1987. If it had tightened policy then, the economic damage would have been considerably less. So why did the bank wait two more years?

Uncertainties about whether it really was a bubble and how asset prices would respond to higher interest rates both played a part. And as in America today, CPI inflation was low (in part because of a strong yen), so politically the bank would have found it hard to take action. But, says Mr Miller, the Bank of Japan also faced another constraint: political pressure from America. The Louvre Accord agreed by the G7 in early 1987 committed Japan to boosting domestic demand to help reduce America's trade deficit.

Mr Miller concludes that pricking bubbles is far from easy. But he argues that there will be times when asset-price bubbles become so large that they pose a threat to the entire economy – and when they do, central banks should raise interest rates to deflate them.

Two enemies, one bullet

A central bank has only one main weapon: interest rates. So if it decides to raise rates to prick a bubble when consumer-price inflation is already low, this could result in falling prices in product markets. But is that necessarily a bad thing? During previous periods of rapid productivity growth, such as the last quarter of the 19th century, average prices did fall. This was a benign sort of deflation, in contrast to the malign sort where output and prices spiral downwards. Perhaps, as argued in an essay in the 1998 annual report of the Federal Reserve Bank of Cleveland, prices should be falling now in America. The essay summarises arguments made by economists in the 1920s and 1930s, which suggest that at times of rapid technological change overall price stability and economic stability may be incompatible.

Indeed, it is possible that if rapid productivity gains are pulling down the costs of production, price stability might be the wrong goal. Earlier in the 20th century, several economists argued that increased productivity growth brought about by technological advances in the 1920s should have caused real incomes to rise as prices fell relative to wages. Instead, a lax monetary policy prevented prices from falling, and nominal wages lagged behind productivity growth. As a result, profits surged, and share prices soared on the false expectation that this happy state of affairs would continue indefinitely.

Notes

1 Armen Alchian and Benjamin Klein, "On a Correct Measure of Inflation", *Journal of Money, Credit and Banking,* vol. 5, 1973.
2 Geoffrey Miller, "The role of a Central Bank in a Bubble Economy", *Cardozo Law Review,* vol. 18, no. 3, December 1996

In a fog

The only certain thing about monetary policy is its uncertainty

ON THE GROUND FLOOR of the Federal Reserve building in Washington you can play an electronic game which offers four tests to judge whether you are suitable to be Fed chairman. You have to decide whether to tighten or loosen monetary policy in response to various events, such as rising inflation or a stockmarket crash. The author got all the answers right and was duly appointed the next Fed chairman.

If only real life were that simple. Because of huge economic uncertainties, central bankers never have the luxury of an obviously "correct" answer to when and by how much to move interest rates. Although they have become more powerful, their ability to use that power effectively is weakened by imperfect knowledge. Their information on the current state of the economy is always out of date and subject to big revisions. There is particular uncertainty about critical measures such as the pace of productivity growth or the size of the output gap. Central banks do not have a trusted model of how the economy works because it never stands still for long enough for them to get a fix on it.

Moreover, their instruments are blunt. Nobody knows exactly how a change in interest rates will affect the economy. And monetary policy is subject to long and variable lags. It typically takes up to a year for interest rates to affect output and 18 months to two years to feed through into inflation. Alan Blinder, an economist at Princeton University and a former vice-chairman of the Fed, offers a nice analogy. You arrive late at night in a strange hotel room that feels chilly, so you turn up the thermostat and make for the shower. Ten minutes later the room is still too cold, so you turn up the thermostat again and go to sleep. At 2am you awake in a pool of sweat in an oppressively hot room.

Much the same happens with monetary policy. If interest rates are set according to the economy's temperature today, then they will probably be raised by too much and kept high for too long. Monetary policy must be forward-looking, taking account of future inflation. Mr Blinder suggests that central banks should follow a strategy of "dynamic programming"[1]. Today's interest-rate decision should be thought of as the first step along a path of future interest-rate decisions. So before a central bank begins a cycle of tightening, for example, it should have some idea about where it is going. At each stage the central bank should project an entire path of future interest-rate decisions with associated paths for key economic variables. If those economic variables turn out as expected, the central bank should continue to follow the planned path. But if the economy slows sooner than expected, the bank should tighten by less than planned, or even cut interest rates.

In recent years central banks have tried harder to head off trouble before it happens. The snag, says Mr Blinder, is that a successful policy based on pre-emptive strikes will appear to be misguided, exposing central banks to criticism. If they successfully tighten policy early, so that inflation does not even start rising, critics accuse them of unnecessarily destroying jobs. This is exactly what happened when the Fed raised interest rates in 1994–95, and succeeded in preventing a rise in inflation. Central banks cannot win. More recently, America's monetary policy seems to have become less pre-emptive because of the new uncertainties about productivity growth and the link between inflation and unemployment. The Fed now seems to require more evidence of rising inflation before it will put up interest rates. This increases the risk that the economy will wake up in a sweat at 2am.

Note

1   Alan Blinder, *Central Banking in Theory and Practice*, MIT Press, 1999.

Endnote

Alan Greenspan stepped down as chairman of the Federal Reserve in January 2006, enjoying great acclaim after 18 years of service. His successor, Ben Bernanke, is well-known in academic circles for arguing that central banks should not raise interest rates to contain asset-price bubbles, unless they threaten to spill over into inflation.

The material on pages 175–180 and 184–195 was first published in a survey in *The Economist* in October 2004. The material on pages 181–83 was first published in *The Economist* in November 1999.

8
GLOBAL CAPITAL

Every so often *The Economist* changes its mind. The first principles on which it relies (liberties should be jealously guarded; markets lightly regulated) cannot always be applied without second thoughts. The unimpeded flow of capital across borders is one such case. Letting people move their money around as they see fit, rather than penning it within national boundaries, would seem a matter of both liberty and efficiency. But cosmopolitan capital has caused unimaginable mischief in one emerging market after another in recent years: Mexico in 1994, East Asia in 1997–98, Russia in 1998, Brazil in 1999 (and again in 2002), Turkey in 2000–01, and Argentina and Uruguay in 2001–02. As the first article says, "It is enough to make a good liberal stop and think."

The Economist's initial enthusiasm for free capital flows is easy to explain. Poor countries have daunting investment needs, and little wherewithal to meet them. Importing capital from the rich world seemed the obvious solution. Indeed, the case for foreign capital in the 1990s resembles the arguments made for foreign aid in the 1960s: it is needed to fill the gap between a country's desire to accumulate and its ability to save. In 1996, private capital flows to emerging markets reached $324 billion, according to the Institute for International Finance, dwarfing the official aid disbursed that year. Such transfusions of money promised a shortcut to prosperity.

Why was this promise not fulfilled? The crisis-hit countries themselves have attracted some of the blame. Their banks lent to the wrong people for the wrong reasons. Their hard-currency pegs created the illusion of strength, but proved brittle when put to the test. And because their financial systems were opaque, outside investors, when touched by doubt, were quick to assume the worst.

Others place the blame on the lenders not the borrowers. They adopt an old motor-racing adage: "It's not the speed that kills, it's the sudden stop." The crisis-hit countries were undone not by their pace of borrowing *per se*. It was only when their debts were called in, not rolled over, that they collapsed. If foreign investors had only kept faith with emerging markets, that faith would have been repaid.

There may be some truth in this. Financial markets are fickle, herd animals, and their collective whims can swiftly change the facts on the ground. If creditors decide that countries are insolvent, they can make them so, by raising the cost of refinancing debts to unbearable levels. But it is of little comfort to the victims of financial crises to know that they were not wholly to blame for their plight. What is to stop them becoming blameless victims again?

Financial autarky is always an option: neither a borrower nor a lender be. But in the years since their crises, emerging markets have rejected this old (and bad) advice, and decided to be both debtors and creditors. They have been careful to match private inflows of capital with official flows in the opposite direction. In 2005, for example, private capital flows to emerging markets reached $358 billion, beating the 1996 record. But at the same time, governments in these countries amassed $410 billion of foreign-exchange reserves, most of them rich-government bonds. Emerging markets now buy as much debt as they sell.

This chapter suggests another, more profitable response to the dangers of cosmopolitan capital: tax it. Chile pioneered implicit taxes on inflows of foreign money, designed to slow them down and lengthen their maturity. Capital controls of this sort inflict costs and distortions on the economy, and go against many of *The Economist*'s better instincts. But if sudden stops are lethal, governments would do well to watch their speed.

A cruel sea of capital

**Global financial integration is supposed to lift countries up.
Sometimes it sinks them. Here is a guide to safer sailing**

THOSE WHO BELIEVE that globalisation throttles democracy, gouges the poor and fouls the environment are bound to regard today's mostly open markets for international capital as evil. However, this does not prove that unimpeded flows of capital are a good thing. The capital market has vindicated its critics and embarrassed its would-be defenders too often of late. It has been responsible for, or at least deeply implicated in, some very costly economic breakdowns. Perhaps the anti-globalists are on to something.

Rapid globalisation has done nothing to undermine the confidence liberals have always placed in trade. No serious economist questions the case for international integration through flows of goods and services, though there is a lively argument over how integration through trade can best be brought about. Trade is good. But even the most enthusiastic advocate of economic integration may be starting to wonder whether unimpeded flows of capital are quite such a blessing.

Economic principles suggest that they should be. Economics relies heavily on the idea that wider opportunities make people better off – or at least that they do not make them worse off. Whatever else trade does, it widens opportunities. When trade barriers come down, people on each side have an opportunity lacking in a closed economy. They can decide to consume goods that they have not produced, and pay for them by producing goods they do not wish to consume. If they believe they are better off as a result, that is what they will do. Otherwise, they will carry on as before.

Essentially the same logic applies to international finance. Just as a closed economy can consume only what it produces, it can invest only what it saves – no more, no less. Trade in capital makes it possible for countries to separate their saving and investment choices. They can invest more than they save by borrowing the difference from abroad; or they can invest less than they save by lending out the surplus. Changes in the price of capital will ensure that global supply and demand match up, just as changes in the prices of goods bring exports and imports into global balance.

Just as nothing forces a country to trade when the economy opens up, nothing forces a country to become a net importer or exporter of capital if its firms and individuals prefer to lend and borrow as they did before. International capital widens choices in just the same way as international trade.

So how can you be worse off if you are given choices you did not have before, without being obliged to take them up? The answer is that you may make choices you come to regret. Experience suggests that even within the borders of a single economy, trade in capital is far more prone to mistakes than trade in goods or services – though why this should be so is not immediately obvious. And if domestic trade in capital is more error-prone than domestic trade in goods, then international trade in capital is even worse. This perhaps is easier to understand: take the mistakes that get made in a domestic context, then multiply them by ignorance due to distance and exchange-rate risk.

The result is plain enough: recurring financial calamity; sovereign debt default; capital flight; currency crisis; bank failure; stockmarket crash. And the harm is by no means confined to the people who made the mistakes, or to the finance industry at large. Financial collapses have an unmatched capacity for projecting their effects right across the domestic economy, and in the worst cases far beyond that, across the region and even across the world.

Even if there were no doubt that the gains from trade in capital are large – on a par with the gains from trade in goods and services – the costs incurred in recent financial emergencies would still give one pause. Financial crises of the sort that hit Latin America in the 1980s, Mexico in 1994 or East Asia in 1997–98 cause recessions equivalent to years of growth forgone. The 1980s were aptly called Latin America's "lost decade". Financial distress is a salient ingredient in Japan's endless economic difficulties, in Europe's slowdown, in the fragility of America's economic recovery. And if things grow suddenly worse in any of these places, finance will spread the damage far and wide.

So trade in capital is different from trade in goods and services in two main ways: in the scope for getting things wrong, and in the punishment that follows. The first is great and the second is fearsome. It is enough to make a good liberal stop and think.

We all make mistakes

What makes finance so prone to error? Financial markets are asset markets: that is, they are markets for streams of payments spread out over time. (Many goods and some services have an extended time dimension too. By definition, the more this is true, the more such goods and services behave like assets. That is why the market for houses behaves a lot like the market for corporate bonds and not much like the market for biscuits.) When you buy an asset you are gambling on the future. Small changes in beliefs about the future can have a surprisingly large effect on the value of the assets concerned.

In other words, because asset prices are bets on a distant and uncertain future, they are inherently volatile. Moreover, investors tend to deal with uncertainty in ways that aggravate the problem. If information about underlying value is absent or obscure, they are likely to become preoccupied with the views of other investors. Sometimes, maybe usually, this is a process that uncovers new information and disperses it. Now and then, however, it degenerates into crowd hysteria.

In extreme cases, the views of other investors are taken seriously even when flatly contradicted by such facts as may be available. That was certainly true during the later stages of the dotcom bubble of the 1990s, and there are countless other examples. From time to time, such mental aberrations are even dignified by being presented as "schools of thought": from "momentum investing" and "greater fool theory" to "the new economy".

Now add to this the possibility of leverage. Thanks to capital markets, investors can place their bets on this distant and uncertain future using borrowed money. Without debt, the most you can lose is everything you have. If you can borrow, on the other hand, there is really no limit to what you can lose, because leverage allows you to punt other people's money as well as your own. Financial markets attract talented and ingenious people. A great deal of effort, it is said, goes into finding ways of pooling and reducing risk. Evidently, however, a good deal also goes into finding ever more complicated ways of building leverage on leverage, and then leveraging some more.

It has been widely noticed that going bankrupt for a few million dollars is no more painful than going bankrupt for a few thousand. This is apt to discourage prudence, and the imprudent, however talented and ingenious, make mistakes.

Debts are also a main reason why mistakes in financial markets, when they happen, can have bigger consequences than errors in an economy's less excitable parts. Losses may cascade across a series of lenders, many of which may not even have realised that they were exposed to the risk. A surprise that is big enough and bad enough may perturb the mood of self-justifying expectations that had up to then been propping valuations across an entire class of investments, and at worst across the economy as a whole.

A particular risk is that a bank may be threatened with failure as a result of its losses. Banks are intrinsically fragile entities, which is why, historically, they have invested so much in the pretence of security and solidity. They promise to give depositors all their money back on demand. As soon as depositors ask a bank to make good on that pledge, the bank (which retains only a fraction of its deposits in ready cash) goes bust. Depositors at other banks may then want their money back too. And because banks provide the infrastructure of payments services in a modern economy, that comes under threat as well.

Financial volatility need not in itself be such a bad thing. Unfortunately, the evidence suggests that financial volatility not only causes bigger ups and downs in output and incomes, it also leads to lower average incomes over time. Latin America's lost decade really was lost.

All this, to be sure, could perfectly well be true of a closed economy. But an economy with financial links to the outside world may, according to circumstances, face much bigger risks. The problems of uncertainty are worse, for the reason already mentioned: distance, measured not just in miles but also in differences in language, business culture and legal environment. This increases the tendency to rely on other investors' judgments rather than one's own. It also increases the scope for risk that is disguised, accidentally or otherwise, and hence the danger that investors will be taken by surprise.

And trading capital across borders usually involves an additional financial market that is especially susceptible to all of the above: the market for foreign exchange. Most if not all of the big financial crises of recent decades have involved banking crises, currency crises or both. In these ways, the global capital market appears to take a big problem – the economic instability that would anyway be caused by purely domestic finance – and make it worse.

If the scope for error in capital markets is so great and the subsequent punishment so brutal, do the benefits of unimpeded global finance, substantial as they may be, justify the risk? The answer is yes – but for many economies it is a close thing. Much depends, as well, on exactly what is meant by "unimpeded".

A close-run thing

Trade in goods and services is simple: what governments need to do, through the World Trade Organisation, through this or that regional trade agreement, or best of all unilaterally, is abolish their barriers. When it comes to finance, there is no such straightforward advice. "Let capital flow where it may" is bad policy. Finance must be intelligently regulated, at home as well as internationally, in ways that ordinary commerce does not require. When capital flows are liberalised, it needs to be done cautiously and within prudent limits. To that extent, global finance must indeed be impeded.

Governments and their advisers are a long way from understanding how this should ideally be done, let alone from putting any such understanding into practice. There is no detailed consensus on the right approach to international financial regulation, any more than there is on the domestic sort: there is plenty of activity, but for the most part it is co-operation without conviction.

The risks of international finance need to be frankly acknowledged, and then reduced so far as possible. That means weighing the costs and benefits of different kinds of capital mobility, and setting policies accordingly. It means abandoning certain orthodoxies of international economic policy. The danger cannot be eliminated altogether, but the remaining risk is worth taking because the potential gains from international capital flows are large, especially for the world's poor countries.

To ignore that potential would be an even greater mistake than to liberalise recklessly. The global capital market is a treacherous aid to economic growth, but in the end, above all for the poor, an indispensable one.

Catching the tide

Why does so little capital flow from rich countries to poor?

SUPPOSE CAPITAL WERE BOTTLED UP in individual countries, not free to flow from one to another. Rich economies would have lots of it. Too much, in a way: the law of diminishing returns would have set in. Poor economies, in contrast, would have less capital than they can put to good use: returns to extra capital there would be higher. Both kinds of country, and the world as a whole, would be better off if people were free to move capital from the one to the other – or so it would seem.

The poor-country capital importers would invest more and produce more. The rich-country capital exporters would invest less, but the income they lost this way would be more than outweighed by the additional income they received from investments abroad offering high returns.

This is the simple theory of international capital flows. Sometimes it works. For sustained periods during the past century or two, capital went where it was supposed to, and made a great difference to the pattern of economic development. In the last quarter of the 19th century, British capital equivalent to 5% of host-country GDP and more flowed out each year to the United States, Canada, Australia and Argentina. France and Germany were big exporters of capital too, though not quite on that scale. The flows paid for a large part of the investment undertaken in the capital-importing countries.

This golden age of financial globalisation ended in 1914. Global financial connections were cut by the first world war, and only briefly repaired in the immediate aftermath. Then, for nearly half a century, from the Depression until the 1970s, international flows of private capital dwindled to almost nothing. In the 1970s, net flows of private capital to the world's poor countries amounted to a little over 1% of host-country GDP. This trickle was sufficient to finance a miserly one-twentieth of what many poor countries spend on investment (and an even smaller share of what they should be spending).

By the end of the 1970s, those meagre figures were increasing, though they still fell far short of the 19th-century boom. And the resurgence, such as it was, ended badly, in the debt crises of the 1980s. By the end of the 1990s, flows had recovered from that setback and endured two more – the Mexican devaluation of 1994 and the East Asian debacle of 1997–98. Taking one decade with another, flows in the 1980s were about equal to flows in the 1970s; during the 1990s, they were substantially larger. By the end of the 1990s, annual flows as a proportion of developing-country GDP were some three times bigger than in the 1970s (see Chart 8.1).

Go with the flow   8.1

Net private capital flows* to developing countries
% of GDP

5.00
3.75
2.50
1.25
0

1970s   1980s   1990s   2000
–03

*Long- and medium-term flows of debt,
FDI and portfolio, net of repayments
Source: World Bank   Figures for 1970-95 are averaged

Nonetheless, measured against the apparent opportunities for productive investment in the developing countries, as well as against the flows a century earlier, they were still small. At the end of 2001 the worldwide stock of cross-border bank loans and deposits was $9 trillion. Of that, only around $700 billion was attributable to developing-country borrowers. The stock of global cross-border investment in securities was some $12 trillion, of which developing-country borrowers accounted for just $600 billion. As in the 19th century, moreover, most of the capital exported by rich countries to poor countries still travels to just a handful of recipients.

Anti-gravity

These figures belie the idea of a steady tide of capital running from rich countries to poor. On average, it is true, creditor countries are richer than debtor countries; in this sense, at least, capital does flow downwards. But there are some notable exceptions even to this broad pattern. Despite its economic slowdown, the United States continues to invest a lot while saving next to nothing: its economy draws in huge amounts of capital from abroad, and its net foreign liabilities currently stand at more than 20% of GDP.

All this raises a question. The most successful developing countries of an earlier era showed that foreign capital can make an enormous difference to their prospects for rapid development. Financial crises notwithstanding, rich-country investors profited too. Why, in that case, does capital today not flow in much larger quantities from rich parts of the world to poor?

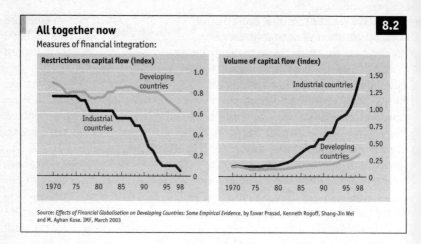

All together now   8.2

Measures of financial integration:

Restrictions on capital flow (index)

Developing countries

Industrial countries

1970 75 80 85 90 95 98

Volume of capital flow (index)

Industrial countries

Developing countries

1970 75 80 85 90 95 98

Source: *Effects of Financial Globalisation on Developing Countries: Some Empirical Evidence*, by Eswar Prasad, Kenneth Rogoff, Shang-Jin Wei and M. Ayhan Kose. IMF, March 2003

One reason is that capital is not the only thing which is lacking in most developing countries. Labour may be plentiful, but workers in poor countries are mostly less well educated and have less training in industrial skills than their rich-country counterparts. In many countries, property rights are insecure and the rule of law is unreliable. The economic infrastructure necessary to get the most out of new investment may not be there. Political risk may be a problem. For these and other reasons, switching capital from countries where there is plenty to countries where there appears to be a shortage yields smaller profits than one would suppose. (America's overwhelming advantages in all these respects help to explain why it attracts so much new capital, despite seeming to have more than it needs.)

Second, most developing countries do not let capital come and go freely. Blanket restrictions on the movement of capital are much rarer than they used to be, but assorted official or unofficial obstacles are still often put in the way of foreign investors. Despite measures to liberalise the capital markets in recent years, they are still far less open to cross-border finance than the typical developed economy (see Chart 8.2).

So where the flow of international capital could do most good – in the developing countries – there is precious little of it. Does that matter? If you take the view that capital flows are more of a curse than a blessing, probably not. Yet history suggests that the most successful developing countries, at least up until the first world war, benefited enormously from foreign capital. And everybody agrees that the flow of capital from one rich country to another is wholly beneficial for both sides. Is anybody suggesting capital controls for the United States? Not even those who consider America's present rate of capital inflow worryingly high. The benefits of access to global capital markets are called into question only for poor countries.

To get an idea of what is at stake, it would be useful to have a rough estimate of the developing countries' gains from capital flows. Unfortunately, no generally agreed estimates exist. The 19th century seems too remote a guide. Careful analysis of the more recent connection, if any, between capital flows and growth in developing countries is still surprisingly sparse, though interest in the subject is mounting. As yet there are relatively few studies, far fewer than of the links between growth and trade, and the results have not settled down to anything resembling a consensus. This is partly because the expansion of rich-to-poor capital flows to significant size is, as noted earlier, a comparatively recent event.

Guessing the benefits

Two other things frustrate efforts to estimate the gains. One is that the main effects of openness to capital can be expected to push in opposing directions: access to capital ought to spur investment and growth, but at the same time it will expose an economy to additional economic turbulence which may slow it down. The net result will be difficult to uncover among all the other factors contending for influence.

Also, "capital flows" is a broad term. It includes quite different kinds of financial transaction: bank lending, short- and long-term; investment in public or private bonds; investment in equities; direct investment in productive capacity. Each has different implications for growth on one hand and exposure to capital-market risk on the other. The gains from capital inflows are going to depend on exactly what kind of capital is flowing. Again, statistical evidence may struggle to provide answers.

Still, one may hazard a guess. According to one recent review of the literature, by Wendy Dobson of the University of Toronto and Gary Hufbauer of the Institute for International Economics, developing countries may have gained roughly as much, overall, from access to global capital markets as from access to trade in goods and services. The authors say it is plausible to suppose that by 2000 developing countries were gaining around $350 billion a year in additional GDP thanks to access to the global market in goods and services. As a result, developing-country GDP was about 5% higher than it would otherwise have been. Drawing on research that aims to separate the effects of different kinds of capital, they calculate that the gain up to now from even the

Downside 8.3		
GDP losses from banking and currency crises		
	1980s	1990s
GDP loss from financial crises in emerging markets, $bn	249	419
Asia	13	260
Latin America	207	123
Africa	15	18
Europe	na	11
Middle East	14	7
Average annual GDP loss in emerging markets, %	0.6	0.7
Asia	0.1	1.4
Latin America	2.2	0.7
Africa	0.5	0.6
Europe	na	0.1
Middle East	0.3	0.1

Source: *World Capital Markets: Challenge to the G10*, by Wendy Dobson and Gary Clyde Hufbauer. Institute for International Economics

limited access to international capital these countries have enjoyed might be about the same.

If the gains from (incomplete) capital-market integration really are as big as that, they would be worth the price of a financial crisis or two. Over the past few decades, admittedly, the world has suffered more than a few. When it did the sums in 1999, the IMF counted 64 banking crises and 79 currency crises since 1970. (That includes some double-counting, because many countries had both kinds of crisis simultaneously.) Most of these were small affairs, national rather than international in character. Over time, however, the role of international capital in spreading financial breakdown across borders has been growing. And when financial crises happen, the toll on incomes is heavy.

Ms Dobson and Mr Hufbauer have gathered estimates of the cost in lost GDP of 24 banking crises and 36 currency crises during the 1980s and 1990s. Research suggests that the calamities of the 1980s cost Latin America an average of 2.2% of GDP a year over the decade. In the 1990s East Asia's financial traumas cost the region 1.4% of GDP a year.

Within these regional averages, of course, some countries suffered much more than others. Indonesia's output, for example, fell by 14% in 1998 alone, against an earlier trend of 7% annual growth: a one-year GDP shortfall of more than 20%. Overall, though, the cost of financial crises for all emerging-market economies worked out at around 0.6% of GDP a year for the 1980s and 0.7% of GDP a year for the 1990s (see Chart 8.3). Set beside Ms Dobson's and Mr Hufbauer's estimated capital-market benefits of 5% of GDP a year, that does not seem too bad.

However, many critics of financial globalisation would challenge these numbers, especially so far as the benefits are concerned. And they have a surprising new ally. A review of the empirical literature by economists at the IMF, traditionally devoted to the cause of open capital markets, finds no consensus that financial integration yields any net benefits in growth at all (even though, the Fund insists, in theory it ought to). Of 14 papers reviewed, only three find that financial integration has a positive effect; another four find that the effects are mixed; and the rest find no effect one way or the other. The IMF's review also looks at the relationship between other measures of economic well-being and different measures of economic openness. Trade improves economic welfare, according to this research. Financial integration has no significant effect.

The absence of a clear conclusion suggests two possibilities. One is that financial integration is indeed a mixed blessing: it has costs as well as benefits, making net benefits (if any) hard to spot. Second, unlike free trade, financial integration may be good for economies only if certain conditions are met. If countries meet these requirements, they gain; if not, they lose. On balance, the effects tend to cancel out. These theories are not mutually exclusive.

Split the difference

There is no need to come to an all-or-nothing judgment about capital flows. The choice is not between completely unfettered flows and financial isolation. According to circumstances, a middle way may be best. The aim should be to reduce the costs of financial integration without casting aside such benefits as there may be.

Hot and cold running money

**One way of increasing the benefits of global capital while
reducing the costs is to alter the mix**

ARE SOME KINDS OF CAPITAL INFLOW better than others? On the
face of it, yes. Borrowing from a bank, for example, is relatively
risky. If, for example, the borrower's income falls, for whatever reason,
he has no choice but to service the debt just as before, even though his
capacity to do so may be less. A bank loan taken out at a floating interest rate, or denominated in foreign currency, exposes the borrower to
additional risks beyond his control. Banks may call in loans, or refuse to
roll over short-term credits.

At the other extreme, foreign direct investment (FDI) looks comparatively safe. In effect, the foreign investor is sharing much of the receiving country's risk. If profits should fall, so will the foreign investor's
income from his investment: the cost of servicing the investment moves
in step with the recipient's economic fortunes. Also, FDI is a lot more difficult to withdraw when times are hard. Investments may have to be
sold at a loss, if they can be sold at all. Somewhere between bank loans
and FDI in terms of risk-sharing are portfolio investments such as bonds
and shares.

Again, however, there are trade-offs which make the choice more
complicated than it seems. A key issue is cost: there is no something for
nothing in international finance. FDI may be a safer source of capital
than borrowing from a bank, but in the long run it is likely to be more
expensive. The reason is simple: in return for shouldering extra risk,
investors require a bigger income. In the end, the share of profits to
which FDI entitles them can be expected to pay a lot more than the
interest payments due on a comparable bank loan.

FDI has other drawbacks. It is much more difficult to arrange. Banks
specialise in bridging the gap between investors and borrowers, bringing them together even though one may know nothing about the other.
FDI demotes the middle-man to an advisory role at most, so the princi-
pals have more to do. Direct investment requires a close long-term relationship between the investor and the company that is invested in.

This is an advantage in some ways. FDI often brings the recipient
useful technical and managerial knowledge, and vital contacts in world

markets, as well as money. But an FDI partnership requires a big invest-ment of time and effort, especially on the investor's side. This will tend to narrow the scope of FDI to large projects in relatively large recipient countries (which can offer the investor a correspondingly big market for its output). Of all the companies or activities in developing countries that could make good use of foreign capital, comparatively few are in a position to attract FDI.

A pity, because the economic evidence, such as it is, seems to confirm that FDI is on balance the most desirable form of capital inflow. Recall the estimate quoted earlier for the developing countries' gains to date from openness to cross-border capital: an improvement of 5% in GDP, roughly on a par with the gains from trade. The studies which yield that number allow separate (albeit rough) estimates to be made for the respective gains from FDI, portfolio flows (bonds and equities) and bank loans. This research suggests that a rise of one percentage point in the ratio of the stock of FDI to GDP will raise GDP by 0.4%. In the decade to 2000, the ratio of FDI to GDP in the developing countries went up from 7% to 21%. That rise of 14 percentage points implies an improvement in GDP of 5.6%.

The evidence on whether portfolio investment affects growth is even more sparse than the evidence on FDI. However, the OECD's Marcelo Soto, whose work was used in deriving the FDI estimate, has looked at both. He found that, within the total of portfolio flows, equity flows have an even bigger positive effect on GDP than FDI, an admittedly strange result. Conversely, bond flows actually have a negative effect. Averaging the two, with a 60% weighting for bonds (to reflect the mix within the portfolio-flows total), suggests an improvement of 0.2% in GDP for each one-point rise in the ratio of portfolio capital to GDP. Between 1990 and 2000, the ratio of portfolio capital to GDP in the developing countries rose from 8% to 14%, implying an improvement in GDP of 1.2%.

According to the same research, bank debt is the one to avoid. It is estimated to reduce GDP by between 0.2% (Mr Soto's figure for loans) and 0.4% (trade-related credits) for every rise of one point in the ratio of bank debt to GDP. The developing countries' stock of foreign bank loans and trade credits increased from 30% of GDP in 1990 to 37% in 2000. That implies a fall in GDP of around 2%.

It just so happens
At best, these figures should be regarded as only a rough guide to orders

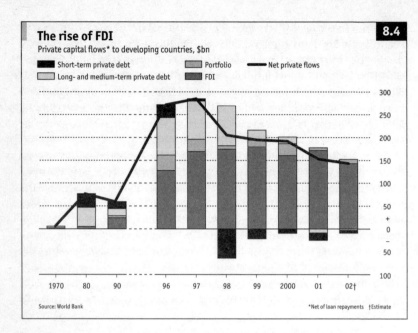

The rise of FDI 8.4

Private capital flows* to developing countries, $bn

- ■ Short-term private debt
- □ Long- and medium-term private debt
- ▨ Portfolio
- ▨ FDI
- ━ Net private flows

Source: World Bank   *Net of loan repayments †Estimate

of magnitude. Nonetheless, they seem to support a preference for FDI over portfolio flows, and a strong preference for either of these over bank-debt flows.

Recent years have seen a dramatic shift in the composition of capital flows to the emerging-market economies. In the light of the evidence on the advantages of different kinds of capital, the change looks like one for the better. Bank lending has fallen sharply. Portfolio investment (bonds and equities) has gone up. And FDI has soared, despite the difficulties in expanding it as quickly as many countries would wish.

In 1980, flows of short-term debt to emerging-market economies amounted to $30 billion, net of repayments. In 1990, the figure was $15 billion. From 1998, flows of short-term debt turned negative; that is, repayments and interest exceeded new loans. FDI inflows moved sharply in the opposite direction: from $5 billion in 1980 to $24 billion in 1990 and $160 billion in 2000. Net portfolio investment increased too, from about zero in 1980 to $26 billion in 2000 (see Chart 8.4).

A variety of factors lie behind this changing pattern. Bitter experience, culminating in the East Asian debacle, has curbed the banks' own appetite for conventional cross-border lending, though perhaps only temporarily. Attitudes have also changed in many of the developing countries. In some of them, financial liberalisation has opened domestic securities markets to foreigners for the first time. In others, access may not yet be free but is at least easier than before. And attitudes to inward direct investment have undergone a transformation. Even countries such as India, which for decades set its face against foreign ownership of local assets, are vying with each other to draw foreign investors in. China's remarkable growth during recent years, fuelled in part by its success in attracting FDI, has not gone unnoticed.

Even if economic policy in industrial and emerging-market countries did nothing further to alter the mix, the trend towards greater flows of FDI and equity finance seems likely to continue. This is not because the lessons from the financial crises of the 1990s have been taken to heart: financial markets have short memories. It is because economic development itself seems to favour this kind of finance.

As the developing countries become more prosperous, their financial and legal systems will become more sophisticated. FDI opportunities will become easier to find and exploit, and domestic financial markets will converge on the standards of depth and organisation familiar in the rich West. As domestic banking systems mature, moreover, they will be able to meet more of the financial needs so far satisfied by bank borrowing across borders. With economic growth and intensifying globalisation, every kind of financial flow might well continue to expand. But the mix of capital types, left to itself, is likely to drift gradually in the right direction.

Faster, faster

Ought governments to be satisfied with that, or should they try to accelerate this trend? The answer is that they should hurry it up. Some suggestions follow as to how they might do it. But first a word of caution: intervention of this kind needs to be done carefully.

If different kinds of capital were a close substitute for one another, there would be little need to hesitate in trying to improve the mix. Policy could aim to reduce cross-border bank flows and increase FDI, say; the expanded FDI would meet all the needs satisfied up to now by cross-border bank finance; capital flows would be safer, and nobody (except the banks) would be any the worse off. The trouble is that different kinds of capital cannot stand in for each other in this way. Many of the borrowers in developing countries that could put foreign capital to good use lack access to FDI, or to equity finance for that matter, and will for the foreseeable future. A strong push against cross-border bank debt could leave most such borrowers stranded. Risky capital from banks may be the only kind they can get.

This danger will be especially great in the poorest, worst-governed countries. Recall that FDI and cross-border equity finance are safer for the borrowing country because the investor shoulders more of the financial risk. In backward countries, foreign investors may simply refuse to do that. Legal systems may offer little or no protection against breach of contract, expropriation or outright theft. Corruption too is often an issue. In such circumstances, a western company with a reputation to lose will think twice before entering into a close economic partnership. To be sure, bank lending to such countries is hardly to be recommended either – but it may be that or nothing. Ruling out bank lending altogether is going to make some worthy borrowers worse off.

All or nothing?

Another risk is that in trying too hard to discourage one kind of capital, governments may inadvertently discourage others too. Maybe cross-border bank finance goes hand in hand with cross-border equity finance and with FDI. Discourage the banks, and far from seeing FDI and equity finance rise, you may see them fall, again leaving the borrowing countries worse off.

On the whole, though, the evidence on these interconnections is encouraging. It certainly does not seem to rule out cautious efforts at reforms to improve the mix. Within domestic financial systems, different aspects of financial development tend to go forward together. Bank finance and stockmarket development, for instance, seem to be closely associated. But there is little sign that cross-border bank finance has any particular significance in this. Certainly, economic policy needs to nurture efficient domestic banking: for its own sake, and also because otherwise equity markets and other aspects of financial deepening may be held back. But so long as governments do not discourage cross-border bank finance in a way that also discourages domestic bank finance, the effects on FDI and securities markets are likely to be slight.

Sudden storms

Financial crises don't come from nowhere. With effort and luck, some can be avoided

ONE WAY TO IMPROVE the capital-flows trade-off – to combine more economic growth with less financial instability – would be to avoid at least some of the financial crises that might otherwise come along. But are they avoidable? They happen so often that it is natural to think that capital mobility and financial distress are inseparable: if a country wants the first, it will have to put up with the second. There is some truth in this. Access to more capital makes bigger crises feasible; every now and then, somewhere in the world, one is going to happen.

Is this because the same mistakes are made again and again, or is each crisis unique? The answer is yes to both: each crisis is unique, and the same mistakes are made again and again. However different the precise circumstances may be in each case, most of the scores of financial crisis seen in the past few decades do have certain central features in common. This is encouraging. Understanding these features and taking steps to deal with them could increase the safety of the global financial system without denying the developing countries the capital they need to grow quickly.

Banks are almost always deeply implicated when a financial crisis occurs – and banking crises are anything but rare (see Chart 8.5 on the next page). Given their role at the centre of any market-based financial system, it could hardly be otherwise. International bank flows, which declined so sharply during the 1990s, can still leave a country financially much more vulnerable than the figures suggest, because bank flows are so much more volatile than other kinds. Bank capital can switch quickly from inflow to outflow, so movements that seem small in absolute terms can exercise disproportionate influence.

Two kinds of banking weakness need to be distinguished: dangers specific to the borrowing country where the crisis starts, and risks that are due to capital moving across borders. As the crisis unfolds, these two interact. And the trouble often starts with financial liberalisation, a process that may aggravate both kinds of weakness. Talk about the perils of liberalisation makes some economic liberals uncomfortable, though financial economists, including many with strong pro-market leanings,

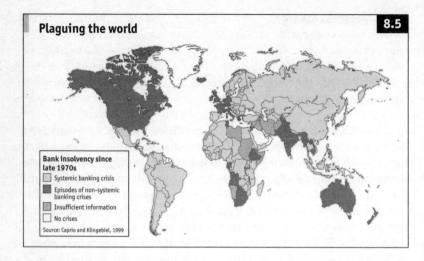

Plaguing the world 8.5

Bank insolvency since late 1970s
- Systemic banking crisis
- Episodes of non-systemic banking crises
- Insufficient information
- No crises

Source: Caprio and Klingebiel, 1999

have been pointing to the dangers of badly handled liberalisation for decades.

Falling standards

Every study of the East Asian crisis of the late 1990s has drawn attention to lax lending standards in the crisis countries. A lending boom preceded the breakdowns, and in each country most of the money went into risky assets such as property and equities rather than into productive investment. In Thailand, Indonesia and Malaysia the stock of lending for property accounted for as much as 40% of all lending before the crisis struck. Creditors were therefore unusually exposed to certain kinds of risk. Higher interest rates, for instance, would lower the value of the assets against which they had lent, at the same time as making some of their loans non-performing.

Government involvement in many of the regions' banking systems made matters worse. Ministries urged banks to lend to specific sectors or firms with little regard for creditworthiness. "Connected lending" – that is, lending to the banks' own proprietors or to affiliated businesses – was tolerated or even encouraged. Ordinary standards of prudent loan appraisal were set aside.

Banks often lacked the resources, human and technological, to apply such standards in the first place. Their lending officers and risk-management systems were stretched beyond the limit of their competence by the sheer volume of business. The same was true of the bank supervisors' resources, such as they were. Not only did the banking authorities lack the skills and the manpower to do an effective job, but they were also usually under the thumb of ministries that were reluctant to see lending curtailed.

"Forbearance" was the rule – meaning permission to keep lending until the problems went away, and to hide the evidence in the meantime. Bad loans were "evergreened": failing borrowers were allowed to service their debt with new loans. Accounting rules allowed such practices to be concealed. Nearly all of the crisis countries turned out to have had vastly greater volumes of non-performing loans on their financial institutions' books than the official figures admitted at the time. The official figure for South Korea's non-performing loans in 1996 was less than 1% of all loans, between one-tenth and one-twentieth of the true position.

In addition to weakly regulated banks, most of the crisis countries had, in effect, virtually unregulated quasi-banks operating alongside. Thailand's finance companies are the most notorious example. South Korea had its "merchant banks": owned by the country's conglomerates, and more or less unregulated, they were at the forefront of credit expansion and of borrowing abroad. Indeed, the government allowed these ex-finance companies to borrow abroad only if the debt was short-term.

All of this was familiar from earlier financial breakdowns, looking back to the 1960s and before. Paradoxically, one of the least familiar aspects of the East Asian crisis, which helps to explain both its severity and the shock it caused around the world, is that many other aspects of economic policy were being handled well, and that the countries concerned seemed in most respects to be thriving.

In fact, East Asia was an extraordinary success story. Investors had every reason to feel confident. Even fiscal policy was mostly under control, which in developing countries is unusual. In a perverted way, it added to the financial danger. Investors believed that if banks and finance companies should fail, governments would be there to sort things out. The record showed that they were competent, and suggested that they had untapped fiscal resources in reserve.

The countries' success added to the dangers in another way: foreign capital was all the more readily drawn in. The sheer volume of additional inflows compounded the difficulties of monitoring and supervision. It added to the mood of optimism, so standards were relaxed still further. And it introduced the exchange rate as a new and potentially destabilising factor. Foreign inflows, while they lasted, supported the local currencies and added to the feeling that all was well. Governments, moreover, had promised to peg their currencies against the dollar; again, the markets assumed that they meant it, and that they knew what they were doing.

This sort of activity is strongly self-sustaining. While a bubble is inflating, reckless lending seems merely bold, and appropriately well-rewarded. Deteriorating credit quality is easy to conceal so long as the price of property and other assets offered as collateral is going up. The growth in lending fuels demand, so economic growth stays high as well. That reinforces the government's reputation for competence, so the boom continues.

Overborrowing syndrome

It is easy to see how this cycle of excess gets out of hand, but what starts it in the first place? Any news that spurs a rush of optimism can get things going. One potential catalyst is financial liberalisation, the very thing that first opens the credit taps. This has been known for decades. A classic text on development finance, by Ronald McKinnon of Stanford University, spelled out the dangers some 30 years ago.

A later volume of Mr McKinnon's again drew attention to the risks. Published six years before the crisis of 1997–98, it recounted South Korea's previous experience with overborrowing in the mid-1960s. Starting in 1965, financial and trade liberalisation had stimulated South Korea's growth, prompting a fundamental reappraisal of the country's prospects by foreign investors (not long before, economists had compared South Korea's prospects unfavourably with the North's). Liberalisation allowed capital to rush in, but the surge was too great; it forced inflation up and left the country struggling with the problem until the early 1980s.

Having started, and grown bigger, why does the bubble eventually burst? All it takes is a shift in perceptions, reversing the one that started it all off. After a few years of overborrowing, balance sheets start to look stretched. At some point, borrowers begin to think enough is enough. Here and there, asset sales begin as firms try to restore financial ratios to something closer to normal. Prices stop rising and then start falling. Inflows of capital slow and the currency comes under pressure.

The central bank would like to defend the currency by raising interest rates, but finds it cannot because the weakness of the banks has suddenly become clear. All at once the abyss opens up, and there is a stampede to get away from it. Panic and forced selling accelerate the decline in property and equity prices into a crash. The government's reputation for competence tanks. As capital flees, pressures on the currency force it to give way.

In the middle phase, while the bubble is inflating, multiple layers of moral hazard are in play. Domestic lenders are not effectively supervised either by regulators or (thanks to explicit and implicit deposit protection) by the markets. Foreign lenders likewise perform their death-defying feats over a safety net extended by their home governments – with some additional assurance of protection from borrowing-country governments and, should things turn really bad, from the IMF.

The promise to defend the currency creates a kind of moral hazard too: an exaggerated sense of safety, leading people to do things which they would otherwise regard as too risky or too costly. Lenders' unwarranted faith in the stability of the currency is important both in inflating the bubble and then in worsening the effects when the bubble bursts.

Looking back at the beginning of the 1990s, with the East Asian debacle yet to come, Mr McKinnon put it like this:

> [We] know that in any purely private capital market each
> individual borrower faces an upward-sloping supply curve for
> finance. That is not really a distortion. The more that is
> borrowed, the riskier the loan gets at the margin. The upward-
> sloping supply curve imposed by private lenders accurately
> reflects the increasing riskiness of the private borrower as he
> increases his exposure.
>
> Consider instead the world of the 1970s and 1980s, where
> governments guarantee all credit flows. The host government
> in the borrowing country guarantees private foreign credits,
> either officially or unofficially. In the lending countries we
> have official export-import banks and deposit insurance for
> the commercial banks. Consequently, the normal upward-
> sloping supply curve for finance did not face individual private
> borrowers in the third world during these two decades of huge
> accumulation of external debts. Because of the government
> guarantees that were involved, they could borrow at a
> virtually flat rate of interest.

Exactly the same thing happened all over again in the 1990s, and not just in East Asia but in many other countries too. Nobody should suppose for a moment that, after East Asia, it cannot happen again. Turkey and Argentina, to name but two, already confirm otherwise.

Is it infectious?

This account of the forces that drive the cycle of optimism, overborrowing (especially from abroad), excessive risk-taking and crisis may seem plausible for any given individual economy – but one of the hallmarks of recent financial stress has been its multinational character. One country gets into financial difficulties, then another and another. This so-called contagion need not be confined to particular regions. The Russian financial crisis of 1998, itself a kind of aftershock from the East Asian crisis, put Brazil and other Latin American economies under pressure almost immediately.

Some economists insist that this apparent contagion is not real. They argue that countries make their own way into a position of financial weakness and vulnerability, essentially in the way just described. They object to the term contagion because it implies that the countries and governments concerned are not to blame. Bad news about a neighbouring or similar economy, they say, merely alerts investors to problems elsewhere the markets had been unaware of, or willing to ignore.

On this view, it is not so much the disease that spreads as awareness of the disease. Financial crises may tend to appear in clusters, but the sources of the problem are fundamentally national in character: that is, they spring from the mistakes of borrowers in, and lenders to, a particular country, not from some global propensity to system-wide breakdown.

It is true that contagion will not bring down a financial system which is strong, and that a crisis needs strictly domestic material to work with. Also, some of the economic shocks that trigger crises in more than one country are global or regional in their effects to begin with, such as a change in world interest rates, or a big movement in the dollar or yen, or a big change in the price of oil. If events of that kind start a cluster of crises, contagion is not to blame (any more than one would call it contagion when an earthquake causes neighbouring buildings to collapse).

The fact remains that even an economy which has been rendered vulnerable by weak supervision, excessive optimism and prolonged overborrowing is not necessarily doomed. If it is lucky, it might pass quietly through that period of danger and emerge on the other side with its vulnerabilities lessened, either by acts of policy or merely as a by-product of advancing economic development. If it is unlucky, it will be affected by bad news just when it is most susceptible. When this happens, it seems reasonable to call it contagion.

A crisis in a neighbouring or similar country might suffice to bring on financial difficulties in just the same way as a purely domestic reappraisal of economic prospects could do: bad news that forces a rethink. Often, cross-border financial flows also come into play, exerting their own direct and powerful influence on events. The evidence points clearly to a "common banker" effect: if two countries have borrowed from the same lender, when one gets into trouble the other can expect to face a squeeze as well, regardless of differences in underlying economic conditions.

There are other channels of contagion too. Equity markets have spells of moving in step, especially in downturns. Rich-country portfolio managers have a tendency to herd together when it comes to investing in emerging markets. When a bank or portfolio manager faces losses in one developing country, it may choose (or be forced by regulators) to sell assets in other markets to shore up its position. If one country devalues its currency, competing exporters come under pressure to do the same, regardless of the effect devaluation might have on corporate and financial balance sheets. All of these factors link economies together.

Because of technology, financial markets move faster than ever before. Partly for the same reason, financial institutions are bigger than ever. When a big rich-country bank changes its mind about the prospects of a particular emerging economy, the effect on asset prices in that economy can be dramatic; all the more so if other rich-country banks decide to join in.

In short, the possibility of contagion certainly adds to the risks of relying on foreign capital, shifting the balance of pros and cons away from openness to capital. For countries that nonetheless still seek access to foreign capital, it underlines the relative attractions of forms that will move only slowly when circumstances change, notably FDI. And it emphasises the dangers of the most mobile and volatile form of capital, short-term bank debt.

Shipbuilding

Developing-country governments still have a lot of work to do if they want to attract the right sort of foreign capital

BETTER BANK REGULATION is as much a task for rich-country as for poor-country governments. But in addition, the developing countries also need to implement many other financial reforms and improvements of their own. Few of them have the capacity to put imported capital safely to work. This capacity is something that governments can build, but a lot needs to be put right before openness to capital can be relied on to bring net benefits rather than net disappointment.

Reducing corruption would be high on the list even if economic efficiency were the only concern. Corruption particularly discourages inflows of FDI, the safest and most productive kind of capital inflow, so relatively speaking it favours bank lending, the riskiest kind of capital (see Chart 8.6).

Work on the connection between corruption and the mix of capital inflows was reviewed in a paper published by the IMF in 2003. However corruption is measured, the answer comes out the same: corruption discourages inward FDI. Indeed, it appears to discourage it even more than do high corporate taxes.

Many developing-country governments, keen nowadays to attract FDI, try to appeal to investors by cutting corporate taxes or by offering subsidies. This often works, but the cost is quite heavy, and goes beyond the mere fiscal outlay or forgone revenue. Governments in most poor countries have to rely on a narrow tax base. They find it difficult to pay for social spending and economic infrastructure while keeping their own borrowing under control. Macroeconomic stability is an important contributor to financial safety. Special tax breaks for FDI may militate against such stability – and run a far greater risk, too, of distorting FDI decisions in favour of inefficient projects. In every respect, curbing corruption is a far better method of attracting FDI.

Reducing corruption is hard but not impossible. Measures include explicit restrictions on connected lending, better accounting standards and greater disclosure of financial information (and not just for the banks). In many countries, legal reforms will be needed as well. A constant theme of much of the recent research on finance and development

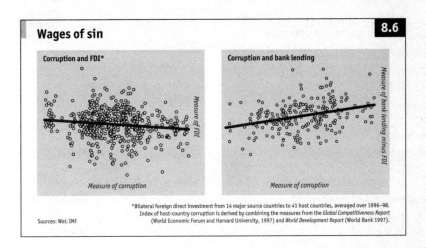

Wages of sin `8.6`

Corruption and FDI*

Measure of corruption

Measure of FDI

Corruption and bank lending

Measure of corruption

Measure of bank lending minus FDI

*Bilateral foreign direct investment from 14 major source countries to 41 host countries, averaged over 1996–98. Index of host-country corruption is derived by combining the measures from the *Global Competitiveness Report* (World Economic Forum and Harvard University, 1997) and *World Development Report* (World Bank 1997).

Sources: Wei; IMF

is the importance of strong property rights. Without them, it is difficult, for instance, to offer collateral against a loan, or to resolve bankruptcies quickly and smoothly.

Faster and more accurate disclosure of information too is desirable in itself, for governments as well as for banks and private companies. A study by Gaston Gelos and Shang-Jin Wei, quoted in the IMF paper, looked at the investments of international equity funds between 1996 and 2000 to see if there was a connection with "transparency", measured in a number of different ways. It examined disclosure not just in the corporate sector but also in the release of official macroeconomic data and in the running of macroeconomic policy. All three aspects of transparency were found to be related to inward portfolio flows, even after allowing for the effect of many other factors (for example, incomes and market liquidity).

And these effects were big. For instance, on the macroeconomic-data measure, transparent countries received a share of global equity investment that was 48 percentage points higher than their market capitalisation (as a share of global market capitalisation) would suggest. Non-transparent countries received a share that was 25 percentage points lower than the same benchmark (see Chart 8.7 on the next page).

The same study found that herding among investors was substantially lower for countries with good disclosure than for the rest – presumably because greater transparency gives investors something more substantial to go on than what other investors are doing. Less herding is a good thing: when investors follow the crowd, they amplify the

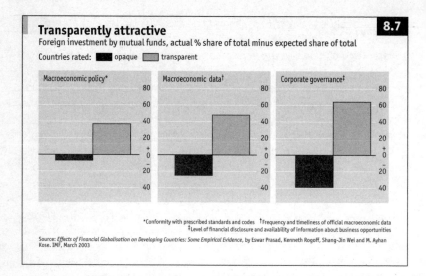

Transparently attractive 8.7

Foreign investment by mutual funds, actual % share of total minus expected share of total

Countries rated: ■ opaque ▨ transparent

*Conformity with prescribed standards and codes †Frequency and timeliness of official macroeconomic data
‡Level of financial disclosure and availability of information about business opportunities

Source: *Effects of Financial Globalisation on Developing Countries: Some Empirical Evidence*, by Eswar Prasad, Kenneth Rogoff, Shang-Jin Wei and M. Ayhan Kose. IMF, March 2003

economic cycle, driving output and asset prices higher in booms and lower in slumps.

Also, in the event of a financial crisis, capital flight seems to be less of a problem in countries with better transparency. Again, this may be because information equips investors to see beyond the short-term emergency to more reassuring long-term fundamentals. "Overall," the study concludes, "the data suggest that an improvement in transparency might very well reduce the so-called sudden-stop phenomenon of 'hot money', and hence increase the stability of the domestic financial market in a developing country."

There is evidence that ownership of the banks and other financial institutions in developing countries matters a lot. Most governments restrict foreign ownership of banks. State ownership, on the other hand, is typically extensive. It would be far better the other way round.

Foreign ownership of banks is just a particular form of FDI. In many ways, therefore, the benefits to the host country of foreign-owned banks are simply the financial-sector equivalent of the broader benefits of FDI. These include not just the initial capital inflow itself but also the introduction of better technology and new management skills, not to mention greater competition for the existing domestic institutions. But in finance there are additional advantages as well. The task of financial regulators is easier if foreigners come into the market and establish new and higher standards. With a heavy presence of foreigners, the government is much less likely to bail out the banks en masse if they get into trouble. Uninsured depositors will accordingly feel that much less secure – which is all to the good, from the standpoint of discipline and monitoring.

Banking-sector FDI also helps to fight corruption. Foreign-owned banks have their reputations at home and around the world to consider, not to mention their home-country regulators, so they will be less susceptible to corruption than incumbent domestic banks. They also have good reason to monitor what domestic banks are doing, and to expose corruption when they find it. From their point of view, improper conduct is a kind of unfair competition that puts them at a disadvantage.

Possibly most important of all, banking-sector FDI promotes diversification, which is a good way of reducing risk. The business of domestic banks in developing countries tends to be heavily concentrated at home. If the local economy turns down, all of their activities are exposed. Foreign banks have a far wider spread of risk, and can call on head office to help if need be.

For every advantage that banking FDI offers the emerging-market economy, state ownership brings with it a corresponding disadvantage. State-owned banks often institutionalise practices that would be called questionable or corrupt if undertaken by private banks. Connected lending, for instance, is not so much a consequence of state ownership as its very purpose: the whole idea is to make lending decisions on the basis of non-economic tests. This means state-owned banks must be expected to make losses, and will have to be sheltered from competition. Regulatory forbearance, in the same way, is not just likely, it is required. Monitoring by depositors and other creditors will be minimal: the promise of bail-out is as clear as it possibly can be. The evidence confirms that countries with the highest proportion of state-owned banks have the highest bank operating costs and the largest proportion of non-performing loans.

In addition to promoting access to information and curbing corruption – where greater foreign ownership can be of great help – developing-country governments need to weigh the case for explicit restrictions on certain kinds of financial activity. In systems that are otherwise clean and well-run, the need for further measures might be limited. Even then, some action may seem advisable, especially since bank regulation is likely to remain far from ideal. But in systems that are neither clean nor well-run, and where governments would find it difficult to put this right by more direct means, narrower restrictions may be necessary. Two kinds of capital stand out: short-term debt, and debt denominated in foreign currency. Short-term foreign-currency debt, combining the hazards of both, is therefore a prime concern.

Unpegged

Today the exchange-rate danger, at least, is smaller than before – not because currencies are more stable, but because the fragility of systems that merely appear to be stable is better understood. Fixed but adjustable exchange rates helped to worsen the plight of the East Asian economies and others in the late 1990s. The promise of a stable currency helped to draw in too much of the wrong sort of capital. Then, when events forced a devaluation, the economies concerned found themselves in trouble twice over – once for overborrowing in the first place, and then again because many of those debts had to be repaid in dollars or other hard currencies which had appreciated in the meantime.

The economic problem is even worse than this, because a heavy burden of foreign-currency debt makes it difficult for the government to cushion an economic slowdown in the orthodox way, by lowering interest rates. If it does that, it is likely to speed the flow of capital out of the country. This will drive the currency down further, increasing the burden of foreign debt yet again and dragging the economy into an even more ferocious recession.

Here, if nowhere else, lessons have been learned. All over the developing world, fixed but adjustable currencies have been replaced by more flexibly managed regimes (either pure floats or, more commonly, managed floats). Under floating-currency arrangements, the foreign investor comes in with a more realistic idea of the exchange-rate risk, and if the economy does get into trouble, the simple one-way bet of withdrawing capital before the currency peg gives way becomes more complicated. That is likely to encourage stability, both by tempering the inflow of capital during upswings of market sentiment and by encouraging long-term flows at the expense of short-term ones.

In other respects as well, international monetary arrangements are improving, albeit more slowly. The IMF, for instance, has a keener sense of the harm that can be done by letting investors believe that it will protect their investments come what may: moral hazard, yet again. A great deal of attention has concentrated lately on making sure that, once a crisis strikes, investors fully share in the losses – and that they will be well aware of this in advance.

But although understanding of the IMF's role has improved, policy for the most part has not. The main reason is that big financial crises are usually political crises as well. It is the way of the world that, at such times, economic principles are swiftly set aside. Generous IMF support, pushed through by powerful members (notably the United States), has often been granted for political rather than economic reasons, and will continue to be.

Also, as the Basel bank-regulation saga confirms, institutional reform that requires international consensus takes years, if it happens at all. Anne Krueger, the Fund's deputy managing director, has proposed a scheme for dealing with "sovereign bankruptcy", which among other things would allow investors' losses on loans to developing countries to be apportioned faster and more predictably. It is a good plan, and has won the support of many expert observers. But many governments, including America's, are not keen. At the moment, its prospects look poor.

Besides, the extraordinary attention paid to reforms of the "international architecture" over the past five years has been out of proportion to its real importance. As has been argued, it is the quality of national financial policy, in rich countries and poor countries alike, that decides the safety of the global capital market. If that policy is wrong, no reform of the IMF or changes to other aspects of the international architecture, however ingenious, is going to make cross-border capital safe and productive.

A slightly circuitous route

Where capital controls make sense

MALAYSIA RESPONDED to the financial crisis of 1997–98 by violating one of the most sacred canons of economic orthodoxy: it imposed exchange controls. The government started supervising all foreign-currency transactions for financial (as opposed to trade) purposes. The policy was draconian, especially by the standards of the financial freedom the country had enjoyed up till then. Suddenly it was illegal to take even $100 abroad. The aim was to allow the authorities to ease fiscal and monetary policy without provoking massive capital flight. Some economists think that the policy was a success, and advocate something similar for other developing countries. A few even see it as a way to prevent crises in the first place, not just to help deal with existing emergencies. Are they right?

They have a point. Liberal economists, who for years rejected the mere possibility that capital controls might make sense, need to acknowledge that the long-standing orthodox prohibition on any and all of them was far too confident. For the IMF, capital-account liberalisation as quickly as possible was until recently an article of faith. The Fund told South Korea to press on with liberalising its capital account even as the crisis of 1997–98 was unfolding.

The Economist, too, long maintained that capital controls are always wrong. Yet the evidence reviewed here shows that the global capital market is a turbulent and dangerous place, especially for poorly developed economies that may be ill-equipped to navigate it. To be sure, capital controls are not the best way to prepare; but for some countries, imposing certain kinds of control on capital will be wiser than making no preparations at all.

In rich economies, with their deep and diversified financial markets, honest and competent regulators, and macroeconomic policies that keep public borrowing and inflation in check, a liberal regime for capital flows works best. Indeed, it works so well that the policy arouses next to no debate. There may be arguments about the details of bank regulation or fiscal policy, but nobody seriously proposes that the United States, say, should introduce exchange controls. Even if it were still possible to control capital flows that way – which it would not be, given the sophistication of America's financial institutions – who would want to? The benefits of financial integration are clear to all investors, and any economic costs vanish by comparison. Moreover, in most rich countries the ability to move capital across borders is seen as a matter of personal liberty. If a government wanted to stop its citizens from moving their savings abroad, it would have a lot of explaining to do.

Timing is all

As a medium- or long-term goal, emerging-market economies too should aspire to regulate cross-border capital as lightly as rich countries do – as a matter both of economic efficiency and of individual freedom. Nor does this mean that they must wait until they are rich before they liberalise capital: that would keep them poor much longer than necessary. What it does mean is that they must improve the standard of their monetary and fiscal policies; deepen, diversify and deregulate their domestic financial systems (not least by allowing foreign ownership of banks and other financial institutions); and upgrade their standards of financial supervision (especially of banks).

Once they are more like rich countries in these three respects, and long before they have closed the income gap, they can liberalise access to foreign capital in comparative safety. All the while they should be encouraging inflows of FDI – not with subsidies, but by curbing corruption and strengthening property rights. When they start to reach those higher standards of economic policy and institutions, the benefits of inward portfolio investment and, later, offshore bank finance will increasingly outweigh the costs as well.

It is a cumulative process, and each step poses difficulties of its own. The need for better bank regulation is nowadays widely understood – but, judging by experience to date, that does not make the underlying dilemma of systemic stability and moral hazard any easier to resolve.

Essentials

The importance of macroeconomic stability, and especially of fiscal conservatism, continues to be underestimated. Yet if a government cannot keep its borrowing in check, it must either force domestic banks to absorb its debt (ruining any chance of creating a profitable, lightly regulated and efficient banking system) or else simply print money, thereby fuelling inflation and destabilising the currency. Now that floating exchange rates predominate, fiscal caution is even more important than before. The simplest principles of public finance are still the foundation for everything else. This is one article of faith the IMF need not renounce.

But until progress in these areas is well under way, some kinds of restriction on inflows (not outflows) of capital will make sense for many developing countries. Chile's well-known system of holding-period taxes subjected imports of capital to a one-year 30% non-interest-bearing deposit. It failed in its stated goal of reducing total capital movements, but managed to tilt the balance away from short-term towards longer-term inflows. In that respect, it was a success worth emulating.

A tax on short-term inflows has the advantages of relative simplicity and transparency. It resists bureaucratic subversion. Moreover, just as tariffs are a more efficient way to restrict trade than import quotas, so taxes are a much less costly way of managing capital inflows than blunt restrictions on quantities. A regime such as Chile's still allows access to short-term capital, albeit at a price.

Over time, it seems the regime became less effective and more subject to evasion, but that is of no great concern. As the financial system becomes more sophisticated, the need to discourage short-term inflows recedes anyway. The important thing is to ensure that standards of supervision rise in tandem with the institutions' growing depth and breadth.

Until recently, financial orthodoxy set its face against restrictions of the Chilean sort. They still make the IMF uncomfortable. In its free-trade negotiations with Chile and Singapore, the United States has also frowned on capital-account restrictions, though it was willing to compromise. Instead of reluctantly acquiescing, rich–country governments and the Fund need to start recommending such policies. If they must, they can tell themselves that holding-period taxes are not really capital controls at all, but simply another form of prudential regulation. In any event, developing countries should be advised to use this method until their financial systems are ready to participate properly in the global capital market.

Rich-country banks will oppose this, because they would be the principal losers from new impediments to short-term bank inflows to developing countries. But, helpfully if incidentally, their opposition might oblige the IMF and its most powerful members to endorse such policies explicitly, instead of merely tolerating them. This would make it clear that the global capital market is not, as is sometimes alleged, being run for the benefit of rich-country banks.

No greater prize

The world's poorer countries have a great deal to gain from the global market for capital, and should do their best to take advantage of it. But they need to approach the opportunity more cautiously than in the past, and better prepared. If rich countries also improve their own financial policies – which they should, in their own interests – the market will become even safer for all its participants. The international market for capital is already vast, but its potential for promoting growth where it matters most has hardly begun to be tapped.

The material on pages 199–231 was first published in a survey in *The Economist* in May 2003.

PART 4

WORLDLY PHILOSOPHY

9

THE USES AND ABUSES OF ECONOMICS

In some ways, this final chapter might have come first. The 15 articles it contains set out the economist's stall, dusting off some of the discipline's trademark insights and showcasing some of its most useful and diverting applications. Is there a unifying theme? Perhaps not. But that is a fair reflection of economics itself. It has become a delightfully eclectic discipline. Indeed, two of the pieces in this chapter, on financial decision-making ("Freud, finance and folly") and pensions ("Pensions by default"), owe as much to the findings of psychology as to the reasoning of economists.

The first article ("State and market") explains why economists are so partial to markets. Their enthusiasm is not unconditional, and the piece spells out the circumstances in which markets might be expected to fail. Interestingly, real-life markets often defy this expectation of failure, overcoming or working around the difficulties that preoccupy blackboard economists. Some things work even better in practice than they do in theory.

One powerful reason to incline towards markets is that the alternatives are less appealing. Contrary to popular wisdom, economists traditionally stack the cards against markets, by assuming that the state is a beneficent social planner, with the citizenry's welfare at heart. The second piece in this chapter ("The grabbing hand") profiles two economists who labour under no such illusions. Their operating assumption is that politicians are venal and vainglorious. Sometimes, sadly, rulers are even worse than that, as the third piece, a satire on Robert Mugabe's Zimbabwe, testifies.

The Mugabe regime has flouted economic logic at almost every turn. But even respectable politicians purvey discredited economic notions, such as the idea that there is only so much work to go round. Known as the lump of labour fallacy, this hoary piece of plausible nonsense is debunked in "One lump or two".

But economics is also a powerful aid to policymakers, as other articles in this chapter demonstrate. It can help antitrust authorities outwit monopoly power and anti-competitive behaviour ("The trustbusters' new tools"), and help governments that want to auction assets, such as oil fields or the public airwaves, obtain the best possible price ("Secrets and the prize"). Sometimes economics serves policymakers best by showing them what not to do, identifying where their interventions are not worth the bother and the expense ("The regulators' best friend").

Economics can save money, but can it also save the planet? This chapter includes three examples of economic greenery. Environmentalists and economists both take a dim view of polluters. Environmentalists despise them on principle. Economists disapprove of them because they do not pay their way. Imposing taxes on polluters forces them to face the true costs of their actions ("Taxes for a cleaner planet"). Alternatively, they can be required to buy (and allowed to sell) the right to harm the environment ("Money to burn?"). Of course, the despoilers of the environment are not always faceless corporations selling the planet for a buck. Sometimes "they" are us. A third article, "Garbage in, garbage out", explains the theoretical appeal and practical difficulties of making people pay for the household rubbish they generate.

This chapter also includes two articles on foreign aid, a cause that comes in and out of fashion. The 22 rich-country governments represented by the OECD's donor committee devoted 0.33% of their annual income to aid in 2005. As a measure of the rich world's commitment to the poor, this sum seems paltry, and The Economist favours making it bigger. But both articles in this chapter also give a respectful hearing to aid sceptics, such as Peter Bauer. Aid money is often squandered, but that is not the worst of it. It can also undermine accountable government in poor countries, skew the incentives of their best civil servants and displace their export industries.

Economics used to be dominated by rival intellectual encampments, firing heavy salvoes at each other on the big questions of employment, interest rates and inflation. Now, the discipline's bright young things (eight of them are featured in "Beyond the stars") seem happy to let the big guns fall silent for a while. Nosing into every corner of life – crime, schooling, parenting, geography, psychology – they have little to unify them except the tools of their trade. They are inquisitive, rangy, unregimented – and all the more interesting for that.

State and market

People are quick to assume that "market failure" justifies action by the government. This piece argues for a strong presumption in favour of markets – not because they always work perfectly (they never do) but because the alternative is usually worse

ACCORDING TO THE CENTRAL DEDUCTION of economic theory, under certain conditions markets allocate resources efficiently. "Efficiency" has a special meaning in this context. The theory says that markets will produce an outcome such that, given the economy's scarce resources, it is impossible to make anybody better off without making somebody else worse off.

Economic theory, in other words, offers a proof of Adam Smith's big idea. In a market economy, if certain conditions are met, an invisible hand guides countless apparently unco-ordinated individuals to a result that is, in one plausible sense, the best that can be done.

In rich countries, markets are too familiar to attract attention. Yet a certain awe is appropriate. When Soviet planners visited a vegetable market in London during the early days of *perestroika*, they were impressed to find no queues, shortages, or mountains of spoiled and unwanted vegetables. They took their hosts aside and said: "We understand, you have to say it's all done by supply and demand. But can't you tell us what's really going on? Where are your planners, and what are their methods?"

The essence of the market mechanism is indeed captured by the supply-and-demand diagram shown in Chart 9.1 (1) on the next page. The supply curve measures the cost to sellers, at any level of output, of selling one more unit of their good. As output grows, the law of diminishing returns forces this extra (or marginal) cost higher, so the supply curve slopes upwards. In the same way, the demand curve measures the benefit to consumers of consuming one more unit. As consumption grows, the benefit from extra consumption falls, so the demand curve slopes downwards.

At the place where the curves cross, a price is set such that demand equals supply. There, and only there, the benefit from consuming one more unit exactly matches the cost of producing it. If output were less, the benefit from consuming more would exceed the cost of producing it.

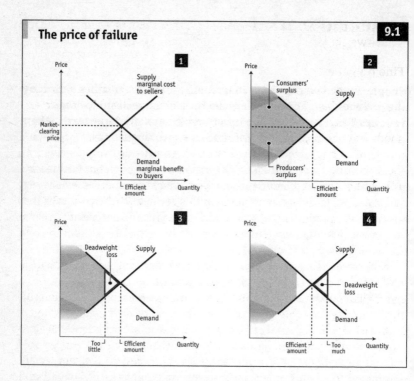

The price of failure 9.1

1
Price

Supply
marginal cost
to sellers

Market-
clearing
price

Demand
marginal benefit
to buyers

Efficient
amount   Quantity

2
Price

Consumers'
surplus   Supply

Producers'
surplus   Demand

Efficient
amount   Quantity

3
Price

Deadweight
loss   Supply

Demand

Too
little   Efficient
amount   Quantity

4
Price

Supply

Deadweight
loss

Demand

Efficient
amount   Too
much   Quantity

If output were higher, the cost of producing the extra units would exceed the extra benefits. So the point where supply equals demand is "efficient".

The shaded area in Chart 9.1 (2) shows the "surplus" created by the market. The upper part is the consumers' surplus: the benefit from consumption (ie, the total area under the demand curve) less what consumers have to pay for it. In the same way, the lower part measures the producers' surplus: revenues received, less the cost of production (the area under the supply curve).

This gain in welfare is at its greatest if consumption and production happen where the lines cross. If, for some reason, consumption and production are less than that, the surplus is smaller and the economy suffers what economists call a deadweight loss, as shown in Chart 9.1 (3).

If production and consumption are more than the efficient amount, the same is true. Producers' surplus is smaller because the extra output has cost more to make than it brings in revenues; consumers' surplus is reduced because the extra consumption has cost buyers more than the benefits it brings. Again, as shown in Chart 9.1 (4), the economy suffers a deadweight loss.

Fine on paper

However, the conditions for market efficiency are extremely demanding – far too demanding ever to be met in the real world. The theory requires "perfect competition": there must be many buyers and sellers; goods from competing suppliers must be indistinguishable; buyers and sellers must be fully informed; and markets must be complete – that is, there must be markets not just for bread here and now, but for bread in any state of the world. (What is the price today for a loaf to be delivered in Timbuktu on the second Tuesday in December 2014 if it rains?)

In other words, market failure is pervasive. it comes in four main varieties:

- **Monopoly.** By reducing his sales, a monopolist can drive up the price of his good. His sales will fall but his profits will rise. Consumption and production are less than the efficient amount, causing a deadweight loss in welfare.
- **Public goods.** Some goods cannot be supplied by markets. If you refuse to pay for a new coat, the seller will refuse to supply you. If you refuse to pay for national defence, the "good" cannot easily be withheld. You might be tempted to let others pay. The same reasoning applies to other "non-excludable" goods such as law and order, clean air and so on. Since private sellers cannot expect to recover the costs of producing such goods, they will fail to supply them.
- **Externalities.** Making some goods causes pollution: the cost is borne by people with no say in deciding how much to produce. Consuming some goods (education, anti-lock brakes) spreads benefits beyond the buyer; again, this will be ignored when the market decides how much to produce. In the case of "good" externalities, markets will supply too little; in the case of "bads", too much.
- **Information.** In some ways a special kind of externality, this deserves to be mentioned separately because of the emphasis placed upon it in recent economic theory. To see why information matters, consider the market for used cars. A buyer, lacking reliable information, may see the price as providing clues about a car's condition. This puts sellers in a quandary: if they cut

prices, they may only convince people that their cars are rubbish. The labour market, many economists believe, is another such "market for lemons". This may help to explain why it is so difficult for the unemployed to price themselves into work.

How harmful?

When markets fail, there is a case for intervention. But two questions need to be answered first. How much does market failure matter in practice? And can governments put the failure right? The rest of this piece deals with the first question.

Markets often correct their own failures. In other cases, an apparent failure does nobody any harm. In general, market failure matters less in practice than is often supposed.

Monopoly, for instance, may seem to preclude an efficient market. This is wrong. The mere fact of monopoly does not establish that any economic harm is being done. If a monopoly is protected from would-be competitors by high barriers to entry, it can raise its prices and earn excessive profits. If that happens, the monopoly is undeniably harmful. But if barriers to entry are low, lack of actual (as opposed to potential) competitors does not prove that the monopoly is damaging: the threat of competition may be enough to make it behave as though it were a competitive firm.

That is why economists are no longer so interested in concentration ratios (the output of an industry's biggest firm or firms as a proportion of the industry's total output). Judging whether markets are "contestable" – that is, whether barriers to entry are high – is thought to be more important.

Many economists would accept that Microsoft, for instance, is a near-monopolist in some parts of the personal computer software business – yet would argue that the firm is doing no harm to consumers because its markets remain highly contestable. Because of that persistent threat of competition, the company prices its products keenly. In this and in other ways it behaves as though it were a smaller firm in a competitive market.

Suppose, on the other hand, that a "natural monopoly" (a firm not subject to the law of diminishing returns, whose costs fall indefinitely as it increases its output) is successfully collecting excessive profits. Then would-be competitors would spare no effort to make the market contestable, through innovation or by other means.

Telecommunications was once considered a natural monopoly.

Today, thanks to new technology and deregulation, it is an intensely competitive business – and in many countries would be more so if not for remaining government restrictions. Economists used to see natural monopolies wherever they looked. Now, thanks mainly to innovation – inspired chiefly by the private pursuit of profit – these beasts are sighted much less often.

Economists have also changed their thinking on public goods. Almost all economists accept that there are such things: national defence and law and order remain the most straightforward examples. But it was once taken for granted that many other products also qualify (if not by being pure public goods, at least by having some of the relevant characteristics), This is no longer so.

The classical example of a public good is a lighthouse. Its services are both non-excludable and "non-rivalrous in consumption", meaning that extra ships can consume its output without the existing users having to consume less. This implies that lighthouses are a pure public good: only the state can provide them. Such a neat example, cited by economists from John Stuart Mill to Paul Samuelson – yet it is at odds with the facts.

As Ronald Coase pointed out in a celebrated paper, from the 17th century many of Britain's lighthouses were privately built and run. Payment to cover costs (and provide a profit) was extracted through fees collected in local ports. The government's role was confined to authorising this collection, exactly as a modern government might provide for a private road-builder to collect a toll.

On the face of it, television broadcasting is another pure public good – again, both non-excludable and non-rivalrous in consumption. Now, thanks to technology, it is straightforwardly excludable: satellite broadcasters collect a subscription, and in return provide a card that unscrambles their signal. With cable and pay-per-view, excludability works with even finer discrimination. And these market-strengthening innovations were not necessary for privately provided television to succeed, despite its public-good appearance. Non-excludable television was and is financed through advertising (another kind of innovation).

Fable of the bees

The same Ronald Coase who attacked the lighthouse myth is better known (and won a Nobel prize) for his work on externalities – the third species of market failure discussed earlier. He argued that, so long as property rights are clearly established, externalities will not cause an inefficient allocation of resources.

241

In fact, few economists would agree: in many cases, unavoidably high costs will prevent the necessary transactions from taking place. Even so, Mr Coase's insight was fruitful. Markets find ways to take account of externalities – ways to "internalise" them, as economists say – more often than you might think.

Bees are to externalities as lighthouses are to public goods. For years they served as a favourite textbook example. Bee-keepers are not rewarded for the pollination services they provide to nearby plant-growers, so they and their bees must be inefficiently few in number. Again, however, the world proved cleverer than the textbooks. Steven Cheung studied the apple-growers of Washington State and discovered a long history of contracts between growers and bee-keepers. The supposed market failure had been effectively – and privately – dealt with.

As for lack of information, the final main source of market failure discussed earlier, here too economists have discovered all manner of private remedies. Recall the used-car example. An easy way round the difficulty is to buy from a seller with a good reputation (one worth protecting), or who offers guarantees. In ways such as this, the information gap can often be filled, albeit at a cost, and sometimes only partially.

More broadly, the new thinking on information in economics sees the institutions of capitalism largely as attempts to solve this very problem. The fact that firms, banks and other institutions exist, and are organised as they are, reflects society's efforts to make best use of scarce information.

Even on economic grounds (never mind other considerations), there is no tidy answer to the question of where the boundary between state and market should lie. Markets do fail – because of monopoly, public goods, externalities, lack of information and for other reasons. But, more than critics allow, markets find ways to mitigate the harm – and that is a task at which governments have often been strikingly unsuccessful.

All in all, a strong presumption in favour of markets seems wise. This is not because classical economic theory says so, but because experience seems to agree.

The grabbing hand

Most economists advocate the helping-hand model of government. Some prefer the invisible hand. Two economists offer what you might call – were it not for the term's tragi-comic associations – a third way

MUCH THE BIGGEST DEFECT IN ECONOMICS as it is commonly practised is what it assumes about government. Mainstream economics has a detailed and elaborate (if not always entirely convincing) theory about why consumers, workers and firms do what they do. Its thinking about what animates the other main actor in economic life – the government – is in contrast laughably thin.

People often complain that it is simplistic for economics to assume that individuals are rational and self-interested. Of course this is a simplification, but it is an enlightening one, and not flatly contradicted in the real world. The corresponding assumption about government – that the state aims to maximise social welfare – is contradicted by the real world about as flatly as you could wish.

A disinterested observer could describe only a small part of what governments do as even an attempt to improve overall welfare. Judging by their largest interventions (taxes and spending), governments are mainly concerned with redistribution: reducing one group's welfare so as to improve another's (at some net cost overall). As Andrei Shleifer of Harvard University and Robert Vishny of the University of Chicago insist in their book, *The Grabbing Hand: Government Pathologies and their Cures*,[1] the assumption behind most economists' thinking about the role of the state is not even simplistic; it is plain wrong.

There is no comparably elaborated body of thought based on the idea that governments are, like individuals, rational and self-interested – in other words, that they are chiefly concerned with winning power, exercising power and hanging on to power. Some great minds (James Buchanan, Gordon Tullock and the late Mancur Olsen, to name three) have applied themselves to public-choice theory, as the branch of the subject devoted to this insight is known, but, so far as mainstream thinking is concerned, to disappointingly little effect.

Why is this? There is (of course) a public-choice explanation: neither producers nor consumers of economics (economists and politicians, respectively) have much interest in seeing such truths exposed. But another reason for the limited influence of public-choice theory is that it has often made itself seem irrelevant. The public-choice literature has taken such a cynical view of politics that it regards the state as beyond redemption. Its prescriptions often boil down to the demand that governments withdraw from almost every aspect of economic life. As a result, the insights of public-choice theory have been too little applied to improving government, as opposed to demanding that it be largely abolished.

Devilish details

Messrs Shleifer and Vishny are trying to put that right. They believe their "grabbing hand" model is a distinctive alternative both to the "helping hand" (market-failure correcting) model of mainstream thinking and to the invisible-hand paradigm of the public-choice school. It is certainly closer to the second than to the first. But what divides it from the invisible-hand approach is its prescriptive content – its emphasis on tilting the balance of political costs and benefits in order to bring public and private interests into closer alignment, leading, they hope, to better (but not always less) government.

Consider a specific example: privatisation. How do the three approaches differ in their thinking? Helping-hand economists are not much interested. Ownership alone matters little, they say: what counts is choosing the right managers and giving them the appropriate incentives. Also, privatisation is bad if it creates a monopoly. Put these together and the prescription is "be cautious", or even "don't bother – focus on what matters".

The invisible-hand approach says that, at least in countries where private markets are established, the government has no business owning any enterprise. The government should simply get out: privatise, and let the market do the rest.

Messrs Shleifer and Vishny agree that ownership matters, that it is no accident that state-owned enterprises are nearly always badly run, and that privatisation is a good thing. But they are interested in details that the invisible-hand people often find too disgusting to contemplate. How did the firm come to be nationalised in the first place? Whose private interests does public ownership serve? How, as a matter of strategy, are these interests to be disenfranchised? Most important, how can privatisation be organised in such a way that, first, it becomes politically possible and, second, the new pattern of private interests supports rather than undermines the public interest?

Having set out this agenda, the authors gather a series of papers published over a number of years to show what kind of results you can expect. The range of material is impressive: the chapters deal with the growth of European cities before the industrial revolution, corruption in post-Soviet Russia, privatisation in eastern Europe, local government in the United States, and more. The authors keep technical apparatus to a minimum. By any standards, let alone the debased standard of most modern economics, the essays are lucid and literate.

Grabbing-hand economics is at best a work in progress – a work barely begun, in fact – rather than an established school of thinking. And it might have been more accurate (though duller) to call it applied public-choice economics, rather than to come down with a touch of third-way syndrome (not this, not that, but something quite new and wonderful). No matter. Good luck to Messrs Shleifer and Vishny. If they are to make a perceptible dent in the reflex statism of orthodox economics, they will need it.

Note

1   Published by Harvard University Press, 1999.

The Zimbabwean model

The pros and cons of opting out of the global economy

ORTHODOX ECONOMISTS sometimes get it wrong. For example, when a government fixes the prices of various goods below what they cost to produce, and fails to provide the necessary subsidy to fill the gap, orthodox theory predicts that there will be empty shelves in the shops. But in Zimbabwe, this is not how things have turned out. Retailers there have indeed run out of all manner of price-controlled goods. But for some reason they can still get hold of toilet paper. So, instead of empty shelves, Zimbabwean shoppers encounter aisle upon aisle of roll upon roll, where the bread, sugar and oil used to be.

Ignore, for a moment, the headlines about murder, torture and election-rigging. For an interesting economic experiment is being conducted in Zimbabwe. To the foes of globalisation, President Robert Mugabe's views are unexceptional. He argues that "runaway market forces" are leading a "vicious, all-out assault on the poor". He decries the modern trend of "banishing the state from the public sphere for the benefit of big business". What sets him apart from other anti-globalisers, however, is that he has been able to put his ideas into practice.

In countries where the IMF calls the shots, governments have to balance their budgets on the backs of the poor. Having told the IMF to get stuffed, Mr Mugabe is free not to do this. By official estimates, Zimbabwe's budget deficit was about 11% of GDP in 2002; the government was frantically borrowing and printing money to cover the shortfall: inflation was 133% in 2002.

Mr Mugabe argues that price rises are caused by greedy businessmen. His solution is price controls. To start with, these applied only to everyday essentials, such as bread and maize meal. Shops were ordered to sell such goods at fixed, low prices. Unfortunately, Mr Mugabe was right about those greedy businessmen. Rather than lose money, they stocked their shelves with toilet paper, or tried to dodge price controls by modifying their products. For example, since bread was price-controlled, bakers added raisins to their dough and called it "raisin bread", which was not on the list. Not to be outsmarted, in November 2002 the government extended price controls to practically everything, from typewriters to babies' nappies.

Some things have to be imported, however, and it is hard to prevent foreigners from profiteering. Mr Mugabe is anxious that petrol, for example, should be affordable; otherwise, people will not be able to get to work. A strong currency should help, so he froze the exchange rate, and denounced as a "saboteur" anybody who suggested devaluation. Since Zimbabwe's inflation is a tad higher than America's, nobody wished to surrender hard currency at the official rate of 55 Zimbabwe dollars to one American dollar. The black market rate is several hundreds to one; the government blames speculators.

To lay hands on foreign currency, Mr Mugabe has no choice but to rob exporters. Those whose products are bulky and hard to smuggle (tobacco farmers, for instance) must surrender half of their hard-currency proceeds to the government, which repays them in crisp new Zimbabwe dollars, at the official rate.

This is not nearly enough, however, to keep Zimbabwe supplied with petrol (the distribution of which is a state monopoly). So, in November 2002, the finance minister announced a clampdown on the black market: all bureaux de change were to be shut. He also asked expatriate Zimbabweans to remit money home via the central bank, which will confiscate almost all of it. For some reason, they prefer informal channels, such as internet-based firms that accept cash offshore and issue friends and relatives back in Zimbabwe with local currency or vouchers for supermarkets.

For most problems, a coercive solution can be found. The government's debt-servicing costs are too high? Force financial institutions to buy treasury bills that yield far less than the rate of inflation. People are running out of food? Confiscate grain from those who have it ("hoarders") and distribute it at an artificially low price through a state monopoly grain distributor. Ordinarily, this would somewhat dampen commercial farmers' incentive to grow food. But since most of them have been driven off their land, what does it matter?

An example to us all

It would be nice to think that the rest of the world has nothing to learn from Zimbabwe. But Mr Mugabe has many admirers. His fellow Africans cheer his defiance of the old colonial powers. Namibia's government has promised a similar land-grab. South Africa, showing comparable paranoia about currency speculators, conducted a pointless investigation into whether banks had conspired to undervalue the rand.

Globally, few policymakers favour going the full Mugabe, but many believe that a little bit of price-fixing won't hurt. Price supports for EU farmers, for example, persist because their governments are rich enough to keep subsidising them, and because the costs are spread across the entire population, who are often unaware that they are being fleeced. Influential charities argue that poor countries should also be paid a "fair" price for their products. Oxfam, for example, contends that the price of coffee is "too low" because multinationals manipulate it. The charity is campaigning for it somehow to be raised.

It may seem harsh, when faced with the misery of an Ethiopian coffee farmer, to argue that it would be more efficient to let the price mechanism deliver its message ("Grow something else") unmuffled. But greater efficiency leads to greater wealth, and vice versa, as Zimbabwe so harrowingly shows. Nowhere has withdrawn so swiftly from the global economy, nor seen such a thorough reversal of neo-liberal policies. The results – an economy that contracted by 35% in five years, and half the population in need of food aid – are hard to paper over.

Endnote

Since this article was published in 2002, Zimbabwe's economy has continued to shrink, and inflation accelerated to 579%, by official estimates, in 2005. In 2006 The Zimbabwean dollar was trading at an official rate of 99,202 to the dollar. The unofficial rate is higher still.

The trustbusters' new tools

Activist competition policy is back in style. Thank big changes in economic thinking

FOR MOST OF THIS CENTURY, "industrial organisation" – the branch of economics that studies competition – has been an intellectual backwater. But now, as trustbusters weigh an unprecedented number of mergers (see Chart 9.2 on the next page) and all sorts of novel business arrangements that would reshape industries from publishing to defence and accounting to aviation, the intellectual tide has turned. The economic ideas of the 1970s and 1980s argued overwhelmingly that government activism in competition was often unwarranted and counterproductive. Now they are giving way to new thinking that justifies tougher antitrust enforcement. That competition authorities seem to be casting a more sceptical eye is partly thanks to these fresh ideas.

Surprisingly perhaps, the controversies surrounding Microsoft plough little new intellectual ground. Although technophiles are prone to assert that advanced technology has changed everything, few new antitrust problems are posed by Microsoft's purported sins, which involve mostly predation against competitors in a supposed effort to monopolise parts of the software industry. If advanced technology has changed competition policy, it is for another reason entirely: that computers have greatly enhanced economists' ability to crunch numbers and model behaviour. The pages that follow describe these new techniques and the thinking that lies behind them.

Never mind the market

No matter the issue at hand, economists, lawyers and judges are wont to begin their analysis of competition by asking a single question: what market are we worried about? Yet, in one of the most startling developments in industrial organisation, economists have now concluded that "the market" does not necessarily matter.

Consider the most basic task of trustbusters: to keep any firm from exercising "market power", the ability to set prices higher than competition would allow. In the past, economists sought to measure market power with the Herfindahl-Hirschman Index, which is determined by adding the squares of the market shares of all firms involved. If the

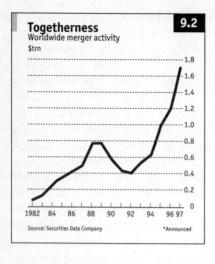

Togetherness `9.2`
Worldwide merger activity
$trn

- 1.8
- 1.6
- 1.4
- 1.2
- 1.0
- 0.8
- 0.6
- 0.4
- 0.2
- 0

1982 84 86 88 90 92 94 96 97

Source: Securities Data Company   *Announced

Herfindahl is low, there are many competitors and exercising market power should be hard; a high Herfindahl, on the other hand, was thought to warn of a concentrated market in which price rises are easier to sustain.

The Herfindahl's great virtue is its simplicity. But that virtue masks two shortcomings. First, there is often no clear way to define what market is at stake. In the investigation of the proposed (but never consummated) alliance between British Airways and American Airlines, for example, the carriers asserted that the relevant market was travel between the United States and Europe (of which their combined share was modest). European Union officials, on the other hand, focused on travel between the United States and Britain (of which their combined share was huge). Second, even when the scope of the market is clear, the relation between the Herfindahl and market power is not. America's soft-drink industry, to take one example, is noted for price competition although only two firms, Coca-Cola and PepsiCo, control three-quarters of sales.

Frustration with the Herfindahl's failings has led economists in a different direction. Instead of calculating market shares, they seek to gauge if an arrangement such as a merger will drive prices higher than they would be otherwise. According to Jerry Hausman, an economist at the Massachusetts Institute of Technology, economists can actually model oligopolistic behaviour and predict what will happen if the merger goes ahead. This became possible with the spread of two technologies during the 1990s: desktop computers with extraordinary number-crunching power and the scanners used at retailers' checkouts.

These techniques were first applied in 1995, when Interstate Bakeries, America's third-largest wholesale baker, proposed to buy rival Continental Baking. Instead of arguing about whether the market for white bread is separate from the market for rye, the government obtained scanner data from a commercial-information company, providing weekly details about average prices and sales volumes for dozens of different breads in various cities.

Thousands of equations later, economists from the Department of Justice concluded that the price of Interstate's sliced white breads strongly affected sales of Continental's Wonder bread, and vice versa, but made little difference to sales of other white breads or other varieties, such as rye. Having shown that each company's brands were the main restraint on the other's prices, the authorities moved to block the merger. In the end Interstate met their objections by selling some of its brands and bakeries.

The empirical analysis went still further with 1997's proposed merger of Staples and Office Depot, two chains of office-supply "superstores" in America. By traditional lights, the merger posed no problems, as thousands of retailers sell office supplies. But when economists hired by the Federal Trade Commission (FTC) scrutinised sales prices and quantities for every item sold by each chain, the computers spotted a pattern: Staples's prices were lower in cities where Office Depot also had a store than in cities where it had none. This was strong and unexpected evidence that the merger would allow Staples to raise prices. A court then blocked the merger.

Some practitioners, such as Greg Werden of the Department of Justice, suggest that when scanner data or similar information is available, defining a market need no longer be part of antitrust analysis. The courts have yet to accept that view. But this econometric approach has greatly influenced America's competition authorities. "It started the agencies focusing on stuff that really matters," says Luke Froeb, an economist at Vanderbilt University in Tennessee. For the first time, they have the ability to predict whether a merger will raise prices for consumers.

That central concern is the legacy of the academics from the University of Chicago who rebuilt industrial organisation in the 1970s and 1980s. Chicago's famously free-market thinkers defined two principles for competition policy. First, they said, governments should stop worrying about size and ask only whether a firm can exert market power. Second, even if a firm gains market power, the effect will usually be temporary, because high profits will attract new competitors. Hence, markets will erode most monopolies more quickly and effectively than will governments.

Incontestable
The Chicago analysis was hugely influential. Some of its tenets, such as

an insistence on rigorous economic analysis and on consumers' well-being as the only meaningful gauge, are still widely accepted. But these tenets are now supporting judgments that are far more interventionist than those that went before.

In the 1980s, under Chicago's sway, American competition authorities would probably have given the bakery and office-supply mergers their blessing. In doing so, they would also have relied on the theory of contestable markets, one of the most publicised economic ideas of the 1980s. Contestability theory still matters today – but in a way that is opposite to its developers' original conception.

To understand contestability, first recall that monopolies are undesirable because they can restrict output and raise prices so as to increase their own profitability at the expense of consumers. But economists showed in the early 1980s that raising prices is not always in a monopolist's interest, because it may attract other firms to enter the market. If entry is easy and costless – in other words, if the market is "contestable" – a sensible monopolist will forestall competition by setting prices as if it were operating in a competitive market, and there will be no economic harm.

Contestability theory was conceived with telecoms in mind – indeed much of the research was sponsored by American Telephone & Telegraph (AT&T), then fighting attempts to dismantle its national telephone monopoly. But the idea was soon applied to other industries, notably aviation. Go ahead and deregulate routes and fares, the theory taught, because even if only one airline flies on a route, it will keep fares low to deter rivals. Contestability offered a rationale for easing anti-monopoly rules in both America and Britain.

In the enthusiasm, however, one condition was forgotten. For a market to be fully contestable, firms must be able to avoid large sunk costs. The newcomer must be able to make a one-way bet, winning if profits are good, but losing nothing if it should decide to retreat.

The real world is not like that. A bakery would have to advertise its brand in a new market – an investment that would be wasted were it to back away. A new office-supply chain would have to continue paying rent even if it were to close its shops. As a firm weighs whether to sink costs, it knows that the high profits that look so enticing now will shrink with competition. And so, taken to its conclusion, contestability theory leads to an arresting result: the greater the sunk costs, the less the incentive for new firms to compete against an incumbent, which therefore can restrict output and raise prices.

The belief that firms would find clever ways to hinder competition was one of the original motives for anti-monopoly laws. This was a threat that the Chicago theorists did not take seriously. Their predilection was that firms do business in whatever way they find most efficient. Other motivations such as harming rivals are not likely to maximise profits, and are therefore improbable. Robert Bork, a Chicago-trained legal scholar, was one of the most influential antitrust thinkers of the 1970s. He argued that vertical restraints, such as "tying" (requiring the purchaser of one product to buy another) and "resale price maintenance" (in which a manufacturer tells retailers what they may charge) are unlikely ever to lead to higher prices and should therefore always be legal.

Of Bork and brokers

Mr Bork says his views have not changed – even though he was an adviser to Netscape, a software firm that accused Microsoft of predatory behaviour. What has changed is the sorts of models game theorists employ, which are far richer and more complex than those used in the 1970s. "The Chicago theories assume perfect competition or perfect monopoly, and nothing in between," says Steven Salop, an economist at Georgetown University Law School in Washington, DC. "The post-Chicago school is based on models of strategic competition among oligopolists."

How, for example, can stockbrokers maintain wide spreads between the price they pay for shares and the price at which they sell them, as occurred until recently on America's NASDAQ stockmarket? Simple game theory suggests that this kind of behaviour will not persist, because each broker will narrow his spread in anticipation of another firm doing so first. But as Derek Morris, head of Britain's Monopolies and Mergers Commission, points out, the "game" in that model is "played" only once. In the real world, where competitors face off again and again, a company that violates shared but unstated understandings might face retaliation. That makes it disinclined to be a rule-breaker. "The static game typically gives you non-collusive pricing," Mr Morris says. "But once you have a time dimension, you have conditions in which tacit collusion may occur."

Predatory behaviour also looks less innocent through the lens of sophisticated game theory. Following the Chicago lead, most economists until recently viewed it as pro-competitive. In its most obvious form, one firm charges unrealistically low prices to drive another out of the market. Low prices benefit consumers, went the thinking, and the predator rarely sustains monopoly profits for long.

This reasoning is correct – in some cases. Enforcers "really do have to worry about scaring off real competition," says Jonathan Baker, chief economist at the FTC. However, by simulating complex interactions among firms, economists are able to show that predatory pricing may be highly profitable. Authorities in both Europe and America are studying allegations that big airlines slash fares and add seats when a discount airline starts service on a given route. Such predation would pay off if, by establishing a reputation for aggressive counter-attacks, a carrier could deter competition on other routes. This argument has yet to be tested in American courts, the economics of predatory pricing is still fairly underdeveloped, and there are few theories to distinguish desirable price competition from undesirable predation.

In addition, the academics of the Chicago school failed to identify some other kinds of predatory behaviour:

- **Raising rivals' costs.** When America's Justice Department moved to block the merger of two aerospace companies, Lockheed-Martin and Northrop Grumman, in March 1998, among its concerns was the firms' role as components suppliers for other defence contractors. After the merger, might not those subsidiaries offer higher prices or less advanced products to Lockheed's rivals? In a highly competitive industry, the rivals could simply find other suppliers. But in an oligopolistic industry, the government feared, a dominant Lockheed might be able to get away with predatory behaviour, forcing up prices for competitors and thus squeezing their profits. The merger was blocked.
- **Reducing rivals' revenues.** A different sort of predation was behind a Microsoft strategy that obliged computer-makers to pay it a royalty on each machine they sold, whether or not it carried Microsoft's software. Frederick Warren-Boulton, a Washington-based economist and former Justice Department official, labels this a "tax" on competitors: customers will be unwilling to pay much for other firms' software, as they must already pay for Microsoft's. Microsoft changed its policy in 1995.
- **Connected markets.** The Chicago school held that if markets are linked, a firm with a monopoly in one cannot boost profits by monopolising another. That is no longer accepted. If Microsoft

monopolises browsers, economists argue, it could prevent competitors such as Netscape from using browsers to challenge its dominant position in operating software. The European Union is examining similar issues in broadcasting, on the theory that if a firm obtains market power in, say, sports programming, it can leverage that into an even more profitable market position in pay-TV. Martin Cave of Brunel University, near London, believes that this idea could open up whole new areas of investigation for the antitrust authorities.

No monopoly of wisdom

None of these types of predation, it is worth pointing out, can succeed in a highly competitive environment of the kind the Chicago theorists assumed. However, economists have concluded that matters are different if a firm has already gained a dominant position in a market. In that case, predation may strengthen the dominant company's position and generate more profits at the consumers' expense.

Economists themselves, of course, are no less entrepreneurial than other folk. Given prompting, they will happily tout the novelty of their work. So it is perhaps inevitable that some of the ideas now being touted as revolutionary insights may be less startling or useful than advertised.

One example is network effects. The notion is that some businesses – internet access, credit cards and computer software, to name three – differ fundamentally from other economic activities because the desire for compatibility makes certain forms of competition impractical or even unwanted. Although this sounds dramatic, the consequences for policy are fairly minor and involve old-fashioned regulation. The question of how to keep the owner of an "essential facility", such as a credit-card approval network, from exploiting its monopoly power is an old one; the European Union's examination of competition in internet access raises questions similar to the investigation that led to the break-up of AT&T by the American authorities.

The new approach to competition by no means heralds a return to the pre-Chicago days when bigness itself was deemed to be an evil. Indeed, it explicitly emphasises market power rather than size, which was anyway only ever an unsatisfactory proxy. Nor does the new approach mean that trustbusters will bring more cases. "You still need to prove something bad is happening and get customers to complain about it," says Robert Litan, a former antitrust official now with the Brookings

Institution in Washington. "You can't make an antitrust case out of fancy economic theories." But the fancy theories will, without doubt, motivate enforcers to investigate business behaviour that hitherto would have raised no eyebrows. They will come to understand new ways in which businesses acquire excessive market power. Consumers should be grateful.

One lump or two?

In parliaments and in pubs, many debates about unemployment, trade and so on are based on misunderstandings about economics. One of the most common is the "lump of labour" fallacy

EVEN AFTER SEVERAL YEARS of economic recovery, one out of 15 workers in the rich industrial world is out of work. There is no shortage of popular explanations for this. Some people blame the introduction of new technology; others the influx of cheap imports from the developing world. One often hears that immigrants are stealing jobs; or that there are fewer jobs for the boys because more women are entering the workforce.

Along with these simple "explanations" comes an outpouring of simple "cures": why not cut working hours so that there are more jobs to go round, or keep out cheap imports or foreign workers? There is a common fallacy at the bottom of both explanations and cures. It is that the output of an economy, and hence the amount of work available, is fixed. Both history and common sense show that it is not. Economists call this the lump of labour (or sometimes the lump of output) fallacy.

Take fears about technology. Workers have fretted about new machines causing unemployment at least since the start of the industrial revolution. In the early 19th century Luddites smashed the power looms that threatened their jobs. And yet although technology has advanced rapidly over the past couple of centuries, unemployment has not risen with it. On the contrary, productivity, output and jobs have all risen together (see Chart 9.3 on the next page). Blacksmiths, coachmen and hand-loom weavers may have disappeared, but the total number of jobs has expanded.

New technology comes in two forms. There is "product innovation": the appearance of wholly new items such as home computers and microwaves, the demand for which creates jobs that did not exist before. And there is "process innovation": new machines and methods for producing existing goods more efficiently. In the short run, process innovation enables a given amount of output to be produced with less labour, and may therefore increase unemployment. But, like product innovation, it also generates extra demand in the economy, which can offset the initial labour-cutting effects.

257

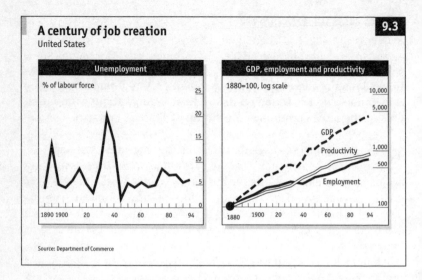

A century of job creation
United States

9.3

Unemployment

% of labour force

1890 1900 20 40 60 80 94

GDP, employment and productivity

1880=100, log scale

GDP

Productivity

Employment

1880 1900 20 40 60 80 94

Source: Department of Commerce

How does this happen? Higher productivity reduces costs, and lower costs will in turn lead to lower prices, higher wages or fatter profits. The first two will boost real incomes, and so raise the demand for goods and workers. Alternatively, if higher productivity feeds into profits, investment will expand, which will also boost output and jobs.

The net effect on employment will depend upon how much prices respond to lower costs, and how sensitive demand is to lower prices. In a world where all consumer desires have been fully satisfied, and so demand cannot rise to match any increase in productive capacity, new technology could lead to permanently higher unemployment. But that world does not exist, and probably never will.

In the past, the demand-generating effects of new technology have always outweighed the labour-displacing effects. Technology has, in the end, created more jobs than it has destroyed. That does not mean that new technology will not raise unemployment in particular occupations or regions. There may also be lags in between the destruction of old jobs and the creation of new ones. But these are not arguments for delaying change: the OECD's *Jobs Study*, published in 1994, found that countries which had shifted the structure of their production most quickly to high-technology sectors had created the most jobs.

The productivity paradox
The lump of labour fallacy is often to blame for confusion about

whether productivity growth (due to more efficient working practices or to new technology) is a good or bad thing. The faster productivity grows, the fewer jobs are created by a given rate of growth. Some people conclude from this that it would be better for jobs if productivity grew more slowly. The trouble is that, in the long run, productivity growth is the only way to increase living standards. History suggests that when governments attempt to preserve jobs by curbing the growth of productivity, they are far more likely to end up increasing unemployment and reducing living standards.

The reason for this is that rapid productivity growth tends to go hand in hand with rapid output growth. In the 1960s, when productivity in OECD economies grew rapidly, unemployment remained low. Only in the 1970s, when the growth in productivity (and in output) slumped, did unemployment rise.

There is another argument against trying to preserve jobs by curbing productivity growth. The demand for labour by firms depends upon the relationship between productivity and wages. Say firms invested less in machinery, and so productivity growth was reduced. Then unless workers also accepted smaller pay rises than before, the cost of hiring the "marginal" worker would now exceed the value of his extra output – so unemployment would rise rather than fall.

The lump of labour fallacy also lies behind paranoia about jobs being "stolen" by low-wage countries. Cheap imports, it is argued, will displace domestic production and so eliminate jobs.

It is true that in a country that imports cheaper low-skill goods from developing countries, the demand for low-skilled workers at home will fall. But this is not the end of the story. As they become richer, developing countries will not just sit on their export earnings, but spend them on skill-intensive goods from rich countries, thereby creating new jobs in those countries. Indeed, if countries specialise in the production of goods in which they have a "comparative advantage", world output will expand.

Although it follows that trade with low-wage developing economies should have little net effect on overall employment in rich countries, such trade will change the job mix. Demand for low-skilled workers (and hence their wages) will fall, and demand for high-skilled workers will rise.

The entry of immigrants or women into the labour force can be analysed in the same way. If the skill distribution of the newcomers is different from that of existing workers, then relative wages will change.

For instance, if immigrants are, on average, less skilled than native workers, they will depress the wages of low-skilled labour.

But there is no reason why an increase in the labour force should permanently increase unemployment. Immigrants or new female workers will spend their wages, thereby expanding demand, output and jobs. In the 1980s, 8m immigrants entered America, one-quarter of the overall increase in its workforce. And yet unemployment fell because many more jobs were created.

Job-sharing

The idea of using shorter working hours, job-sharing (splitting one full-time job into two part-time ones) or early retirement as a cure for unemployment has become popular in recent years. It might seem wrong that even as many people long for work, others spend too long in the office – to the detriment of family and health. One-quarter of British men work more than 48 hours each week. Why not share out work more evenly?

In 1994 Volkswagen, a carmaker, decided, instead of reducing the number of people it employed, to introduce a four-day week. Some European governments have encouraged job-sharing by offering firms incentives such as rebates on employer social-security contributions.

Most such schemes have had disappointing results, for a familiar reason. It is quite true that if there were a fixed amount of work to be done in the economy, there would be more jobs to go round if those who had them worked fewer hours. But – the lump of labour fallacy strikes again – the amount of work to be done is not fixed. Neither theory nor experience support job-sharing as a way to reduce unemployment. It is flawed in three ways:

- Shorter hours will create more jobs only if weekly pay is also cut, otherwise costs per unit of output will rise. Many workers may like the idea of more leisure, but resist a cut in their pay-packets.
- Not all labour costs vary with the number of hours worked. Fixed costs, such as recruitment, training and canteens, can be substantial, so it will cost a firm more to hire two part-time workers than one full-timer. There is therefore a risk that a cut in the working week may raise average costs per unit of output and so cause firms to buy fewer total hours of labour.
- A cut in average working hours will not affect the relationship between inflation and unemployment. In other words, the

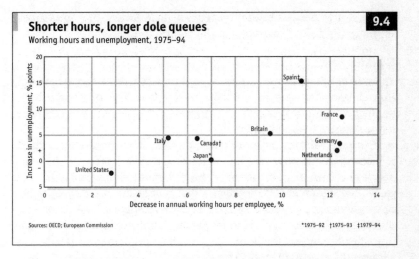

Shorter hours, longer dole queues   9.4
Working hours and unemployment, 1975–94

Sources: OECD; European Commission   *1975–92 †1975–93 ‡1979–94

unemployment rate consistent with stable inflation – which economists call the "non-accelerating-inflation-rate of unemployment", or NAIRU – will remain unchanged. According to theory, if unemployment is above this rate, then it can be reduced by stimulating demand without fear of pushing up inflation. But once the jobless rate drops below this critical level, inflation will rise.

A fall in unemployment brought about by job-sharing would have the same inflationary consequences as a fall generated by an increase in demand, but without the benefit of higher output. Suppose that job-sharing succeeds in reducing unemployment below the NAIRU. Inflation will rise, which will then force the government to tighten its monetary or fiscal policy. That will push unemployment back up to the NAIRU; so the jobless rate will be back where it started, but output and total income will end up lower. The same argument applies if early retirement is used to reduce unemployment.

Nor does the empirical evidence support shorter hours as a cure for unemployment. Chart 9.4 shows that, if anything, unemployment has risen more sharply in countries where hours worked have fallen most.

Perhaps the most damning fact of all is that if shorter hours and longer holidays really were a simple cure for joblessness, then Europe should enjoy the world's lowest unemployment rate, since its workers toil for far fewer hours each year than their American and Japanese counterparts. Instead, Europe has the highest jobless rate.

A better way

There is nothing wrong with firms and trade unions freely negotiating shorter hours for less pay. But if governments try to create jobs by imposing compulsory limits on working hours, they are more likely to reduce than increase employment.

In a way, calls for a shorter week, popular in Europe, reflect a desire to quarrel about how to share a fixed-size cake instead of baking a bigger one. This distracts attention from the underlying causes of European unemployment. Only policies that reduce the NAIRU can reduce unemployment permanently. The OECD's *Jobs Study* in 1994 argued that the best way is to make labour markets work more efficiently, with more flexible wages, lower minimum wages, less generous jobless benefits and a better-trained workforce.

If new technology or foreign competition do lead to net job losses it will not be because the lump of labour has become a fact rather than a fallacy, but because labour is not sufficiently mobile between sectors and regions, or because relative wages have failed to adjust. Not only will work-sharing fail to address these rigidities, it could actually do real harm. Working less hard may well appeal to cosseted continental Europeans, but they should not delude themselves into believing that it is a magic solution.

Secrets and the prize

James Mirrlees and William Vickrey won the 1996 Nobel prize in economics for helping to answer an important question: how do you deal with someone who knows more than you do?

B Y APPEARING TO TRUMPET selfishness as the path to prosperity, economists have done much to earn their reputation as dismal scientists. The award of the 1996 Nobel economics prize, however, should redress the moral balance a little: its two co-winners were honoured for demonstrating the importance of getting people to tell the truth.

Specifically, the two economists – James Mirrlees who moved to Cambridge University after a quarter-century at Oxford, and William Vickrey, who has spent most of his career at Columbia University – have made pathbreaking discoveries in the economics of asymmetric information: the study of transactions in which some of the parties involved know more than the others.

Anyone who has bought a used car will know how much this matters. In fact transactions involving asymmetric (or private) information are everywhere. A manager cannot tell how hard employees are working; a government selling oil-drilling rights does not know what buyers are prepared to pay for them; a lender does not know how likely the borrower is to repay.

Private information can distort people's incentives and make it harder for them to pursue their objectives efficiently. (Try selling a used car when nobody trusts you.) The problem facing economists therefore is to understand how people can minimise these distorting effects.

Although Messrs Mirrlees and Vickrey worked independently (indeed they had never met), some of their most important research focused on a similar problem: designing an optimal income-tax system. The ideal system must balance two competing objectives: equity and efficiency. In a paper published in 1945 Mr Vickrey showed that governments must take into account private information in order to strike the right trade-off. To see why, imagine a taxman who cared only about equity, and ignored incentives. He would take money from the rich, and give some back to the poor, until he had raised the revenue he wanted and equalised people's after-tax income.

However, since more productive workers can earn more for a given amount of effort, extra effort on their part would be taxed at a higher rate than other people's. Under a pure-equity tax scheme, therefore, the most productive people will not work hard enough.

If the government knew how productive each worker was, it would be possible to get around this problem: the authorities could simply force more productive people to work harder than others (which would increase efficiency), and then redistribute everyone's income as before. But the government does not know people's productivity, only their income. Because of this, a pure-equity tax scheme will not work: everyone will underplay their abilities in order to lower their tax bill. Mr Vickrey showed that designing the optimal tax scheme, while accounting for these incentive effects, was far trickier than had previously been imagined.

The truth helps

Enter Mr Mirrlees, who in the late 1960s found a solution to Mr Vickrey's problem. His most important insight was that an optimal tax system must be what economists now call "incentive compatible". That is, it must give people an incentive to tell the truth, as it were, about their productivity through their choice of how hard to work. So if the government designs a tax scheme in which it wants more productive people to work harder, it must choose tax rates that induce them to do so.

Since governments never do anything optimally, these findings have not yet been fully exploited. Over the past few decades, however, the insights gained from optimal-tax theory have been applied to many other fields.

Mr Mirrlees's theory has been put to work in the study of insurance. Just as governments cannot observe people's productivity, insurers cannot observe whether their customers have taken proper precautions. By charging deductibles, and making claimants bear a portion of losses, insurers can align their incentives properly. If the premiums reflect the risks that would occur in the event of precautions being taken, the customer must face big enough losses to induce him to take them. Building on Mr Mirrlees's research, economists have been able to improve greatly their understanding of insurance markets.

Similarly Mr Vickrey made important advances in auction theory, which also involves information asymmetries. The problem that the auctioneer must solve is to induce potential buyers to "tell the truth" when they bid: that is, to say what the item being sold is truly worth to them. Mr Vickrey showed that with sealed bids, an auction that awards the item to the highest bidder, but forces him to pay the second-highest price, induces him to do so no matter what strategy he thinks other bidders will follow.

Such a "Vickrey auction" not only awards the prize to the party who can make the most of it, but in most cases it allows the seller to obtain at least as high a price as with any other auction. These ideas have been used to sell everything from oil fields to bands of the broadcasting spectrum.

By providing insights into these and other problems, the 1996 laureates have created the foundations for a thriving field in economics. Economists are not only discovering new ways to cope with asymmetric information, but they have also come to see that many accepted business practices have evolved to solve precisely this problem. You may still have to deal with selfish people; but at least you can get them to tell you the truth.

The regulators' best friend?

Europeans embrace the logic of cost-benefit analysis just as some Americans grow suspicious of it

ACCORDING TO ONE OF THE EUROPEAN COMMISSION'S pettifogging regulations, cucumbers sold in the single market cannot be too curvy. According to another proposal, packets of coffee and chicory must conform to weights specified in Brussels.

The first regulation is largely apocryphal, a myth propagated by Eurosceptic newspapers in Britain and debunked by the commission's team of counter-spinners. But the second regulation is quite real. It was one of several examples of regulatory overkill lambasted by Günter Verheugen, a vice-president of the commission, in a speech in April 2005. Mr Verheugen wants to withdraw such needless regulations, simplify others and subject new proposals to "solid cost-benefit analyses".

Cost-benefit analysis – which typically quantifies the attractions and drawbacks of a regulation, converts them into dollars or euros, then tots them up – sounds both dull and innocuous. But its findings can be revealing. For example, Robert Hahn, a scholar at the American Enterprise Institute in Washington, DC, calculates that over 40% of American regulations impose costs that outweigh the benefits they confer.[1] What might a similar review of the European Union's regulatory rule-book reveal? How many of the 90,000 pages of the *acquis communautaire* might be safely torn out, to the net benefit of the union?

The findings of Mr Hahn and other cost-benefit analysts in America have not passed unchallenged, however. A number of critics doubt the worth of the techniques and distrust the motives of the practitioners. They say that America's current administration is guilty of "regulatory underkill" and that cost-benefit analysis is its weapon of choice.

Whether or not this is fair to President George Bush's administration, is it fair to cost-benefit analysis? Is the method fatally flawed and intrinsically anti-regulatory? The Centre for Progressive Regulation (CPR), a think-tank that shelters many sceptics, thinks so. It objects to two features in particular: the "translation of lives, health, and the natural environment into monetary terms" and "the discounting of harms to human health and the environment that are expected to occur in the future".[2]

Those who question cost-benefit analysis doubt that a price tag can ever be put on life. How could one seriously count the cost of death and injury caused by road accidents, for example? But, as Robert Frank, an economist now at Cornell University, has pointed out, even the fiercest critics do not get their brakes checked every morning. They have more pressing uses of their time. Road safety, then, does have an opportunity cost, and an economist will want to know what it is. Thus, when the CPR accuses economists of "pricing the priceless", most economists would plead guilty as charged. They devote considerable effort, and not a little ingenuity, to discovering the implicit price of many things that are not traded directly in arm's-length markets.

As the critics allege, cost-benefit analysis works like a kind of universal solvent. It breaks qualities down into quantities, differences of kind into differences of degree, gold into base metal. A safe childhood, a breathtaking view, a clean pair of lungs – all are reduced to fungible "dollar-equivalents". In doing so, the method forces into the open trade-offs that many would rather not face too squarely. Should taxpayers' money be devoted to keeping grandmother alive for an extra month in an intensive-care unit? Or would it be better spent reducing the risk of asthma faced by deprived children in the polluted inner city? Such comparisons may seem crass. But they are democratic.

The less sweet hereafter

Accused of pricing the priceless, economists are charged with under-pricing the future as well. Most practitioners of cost-benefit analysis assume that gains in the hereafter are worth less today than gains in the here-and-now. They discount future benefits, including lives saved, in much the same way that they discount future profits or costs.

But are lives saved 12 months' hence really worth less than lives saved this year? To say so, the critics argue, is to make a false analogy between financial resources, which can be borrowed from, or invested for, the future, and human life, which cannot. By discounting future lives, economists also further an anti-regulatory agenda, the critics allege. After all, the costs of most health and safety regulations arrive upfront. The benefits can take time to emerge.

Discounting future lives is indeed awkward, and some economists have fretted about it for decades. But it is not necessarily anti-regulatory. If regulators discounted costs, but not lives saved, they would defer action indefinitely, Mr Hahn points out. The benefits would be the same if they waited a year (or a decade, for that matter) but the costs would always be less.

Cost-benefit analysis does not always argue for less regulation. It weeds out regulations that do not pay their way, but it can also identify measures not on the statute books, that should be. For example, defibrillators installed in workplaces might be a cost-effective way to save victims of heart attacks. The White House's Office of Management and Budget sent about a dozen letters to the agencies it oversees prompting them to investigate such potentially beneficial regulations.

Fundamentally, it is not "anti-government" to weigh the costs of public action. On the contrary, the "regulatory excess" Mr Verheugen sees in the EU has doubtless damaged the prestige of Brussels. Some regulatory circumspection might even rehabilitate it. If the EU had not mandated the weights of chicory packets, perhaps people would not so readily believe that it regulates the curvature of cucumbers.

Notes

1 "In Defence of the Economic Analysis of Regulation", American Enterprise Institute.
2 "Cost-Benefit Analysis", available at www.progressiveregulation.org

Money to burn?

Controlling global warming will be expensive. Emissions trading is an intelligent way to lower the cost

LIMITS ON THE EMISSIONS of the "greenhouse gases", notably carbon dioxide, that have caused the gradual rise in the earth's temperature are an obvious way to tackle the problem of global warming. But as the December 1997 meeting of 150 nations in Kyoto, Japan, made clear, introducing limits is far from straightforward. Witness the fact that while emissions of greenhouse gases are rising fastest in poorer countries, these nations, do not have to try to curb their output.

The justification for this exemption is that, for poor countries, escaping poverty must come first. Fair enough – except that if poor countries do not reduce their emissions of greenhouse gases, overall emissions worldwide will rise, even if wealthier countries succeed in scaling back the use of coal-burning power plants and petrol-driven cars. Is there a way out of this impasse? Economists think there is: tradeable emissions permits.

Economists, of course, are usually keen on markets. Here, as in many cases, they see possibilities in creating a market where none exists. There is a precedent in America, where a law allowing power companies to trade their right to emit sulphur dioxide has proved highly successful. The government determines what the allowable emissions from each power plant are. Those plants that can clean up cheaply, and thus emit less than allowed, are then free to sell their unused rights to those for whom pollution control would be costly. Overall, this has cut sulphur emissions faster and more cheaply than anyone predicted.

Permit us to pollute

American and European delegates in Kyoto wanted to explore a similar approach for greenhouse gases, starting with carbon dioxide. Under this concept, each of the 33 countries which must curb emissions would accept a target and a standard for determining how much it is emitting – two items that are basically settled already. Each government could allocate its allowable emissions to different uses. On average, about half of these come from dispersed sources, such as cars and home heating systems, that would be hard to monitor with a permit system (see Chart 9.5). Each government would divide the remainder of its allowable

269

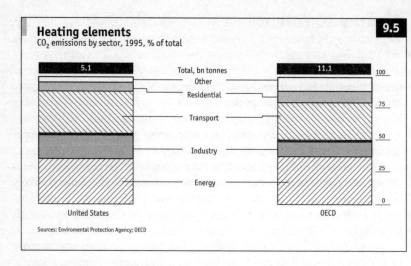

Heating elements 9.5
CO$_2$ emissions by sector, 1995, % of total

Total, bn tonnes
5.1 — 11.1

Other
Residential
Transport
Industry
Energy

United States
OECD

Sources: Enviromental Protection Agency; OECD

emissions among the handful of big industries, such as oil refineries and steelworks, that spew out greenhouse gases in large amounts. Allocations would be made annually, and would diminish over time.

On a national basis, emissions trading would be straightforward. An ageing coal-fired power station might conclude that it would be cheaper to buy extra emissions capacity than to switch fuel sources. It finds a nearby power plant that has switched to clean coal and therefore is emitting less than its entitlement. They make a deal. The national emissions targets are still met, just redistributed.

Trading could work across borders as well. Suppose a German coal-fired power station finds that meeting its allocation of emissions is unexpectedly expensive. It might contract to buy the unused emissions of a Russian chemical plant working far below capacity. This leaves some tricky accounting: German emissions will rise, perhaps alarming environmentalists, even though those in Russia will fall. What matters, however, is that global emissions are being limited in a cost-effective way, with the cuts being made where they are cheapest.

A subset of emissions trading is "joint implementation", in which one country does something that reduces carbon dioxide levels in another country, perhaps replanting a logged-out forest or modernising a smoke-belching smelter, and applies part of that reduction against its own commitments. Many such projects would probably involve poorer countries, because they have more opportunities for inexpensive emissions reduction.

Determining which activities should get credit would not be easy; why give a paper company credit for planting trees, for example, when its business requires it to do so anyhow? But if the details can be worked out, enormous benefits beckon. If poorer nations accept the principle of a full-blown international permit-trading system – which would require overall limits on emissions – it could turn out to be a money-spinner for them. By some, admittedly speculative, estimates, they could receive more money from such a scheme than they now do from aid programmes.

An emissions-trading scheme would have other benefits. The prices at which emissions rights are bought and sold would give policymakers a useful gauge of the cost of emissions reduction. In addition, a trading mechanism offers certainty about how far emissions will be cut, an advantage that the main alternative, taxing carbon, cannot offer.

Nonetheless, the idea of international emissions trading remains controversial. One objection is that it could allow rich countries to avoid taking domestic action to curb greenhouse gases. The answer to that is: so what? Global emissions are still being reduced. Another complaint is that emissions trading does nothing to address emissions from homes or vehicles. This is true, but the implication is simply that different ways of controlling emissions should be adopted for these sources.

The real problems are not theoretical but logistical. America's sulphur-reduction programme has an enforceable target and a limited number of players. The measurement and monitoring systems are effective. The bureaucracy has resisted pressure to hand out more pollution rights to companies that complain about the difficulty of reducing emissions. All of those things have to happen to make an emissions-trading system work.

But that is an argument for caution, not for whiting the idea out of the environmental picture. There is reason to think that global emissions trading might work. And if, in the end, it does not? Little harm would have been done. The risks are negligible, and the potential economic benefits very large.

Endnote

The Kyoto Treaty came into force, without America, in February 2005. The European Union established a union-wide emissions-trading regime a month earlier.

Taxes for a cleaner planet

Enthusiasts for green taxes promise a double blessing: a better environment and a healthier economy. Is this too good to be true?

THE EARTH SUMMIT in New York in June 1997 showed how easy it is to talk about cleaning up the planet – and how difficult it is to do it. Few governments have kept the promises they made in 1992 in Rio de Janeiro to cut emissions of greenhouse gases. Few seem keen to try much harder.

There is, however, no lack of ideas for making a greener world. Some governments, mainly in Europe, have been trying out economic tools, particularly taxes on pollution. The argument for these levies is seductive. Their keenest advocates say that environmental taxes will be good not only for the earth but also for the economy as a whole. Although there is some truth in this, green taxes are not the environmental and economic panacea they may seem.

Regulation may be the most obvious way to cut pollution. Governments can simply ban dirty activities, or force companies to use "clean" technology, such as catalytic converters in cars or desulphurisation equipment in coal-fired power stations. But regulation tends to make polluters use a specific technology, rather than investing in cleaner production methods, and it often forces all polluters to undertake the same sort of clean-up although individual clean-up costs vary enormously. Economic theory suggests that market mechanisms can offer more efficient ways to resolve the problems.

To economists, pollution gets out of hand because the prices of goods and services do not reflect the costs of environmental degradation. The passengers in the aeroplane flying low overhead do not pay for the disturbance the engine noise causes on the ground. Car buyers pay for labour, steel and paint, but the price sticker may not reflect the full cost of the noxious goo the car factory spills into a river. Drivers, of course, spread exhaust fumes as they motor along. The costs are borne by others, perhaps for many years, in the form of discomfort, health damage, and the loss of the pleasures and benefits of a clean environment.

The point is not that there should be no pollution at all. It is worth putting up with some, in exchange for the benefits of economic activity.

Rather, the objective is to make polluters face the true costs of what they do. Taxation is a way to do that.

Some economists add to this a second argument. Without green taxes, governments have to raise revenue through other taxes. But these have an economic cost. Income taxes reduce the incentive to work; payroll taxes reduce the incentive for employers to take workers on. With the revenue from green taxes, governments can cut other taxes and still raise the same total amount. In particular, cutting the taxes clogging up the labour market should create jobs. Hence green taxes have a "double dividend": not only do they reduce the distorted price signals about the cost of using the environment, but they also allow distortions elsewhere in the economy to be alleviated.

To some governments, these arguments are proving persuasive. Although regulation remains the most usual form of environmental policy, green taxes are gaining ground. Several countries have raised petrol taxes, and now tax leaded petrol far more heavily than unleaded fuel. Sweden taxes batteries; Belgium has a levy on disposable razors; Italy taxes the polythene in carrier bags; charges for household rubbish collections are now common in America. Keenest of all, Denmark, Finland, the Netherlands, Norway and Sweden now tax emissions of carbon dioxide, the main greenhouse gas.

Moreover, green-tax revenues are being recycled in the hope of yielding the double dividend. The Danes, Dutch, Finns and Swedes are all using revenues from environmental taxes to reduce taxes on labour. Britain's tax on the disposal of waste at landfill sites is being used to pay for a small cut in payroll tax.

A free, green lunch

But how much can green taxes achieve? Although a welcome addition to the fiscal armoury, they are far from being a cure-all. For starters, there may not be much scope for using green taxes to cut labour taxes and boost employment. Taxes on polluting industries will raise the price of their output, cutting consumers' demand for their products – this is, after all, precisely the purpose of the taxes – and hence the industries' demand for labour. Higher prices, in turn, leave people with less to spend on other things, costing jobs elsewhere, at least in the short term.

A second difficulty is that there is a trade-off between the efficacy of green taxes as instruments of environmental policy and their power as revenue-raisers. Taxes that cut pollution dramatically will not yield much revenue in the long run. If companies responded to a sulphur tax by eliminating sulphur emissions, say, the tax revenue would fall to nil. Governments would have to go back to more conventional sources of revenue.

This is likely to happen when clean, lightly taxed substitutes can replace heavily taxed goods. Thus the OECD says that in Sweden, where dirtier automotive diesel has been taxed relatively heavily since 1991, almost all diesel is now of the cleanest type and sulphur emissions from diesel vehicles have fallen by 75%. In Norway, the carbon-dioxide tax has prompted a switch away from fossil fuels, cutting emissions from power stations and factories by one-fifth since 1991.

In other instances, however, substitutes are harder to find. Green taxes are then promising sources of revenue, but will do little in themselves to change people's behaviour and reduce pollution. Higher petrol taxes and prices, for example, have done little to curb car use in OECD countries. Even in Norway, the carbon-dioxide tax has cut emissions from vehicles by perhaps 2–3% a year.

So are green taxes a good thing? Yes: they signal to polluters that the environment is valuable, and a tax system that includes them will distort economic activity less than one that does not. But governments should not need greenery as an excuse to make labour taxes less damaging. Like environmental protection, that is worthwhile anyway.

Garbage in, garbage out

Charging families for each bag of rubbish they produce seems environmentally sound and economically sensible. It may not be

SOME RITUALS of modern domestic living vary little throughout the developed world. One such is the municipal refuse collection: usually once a week, your rubbish bags or the contents of your bin disappear into the bowels of a special lorry and are carted away to the local tip.

To economists, this ceremony is peculiar, because in most places it is free. Yes, households pay for the service out of local taxes. But at the margin the price is zero: the family that fills four bins with rubbish each week pays no more than the elderly couple that fills one, and if it puts the odd plastic bag of trash atop the bins it pays nothing extra. Yet the marginal cost of rubbish disposal is not zero at all. The more people throw away, the more rubbish collectors and trucks are needed, and the more the local council has to pay in landfill and tipping fees.

This looks like the most basic of economic problems: if rubbish disposal is free, people will produce too much rubbish. The obvious economic solution is to make households pay the marginal cost of disposing of their waste. That will give them an incentive to throw out less and recycle more (assuming that local governments provide collection points for suitable materials). But as Don Fullerton and Thomas Kinnaman, two American economists, have found, this seemingly easy application of economic sense to an everyday problem has surprisingly intricate and sometimes disappointing results.

Over the past few years several American towns and cities started charging households for generating rubbish. The commonest system is to sell stickers or tags which householders attach to rubbish bags or cans. Only bags with these labels are picked up in the weekly collection. The price of a sticker or tag is, in effect, the marginal price the household pays for creating another bag of rubbish.

In a paper published in 1996[1] Messrs Fullerton and Kinnaman studied the effects of one such scheme, introduced in July 1992 in Charlottesville, Virginia, a town of about 40,000 people. Residents were charged 80 cents for each sticker. This may sound like the sensible use of market forces. In fact, the authors conclude, the scheme's benefits did not cover the cost of printing stickers, the sticker-sellers' commissions and the wages of the people running the scheme.

True, the number of bags or cans collected did fall sharply, by 37% between May and September 1992. But this was largely thanks to the "Seattle stomp", a frantic dance first noticed when that city introduced rubbish pricing. Rather than buy more tags, people simply crammed more garbage – about 40% more – into each container. This is inefficient: compacting is done better by machines at landfill sites than by individuals, however enthusiastically. The weight of rubbish collected in Charlottesville (a better indicator of disposal costs than volume) fell by a modest 14%. In 25 other Virginian cities where no pricing scheme was in place, and which were used as a rough-and-ready control group, it fell by 3.5%.

Less pleasing still, some people resorted to illegal dumping rather than pay to have their rubbish removed. This is hard to measure directly. But the authors, observing that a few households in the sample stopped putting rubbish out, guess that illegal dumping may account for 30–40% of the reduction in collected rubbish. The one bright spot in all this seems to have been a 15% increase in the weight of materials recycled, suggesting that people chose to recycle free rather than pay to have their refuse carted away. But the fee may have little to do with the growth in recycling, as many citizens were already participating in Charlottesville's voluntary recycling scheme.

It would be foolish to generalise from this one case, but the moral is clear: economic incentives sometimes produce unforeseen responses. To discourage dumping, for instance, local councils might have to spend more on catching litterers, or raise fines for littering, or cut the price of legitimate rubbish collection.

Not daft, just difficult

In a study in 1997,[2] comparing 100-odd cities that use garbage pricing with more than 800 that did not, Messrs Fullerton and Kinnaman explored the economics of rubbish in more detail. One conclusion from this broader study is that pricing does reduce the weight of rubbish – but not by much. On average, a 10% increase in sticker prices cuts quantity only by 0.3% or so.

This figure is lower than in other studies covering fewer towns, but is it so surprising? To cut their output of rubbish by a lot, people would have to buy less of just about everything. A tax of a few cents on the week's garbage seems unlikely to make much difference. And other factors, such as income and education, seem to matter every bit as much as price. In richer towns people threw out more rubbish than in poorer ones: the rich not only have more garbage to remove, but their time is too valuable to them to be spent recycling or dumping.

Messrs Fullerton and Kinnaman add a further twist. One expected effect of garbage pricing might be that, as in Charlottesville, people recycle more of their rubbish rather than pay for its removal with the weekly collection. Indeed, every town in the study with a pricing scheme (as well as hundreds without) had recycling bins in its streets. This looks right, say the authors – until they take into account the fact that towns with garbage-pricing policies are more likely to have "greener" citizens who recycle more in any case. Strip out this effect, and it seems that pricing rubbish collection has no significant effect on recycling at all.

Does all this mean that the idea of charging households for the rubbish they generate is daft? Not at all: free disposal, after all, is surely too cheap. But the effects of seemingly simple policies are often complex. Intricate economic models are often needed to sort them out. And sometimes, the results of this rummaging do not smell sweet.

Notes

1 Don Fullerton and Thomas Kinnaman, "Household Responses to Pricing Garbage by the Bag", *American Economic Review*, September 1996.
2 Don Fullerton and Thomas Kinnaman, "Garbage and Recycling in Communities with Curbside Recycling and Unit-Based Pricing", NBER working paper No. 6021, April 1997.

Freud, finance and folly

Human intuition is a bad guide to handling risk

PEOPLE MAKE BARMY DECISIONS about the future. The evidence is all around, from their investments in the stockmarkets to the way they run their businesses. In fact, people are consistently bad at dealing with uncertainty, underestimating some kinds of risk and overestimating others. Surely there must be a better way than using intuition?

In the 1950s and 1960s, a group of researchers at American universities set out to find a more scientific method. They created a discipline called "decision science" which aimed to take the human element out of risk analysis. It would offer a way of making soundly based decisions for a future fraught with uncertainties. This would involve using computer models for forecasting, estimating the probabilities of possible outcomes and determining the best course of action, thus avoiding the various biases that humans brought to decision-making. Such models, the researchers thought, would provide rational answers to questions such as whether to build a factory, how to combat disease and how to manage investments.

Business schools soon adopted their teachings, and even some policymakers were persuaded. Decision science's heyday may have been the Vietnam war when Robert McNamara, then America's defence secretary, used such techniques to forecast the outcome of the conflict (though, as it turned out, without much success). But mostly the approach did not quite catch on. Decision-makers, whether in business or politics, were loth to hand over their power to a computer. They preferred to go with their gut instincts.

Think like a machine

Daniel Kahneman, now a professor at Princeton, noticed as a young research psychologist in the 1960s that the logic of decision science was hard for people to accept. That launched him on a career to show just how irrationally people behave in practice. When Mr Kahneman and his colleagues first started work, the idea of applying psychological insights to economics and business decisions was considered quirky. But in the past decade the fields of behavioural finance and behavioural economics have blossomed, and in 2002 Mr Kahneman shared a Nobel prize in economics for his work.

Today he is in demand by organisations such as McKinsey and Part-nerRe, and by Wall Street traders. But, he says, there are plenty of others that still show little interest in understanding the roots of their poor decisions. The lesson from the analyst's couch is that, far from being random, these mistakes are systematic and predictable:

- **Over-optimism**. Ask most people about the future, and they will see too much blue sky ahead, even if past experience suggests otherwise. Surveys have shown that people's forecasts of future stockmarket movements are far more optimistic than past long-term returns would justify. The same goes for their hopes of ever-rising prices for their homes or doing well in games of chance. In a study of Dutch game-show contestants, people's estimates of their odds on winning were around 25% too high. Americans are perhaps the most optimistic: according to one poll, around 40% of them think they will end up among the top 1% of earners.

  Such optimism can be useful for managers or football players, and sometimes turns into a self-fulfilling prophecy. But most of the time it results in wasted effort and dashed hopes. Mr Kahneman's work points to three types of over-confidence. First, people tend to exaggerate their own skill and prowess; in polls, far fewer than half the respondents admit to having below-average skills in, say, love-making or driving. Second, they overestimate the amount of control they have over the future, forgetting about luck and chalking up success solely to skill. And third, in competitive pursuits such as betting on shares, they forget that they have to judge their skills against those of the competition.

- **The anchor effect**. First encounters tend to be decisive not only in judging the character of a new acquaintance but also in negotiations over money. Once a figure has been mentioned, it takes a strange hold over the human mind. The asking price quoted in a house sale, for example, tends to become accepted by all parties as the "anchor" around which negotiations take place, according to one study of property brokers. Much the same goes for salary negotiations or mergers and acquisitions. If nobody has much information to go on, a figure can provide comfort – even though it may lead to a terrible mistake.

- **Stubbornness**. No one likes to abandon a cherished belief, and the earlier a decision has been taken, the harder it is to give up. In one classic experiment, two groups of students were shown slides of an object, say a fire hydrant or a pair of spectacles. The slides started out of focus and were gradually made clearer until the students could identify the object. Those who started with a very blurry image tried to decide early and then found it difficult to identify it correctly until quite late in the process, whereas those who started less out of focus kept a more open mind and cottoned on more quickly.

The same sort of thing happens in boardrooms or in politics. Drug companies must decide early to cancel a failing research project to avoid wasting money, but find it difficult to admit they have made a mistake. Bosses who have hired unproductive employees are reluctant to fire them. Mr Kahneman cites the example of Israel's failure to spot growing threats in the lead-up to its 1973 war with its Arab neighbours. Part of the explanation was that the same people who had been watching the change in political climate had to decide on Israel's response. Similar problems have arisen in recent counter-terrorism work in America. In both cases, analysts may have become wedded early to a single explanation that coloured their perception. A fresh eye always helps.

◪ **Getting too close**. People put a lot of emphasis on things they have seen and experienced themselves, which may not be the best guide to decision-making. For example, many companies took action to guard against the risk of terrorist attack only after September 11th, even though it was present long before then. Or somebody may buy an overvalued share because a relative has made thousands on it, only to get his fingers burned.

In finance, too much emphasis on information close at hand helps to explain the so-called "home bias", a tendency by most investors to invest only within the country they live in. Even though they know that diversification is good for their portfolio, a large majority of both Americans and Europeans invest far too heavily in the shares of their home countries. They would be much better off spreading their risks more widely.

◪ **Winning and losing**. Fear of failure is a strong human characteristic, which may be why people are much more concerned about losses than about gains. Consider the following bet: with the flip of a coin, you could win $1,500 if the coin turns up heads, or lose $1,000 on the tails. Now describe it in another way: with heads, you keep all the money you had before the bet, plus $1,500; with tails, you also keep everything, except $1,000. The two bets are identical, and each one, on average, will make you richer by $250 (although that average will be little consolation to the punter who has just lost $1,000). Even so, people will usually prefer the second bet.

Behavioural economists say that is because the prospect of losses seems far more daunting in isolation, rather than in the context of looking at your entire wealth, even if the average outcome is the same. This sort of myopia in the face of losses explains much of the irrationality people display in the stockmarket.

- ▱ **Misplaced priorities.** More information is helpful in making any decision but, says Mr Kahneman, people spend proportionally too much time on small decisions and not enough on big ones. They need to adjust the balance. During the boom years, some companies put as much effort into planning their Christmas party as into considering strategic mergers.

- ▱ **Counterproductive regret.** Crying over spilled milk is not just a waste of time; it also often colours people's perceptions of the future. Some stockmarket investors trade far too frequently because they are chasing the returns on shares they wish they had bought earlier.

Mr Kahneman reckons that some types of businesses are much better than others at dealing with risk. Pharmaceutical companies, which are accustomed to many failures and a few big successes in their drug-discovery programmes, are fairly rational about their risk-taking. But banks, he says, have a long way to go. They may take big risks on a few huge loans, but are extremely cautious about their much more numerous loans to small businesses, many of which may be less risky than the big ones.

Pensions by default

Behavioural finance offers a tempting alternative to voluntary and forced saving for old age

GOVERNMENTS AROUND THE WORLD want workers to save more for their pensions. Alarmed at the impending strains on public budgets as the post-war baby-boom generation nears retirement, they are anxious to limit the load on already stressed tax-financed pay-as-you-go pension systems.

But in turning this policy goal into reality they face an awkward dilemma. Left to their own devices, many workers do not save enough for their retirement, if they save at all. Exhortation falls on deaf ears; even generous tax incentives are ignored. But if the voluntary approach is ineffective, compulsion is an invidious alternative. Although individuals will control the savings they are forced to make, many will resent mandatory contributions and regard them as a tax increase.

Politicians would love to avoid this dilemma. Fortunately for them, economists are now offering them a way to do that: simply make enrolment into funded pension schemes automatic. At present, most workers have to opt in to retirement-saving plans. With automatic enrolment, they have to opt out. This flick of the switch makes pension saving the default option while retaining the voluntary principle.

The simplicity of the policy is deceptive. It is grounded in some quite subtle findings of behavioural finance. This branch of economics, which draws upon psychology and experiments, shows that people are not always rational, especially when it comes to saving. Although they may want to save for old age, they never get around to it because they lack the self-control to put their good intentions into effect in the short term.

The economic interpretation of this tendency to procrastinate is that in trading off present and future consumption people apply a higher discount rate in the short term than in the long term, rather than the same rate assumed in mainstream economics. Given the choice between $1,000 now and $1,100 next year, an individual may well take the money at once. But, asked to choose between $1,000 in 2025 and $1,100 in 2026, the same person might choose to wait a little longer for the larger sum.

Behavioural finance also shows the surprising extent to which people are swayed by the way that choices are framed. If, when they come to invest, most of the funds offered by the retirement plan are equities, then they will put most of their savings into stocks. If, on the other hand, most of the funds offered are bonds, then they will put most of their money into bonds.

What this suggests is that re-framing decisions about retirement saving through better-designed default rules can be surprisingly effective. Automatic enrolment puts the onus on the worker to opt out rather than to opt in. This is a change of form rather than substance. Yet in one American firm, this switch raised the enrolment rate into its 401(k) plan – the main vehicle for employer-sponsored retirement saving – from 49% of newly eligible employees to 86%.

Save more today

Once workers are enrolled, pre-commitment can be used to raise saving rates. For example, Richard Thaler, of the University of Chicago, and Shlomo Benartzi, of the University of California, Los Angeles, have proposed a programme (called "Save More Tomorrow") that makes use of the lower discount rates people apply to future saving decisions than to those in the present. A study of one firm by Mr Thaler and Mr Benartzi has shown that pre-commitment by workers to allocate a portion of their future pay rises to their pensions raised their average contribution rate from 3.5% of pay to 13.6% over a 40-month period.

The success of such private-sector schemes is prompting interest among government reformers too. New Zealand is leading the way. From April 2007, all new employees will be automatically enrolled into "KiwiSaver", a retirement-saving scheme run by the tax authority, at a default contribution rate of 4% of pay. Workers have three weeks to opt out. If they stay in, they can take contribution breaks. They can save at a higher rate of 8% and choose a fund manager, although there will also be a default option for their investments.

Britain may follow New Zealand's lead. An independent commission reviewing the country's troubled pension system has been considering compulsory savings. However, the government is already taking steps to encourage automatic membership of company pension schemes. A more ambitious national programme, along the lines of New Zealand's reform, could be a politically alluring alternative to compulsion.

There are potential snags. American companies that put new employees automatically into 401(k) plans generally choose a low contribution rate and a safe but low-return investment fund. This is because they want to avoid blame if things go wrong. If governments press for retirement saving by default, they will have to wrestle with this conundrum as well.

Furthermore, it is uncertain whether individuals will respond to a national scheme with the same readiness that they do to corporate plans. One interpretation of workers' responsiveness to employer-sponsored automatic enrolment is that they see it as an endorsement by the company – which is, of course, precisely the worry that many firms have about it. But the evidence, in Britain at least, is that employees in occupational schemes are much more likely to trust employers about pensions than they are governments.

These snags are unlikely to put politicians off. After all, in formulating pension policy they are also susceptible to the psychological flaws highlighted by behavioural economics. The temptation is always to procrastinate. Not the least of the attractions of automatic enrolment is that the policy addresses the politics as well as the economics of pension reform.

A voice for the poor

As Friedrich Hayek was to socialism, Peter Bauer is to foreign aid

A s SOCIALISM AND CENTRAL PLANNING gave way to resurgent market forces in the second half of the 20th century, three great economists were brought in from the ideological wilderness. Friedrich Hayek, who in 1944 predicted the demise of command economies in *The Road to Serfdom*, was later to inspire the free-market policies of Ronald Reagan and Margaret Thatcher. He also inspired Milton Friedman, a fierce advocate of free markets and monetarism at a time when Keynesian demand management was the order of the day. Mr Friedman has given his name to a new biennial prize "for the advancement of liberty", which was awarded on May 9th 2002 to the least famous of the three, Peter Bauer.

Born in Budapest in 1915, the young Mr Bauer came to Britain in 1934, taught at Cambridge and the London School of Economics, and was made a peer in 1982. Lord Bauer's work applies classical economics to questions of poverty and development, where conventional wisdom, for 30 years after 1945, was remorselessly hostile to market solutions.

After the second world war, a new "development economics" came to dominate policymaking in poorer countries, often at the urging of international institutions such as the World Bank. It argued that poor countries were victims of a vicious circle of poverty, doomed to remain poor because they lacked the income that provided savings which, when invested, generated economic growth. The answer? Rich countries should provide the capital, in the form of foreign aid. To use the capital efficiently, poor-country governments should plan their economies and create new industries to substitute for foreign imports. And to give these nascent industries a chance, competition should be restricted through monopoly rights and barriers to foreign trade.

Both the theory and its practice appalled Lord Bauer. His studies of smallholdings in the Malaysian rubber industry and of the importance of small-scale traders in West Africa had convinced him that there could be wealth creation, even in subsistence economies, if only market forces were allowed to work. Trade barriers and monopolies merely destroyed entrepreneurialism.

In his blunt way, Lord Bauer set out alternative theories that, from the

1950s to the 1970s, were heresy. All countries had started poor, he argued. If the vicious-circle theory were true, mankind would still be living in the stone age. Opportunities for private profit, not government plans, held the key to development. Governments had the limited though crucial role of protecting property rights, enforcing contracts, treating everybody equally before the law, minimising inflation and keeping taxes low. It was a tragedy that countries neglected this role.

Above all, Lord Bauer argued, there would be no concept of the third world at all were it not for the invention of foreign aid. Aid politicised economies, directing money into the hands of governments rather than towards profitable business. Interest groups then fought to control this money rather than engage in productive activity. Aid increased the patronage and power of the recipient governments, which often pursued policies that stifled entrepreneurship and market forces. Indeed, aid had proved "an excellent method for transferring money from poor people in rich countries to rich people in poor countries."

Why so much aid, then? Western post-colonial guilt, Lord Bauer claimed, before debunking the notion that countries are poor because they were exploited by former colonialists. They are generally better off now than they were before colonialism. The most developed of the poorer countries are those that have the most interaction with rich countries, through trade and the exchange of ideas.

Today, many of Lord Bauer's views on aid and development are part of a new conventional wisdom. Even the World Bank admits that creating the right conditions for markets to flourish is the key to economic development, and that until recently much of the money that it has supplied has been badly used. Lord Bauer is not convinced that he has won, though, for government-to-government aid has increased, not decreased. Even though there is now more public questioning of aid, he is not optimistic about further change. There are so many vested interests behind foreign aid, "regardless of its effects".

Some of his other views remain out of the mainstream, at least for now. Lord Bauer opposes policies aimed at reducing income inequality. This is not because he favours inequality – although he thinks it often reflects fair pay for output produced – but because policies designed to promote equality usually infringe personal liberties to such an extent as to slow economic development. If, as often happens, development happens to reduce inequality, then so much the better.

Nor does Lord Bauer favour population control. Worries about population growth, he says, reflect a patronising view that the poor are incapable of making sensible choices about having children. The much deplored population explosion "should be seen as a blessing rather than a disaster, because it stems from a fall in mortality, a *prima facie* improvement in people's welfare". At the same time, he argues, there is no correlation between population growth (or even density) and poverty. The population of the western world has more than quadrupled since the mid-18th century, yet real income per head has increased at least fivefold.

In short, economic development rests on people having the right desires and aptitudes, and on a political and legal system that allows people to act on them. In this, the poor are no different from anybody else. Formerly heretical insights such as these put Lord Bauer in a class of his own as an economist, says Amartya Sen, a darling of the aid and development world and both a former student and a sparring partner of Lord Bauer's. His blunt lack of political correctness may have prevented Lord Bauer from sharing the Nobel prize awarded to Mr Sen in 1998. The Milton Friedman prize should provide some consolation – not to mention $500,000.

How to make aid work

Aid to poor countries has largely failed to spur growth or relieve poverty. It can work – but only if aid is limited to countries that are pursuing sound economic policies. More donors should try it

OVER THE PAST 50 YEARS rich nations have given $1 trillion in aid to poor ones. This stupendous sum has failed spectacularly to improve the lot of its intended beneficiaries. Aid should have boosted recipient countries' growth rates and thereby helped millions to escape from poverty. Yet countless studies have failed to find a link between aid and faster economic growth. Poor countries that receive lots of aid do no better, on average, than those that receive very little.

Why should this be? In part, because economic growth has not always been donors' first priority. A sizeable chunk of Saudi Arabian aid, for example, aims to tackle spiritual rather than material needs by sending free Korans to infidels. During the cold war, the Soviet Union propped up odious communist despots while America bankrolled an equally unsavoury bunch of anti-communists. Keeping thugs like North Korea's Kim Il Sung and Liberia's Samuel Doe in power hardly improved the lives of their hapless subjects. Even today, strategic considerations often outweigh charitable or developmental ones. Israel gets the lion's share of American aid largely for historical reasons, and millions of American voters support it. Egypt gets the next biggest slice for recognising Israel. Russia and Ukraine receive billions to ensure that they do not sell their surplus nuclear warheads.

Even where development has been the goal of aid, foul-ups have been frequent. Big donors like to finance big, conspicuous projects such as dams, and sometimes fail to notice the multitudes whose homes are flooded. Gifts from small donors are often strangely inappropriate: starving Somalis have received heartburn pills; Mozambican peasants have been sent high-heeled shoes. Poor research can render aid worthless: a fish farm was built for Mali in canals that were dry for half the year. The Turkana nomads of north-western Kenya, long pestered with ill-planned charitable projects, refer to foreign aid workers and their own government alike as *ngimoi*: "the enemy".

Aid faces further hurdles in recipient countries. War scuppers the best-laid plans. A shipment of vaccines was destroyed in Congo when rebels cut the power supply to the capital, shutting down the refrigerators where the medicines were stored. In Afghanistan, Taliban zealots closed aid-financed hospitals for employing female doctors. Less spectacularly but more pervasively, corruption, incompetence and foolish economic policies can often be relied on to squander any amount of donor cash. One example, Zambia, speaks for many.

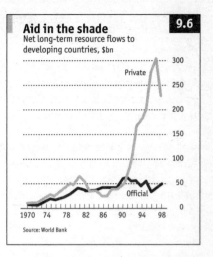

Aid in the shade   9.6
Net long-term resource flows to developing countries, $bn

At independence in 1964, Zambia seemed poised for success. The second-richest country in Africa, it had a popularly elected government committed to helping the poor, big copper mines and a generous stream of aid. Most donors believed that the main obstacle to third-world development was lack of capital, and that giving poor governments cash to invest would spur rapid growth. It was not so simple.

Zambia's first president, Kenneth Kaunda, set up a one-party socialist state and nationalised everything from dry-cleaners to car-part retailers. His officials told farmers what to grow, bought their crops and sold them at heavily subsidised prices. Mr Kaunda assumed that the copper mines would provide an inexhaustible source of revenue, however badly managed. Zambians came to see government loans as a perk of freedom from colonial rule.

In the mid-1970s, the price of copper tumbled, and it became harder to pay for all this. Foreign donors picked up the slack. As Mr Kaunda's economic policies grew worse, aid climbed steadily, reaching 11% of real GDP by the early 1990s. IMF loans were tied to free-market reforms, but these were enacted reluctantly and frequently reversed.

Donors agitated for free elections and in 1991 Frederick Chiluba, a former union leader and avowed economic reformer, became president. Aid began to flow again, but Mr Chiluba's zeal to privatise was soon dampened by the discovery that state-owned firms provided ministers with lucrative opportunities for patronage. Corruption became as great a brake on growth as socialism was under Mr Kaunda. William Easterly, a former World Bank economist, says that, if aid had

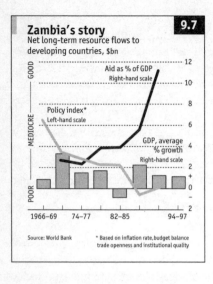

Zambia's story `9.7`
Net long-term resource flows to
developing countries, $bn

Source: World Bank   * Based on inflation rate, budget balance
trade openness and institutional quality

had the predicted accelerating effect on growth between 1961 and 1994, Zambia's income per head would now be more than $20,000. In fact, it has dawdled at less than $500.

Growth and poverty

GDP is not a foolproof measure of well-being. Wealth may be unevenly spread, so that a high average disguises widespread wretchedness. Nor does GDP take account of the hidden costs of pollution, for example. But when GDP grows, social indicators tend to improve with it.

In Thailand, where income per head tripled between 1966 and 1990, the proportion of the population living in poverty fell from more than half to just 2%. Infant mortality fell by two-thirds. Slower-growing countries did less well: in India, income per head doubled, infant mortality fell by half and half the population stayed stuck in poverty. In no-growth countries such as Ethiopia, all the advances in modern medicine and the efforts of foreign donors could not effect more than a 27% drop in infant mortality over the same period.

Until recently, the fastest-growing emerging economies were clustered in East Asia whereas the disaster zones were disproportionately African. This led many to conclude that culture was the best predictor of economic success. Actually, sound policies and institutions, backed by liberal helpings of aid, are usually a better guide.

Take Botswana. Zambia's neighbour was, at independence in 1966, one of the world's poorest countries. One British official called it "a useless piece of territory". To begin with, aid financed virtually all government investment and much of its recurrent expenditure too. Then prospectors found diamonds under the Botswanan desert. Unlike many African governments, Botswana's did not squander the windfall. Diamond dollars were ploughed into infrastructure, education and health. Private business was allowed to grow; foreign investment was welcomed. Aid projects were approved only if they were sustainable and did not duplicate the work of others.

From 1966 to 1991, Botswana's economy grew faster than almost any other in the world. It helped that its government was unusually honest and competent. Cabinet ministers did not award themselves huge pensions, mansions and public contracts. In Zambia, government bigwigs drive Mercedes limousines. Those in Botswana choose locally assembled Hyundai sedans. Even the president, Festus Mogae, has been seen doing his own shopping.

Botswana abolished exchange controls in 1999. Its budget is usually in surplus and GDP per head tops $4,000. The country remains vulnerable to swings in the price of diamonds, but it has made a better job of diversifying than most developing-country mineral producers. Their task completed, donors are packing their bags.

Cash advances or advice?

The reason that aid has worked in Botswana but not in Zambia is simple. Botswana had good economic policies, soundly administered. Zambia did not. In countries with poor management, aid is sometimes stolen. Its effectiveness is often limited anyway because it tends to displace, rather than complement, private investment. In countries with good management, aid "crowds in" private investment: if an economy is growing fast, the returns on road-building or setting up a new airline are likely to be high. A poorly managed, stagnant economy offers private investors fewer opportunities.

It seems clear that aid should be directed towards countries with good management and lots of poor citizens. Yet many donors continue to behave as if it were not. Bilateral aid has tended to favour allies and ex-colonies. A 1998 study by Alberto Alesina and David Dollar found that a former colony with a closed economy received about twice as much assistance as a non-colony with an open one. Undemocratic ex-colonies also received twice as much as democratic non-colonies. On some figures, countries with poor management got just as much bilateral aid as those with good management. (Nordic aid was an exception to this dismal trend.)

Can aid persuade countries with bad policies and institutions to adopt good ones? It is not easy. For years the IMF and World Bank have made their loans conditional on policy reform, but the record is mixed, to put it kindly. Governments often agree to cut subsidies or tackle corruption, but later backtrack. Zimbabwe's president, Robert Mugabe, frequently promised one thing to donors and the opposite to domestic interest-groups. Kenya's Daniel arap Moi was skilled at selling the same reforms several times. Even when recipients blatantly flout aid conditions, donors often hand over the money anyway, for fear of sparking an economic collapse or even bloodshed.

Good policies cannot be imposed on unwilling pupils. Attaching conditions to aid can strengthen the arm of governments that are trying to push through wise but unpopular measures. Broadly, however, reforms rarely succeed unless a government considers the reform programme essential, and its own. A study by David Dollar and Jakob Svensson found that elected governments were much more likely to implement reforms than unelected ones, and new regimes more likely than old ones.

For countries with foolish leaders, a better approach than offering money is offering ideas. The architects of successful reforms in Indonesia in the 1970s, and in several Latin American countries in the 1980s and 1990s, were largely educated abroad, often at aid-givers' expense. The crash course in market economics given to top African National Congress members before they won South Africa's first all-race elections in 1994 helped turn them from Marxists into fiscal conservatives. Ethiopia's new leaders took degrees in business administration in the mid-1990s.

Rethinking aid

A condition of the G8's debt-relief plan is that the cash it frees be spent on worthy things like education and health. The World Bank is well aware of the difficulties in ensuring that this actually happens but many donors are not. Aid-givers often finance specific projects, such as irrigation and the building of schools. Since the schools are usually built and the ditches dug, donors are satisfied that their money has served its intended purpose. But has it? Probably not.

Most evidence suggests that aid money is fungible – that is, that it goes into the pot of public funds and is spent on whatever the recipient wants to spend it on. If donors earmark money for education, it may cause the recipient government to spend more on education, or it may make available for something else the money that it would otherwise have spent on education.

If the government is benign, the alternative may be agriculture or tax cuts. If the government is crooked, donors' funds may be spent on shopping trips to London for the president's wife or fighter planes to strafe unpopular minorities. The important factor is not the donor's instructions but the recipient's priorities. A 14-country study published by the

World Bank in 1998 showed that each extra aid dollar aimed at agriculture, for example, actually decreased total agricultural spending by five cents.

This does not mean that donors should never support specific projects. Sometimes the real value of a donor-financed dam or telephone network lies in the technology that is transferred, and the advice given on how to operate and maintain the infrastructure. But the fact of fungibility suggests that aid-giving could be greatly simplified if most took the form of unconditional "balance-of-payments support". That is, cash.

Rich countries should be much more ruthless about how they allocate their largesse, whether earmarked or not. Emergency relief is one thing. But mainstream aid should be directed only to countries with sound economic management. The debt-relief plans, to their credit, do this. More donors should follow suit. Aid should also favour countries with large numbers of very poor citizens. India, Vietnam, Mozambique and Uganda, among others, meet both conditions. Many countries that receive substantial aid, such as Kenya and Russia, do not.

According to the World Bank, an extra $10 billion in aid could lift 25m people a year out of poverty – so long as it went to poor countries that manage their economies well. The same sum spread across the current cast of aid recipients would lift only 7m out of destitution. In other words, aid could work if it were properly directed. And if taxpayers in rich countries saw their money actually doing some good, they might be happy to give more of it.

Journey beyond the stars

The brightest young economists are outgrowing their discipline's traditional boundaries

IN 1988 *The Economist* published an article about the eight best young economists in the world, academics in their mid-30s or younger who had already achieved star status within their profession. Gratifyingly, the following decade saw these men – and they were all men – achieve a great deal beyond the groves of academe. Three are household names, at least in households that take a financial newspaper.

This talent for picking winners encouraged us to try to repeat the exercise. Who, we wondered, were the young stars of 1998? Who were the economists 35 and under tipped by the cognoscenti for future Nobel prizes? As before, our methods were informal: we canvassed opinion among older economics professors, including our earlier stars. Unfortunately, this time the search was far less successful. There is little consensus among older economists on who the young stars of the profession are, or whether there are any at all.

This void raises interesting questions. Are today's economists less talented than their immediate predecessors? Was there something special about the 1980s that encouraged stardom in the profession? Has economic research reached a turning point? Or a dead end? The answers (no, yes, yes, no) come from understanding that the abundance of stars in 1988 and the seeming scarcity in 1998 share a common cause.

Where do stars come from? Astronomers will tell you that they are born in the collapse of primordial clouds of gas and dust. And what causes these collapses? Some sort of external shock. So stars can be born in profusion when a shockwave passes through rich, fertile clouds – but not when it passes through emptier space. A similar idea explains the profusion of economic stars in the 1980s and their relative scarcity in the 1990s. The effects of new analytical tools developed in the 1970s spread out from the profession's core like a shockwave. In the 1980s the shock passed through the study of economic policy, a rich breeding ground in which it triggered the formation of a cluster of hot, bright stars.

But this did not dissipate the shockwave's energy. It travelled on into areas less predisposed to the formation of stars. Instead it now creates elegant nebulae, fascinating to professionals but hard for the layman to pick out unaided. Unlike the stars of the 1980s, the impressive young academics of the 1990s were using the tools of economics in fields on or beyond the traditional borders of their discipline. In a world of global economic crises, where the traditional issues of economic policy are central to finance, business and politics, where professional economists are increasingly important in banks and bureaucracies, where ever more newspaper pages and cable channels are devoted to articles about economics and finance, today's creative young economists tend to eschew the big traditional themes of economics.

Où sont les Krugmans d'antan?

With the development of "rational expectations" theory in the 1970s – a reaction against Keynesian thought which formalised the idea that people learn from their mistakes – economics became dominated by "New Classicists". They inhabited a highly formalised mathematical world of perfect competition, perfect information and perfect rationality, a world their techniques explained to them with great clarity. Since this world did not exist outside the economists' models, though, the discipline seemed in danger of becoming irrelevant.

This danger was seen off in the mid-1980s, largely thanks to an extraordinarily talented group of young economists, most of whom were at Harvard University or the Massachusetts Institute of Technology. This group, from which many of our young stars were chosen, applied the sophisticated analytical tools of the rational expectations revolution to the real world, a world where people had imperfect information and where markets sometimes failed. They were the first generation both to be steeped in rational expectations and to care deeply about economic policy, and the combination was fruitful.

Ten years later, it was striking how many of the eight we chose then have made an impact well beyond the ivory tower, and how few were still involved in active economic research. Larry Summers and Jeffrey Sachs epitomise the trend. Mr Summers spent the 1990s on the inside of international economic policy, first as chief economist at the World Bank, thereafter at the American Treasury. Mr Sachs came to fame – some might say infamy – as the architect of Poland's "shock therapy" economic reforms in 1990. Since then he has been a more or less formal adviser to numerous developing and transition economies. His relentless advocacy, stinging public critiques (most notably of the IMF) and passionate zeal are frowned on by some of his more sober academic colleagues, but there is no doubt that he has affected policy decisions from Bulgaria to Bolivia, and further down the alphabet too.

Mr Sachs was not the only one of our stars called from the ivory tower by communism's collapse. Andrei Shleifer, also at Harvard, who made his name with research into financial-market behaviour, exercised significant influence on economic policy in his native Russia, playing a central (and controversial) role in the country's privatisation programme. He has continued to produce interesting research, with particular insights into corruption and corporate governance, though it has been something of a sideline.

Paul Krugman wields power with his pen rather than his policies. With several bestselling books, and regular columns in newspapers and magazines, he influences the chattering classes as no other economist, for example with his advocacy of capital controls in Asia.

Gregory Mankiw, another Harvard man, has also concentrated on writing rather than researching and has become considerably richer as a result. He secured his academic standing with investigations into the relationship between long-term and short-term interest rates, but has turned his hand to producing textbooks. His first, *Macroeconomics*,[1] is a bestselling text for intermediate undergraduates. It led to a $1.4m advance for an introductory textbook, *Principles of Economics*,[2] and sales figures suggest the advance was well spent. Sanford Grossman, at the Wharton Business School, also left research for more lucrative pursuits. With a reputation based on models of information's role in financial markets, Mr Grossman formed his own trading company; of our original eight he is now far and away the most wealthy.

The two remaining stars of 1988 spent most of the subsequent decade continuing their research. While Alberto Alesina is an occasional policy adviser and newspaper columnist in his native Italy, he has put most of his effort into following up his groundbreaking analysis of the economic effects of the electoral cycle with further academic work on the links between economics and politics. He has examined the political channels through which inequality may hurt economic growth; through painstaking empirical research he has shown that fiscal cutbacks need not be recessionary and can be politically popular. The last of our eight, Jean Tirole, already a leading microeconomist in 1988, still produces staggering amounts of top-notch research. But more than any of the other stars, Mr Tirole has stayed faithful to the ivory tower, and to traditional microeconomics. Perhaps as a result he is one of the least well known of the bunch.

It is no great surprise that the research stars of 1988 are no longer at the cutting edge. Many a Nobel laureate built his reputation on one or two great papers, and then spent several decades producing nothing new. But it is intriguing that they are still seen as the profession's young hot-shots. Several older professors, when asked to name the top young economists, suggested members of our cast of 1988 – below this cohort, they felt, there was simply no similarly talented group of researchers.

Economic imperialism

Several professors suggested that the economics profession may no longer attract such talents. In the years 1988–98 investment banks and consultancies offered the brightest undergraduates starting salaries that far exceed the pay of a tenured professor. Goldman Sachs can be more appealing than graduate school, and Wall Street increasingly provides young economists with professional satisfaction as well as money, particularly if they are interested in macroeconomic and market issues. So there is a new demand for talent. Against that, however, must be set a new source of supply: the globalisation of higher education now allows America's top universities (which are still home to most cutting-edge research) to draw from a vast pool of applicants.

An alternative explanation for a perceived lack of stars is that the level of talent available fluctuates; sometimes there is a lot, sometimes there isn't. This may have some truth; but a more compelling explanation is that the young stars in the 1980s had a well defined and compelling research agenda – the application of rational expectations to the policy world – which is now more or less complete. So today's best young academics need to look further afield for their questions, providing insight, elegance and, in some cases, real-world relevance beyond their discipline's traditional borders. It is fine research – but in areas where older economists find it hard to see star potential.

The application of economic tools to questions in other disciplines is not new. The University of Chicago's economists are particularly fond of looking into law and the social sciences. It was there that, in the 1950s, Gary Becker first used economic tools to understand the behaviour of the family. He has since pioneered the use of economics in sociology, and picked up a Nobel prize along the way. Today's young economists are following his lead into subjects traditionally studied by sociologists, political scientists, educationalists, epidemiologists and even criminologists. This trend is epitomised by the work of five young researchers who study subjects as diverse as AIDS transmission, drug-gang finances and the demand for religion.

Michael Kremer, of MIT [now at Harvard], won early recognition for two papers written as a graduate student. One of these, "The O-ring Theory of Economic Development",[3] suggested a new way for economists to look at the production process. Traditional "production functions" allow firms to substitute quality for quantity. Mr Kremer recognised that in many complex modern processes that was not the case. Mistakes in any one of a number of tasks can dramatically reduce the value of the final product: the temperature sensitivity of the O-rings in its solid-rocket boosters destroyed the space shuttle *Challenger*. This framework helps explain a number of modern economic phenomena, from rising income inequality to the fact that there are more small firms in poor countries.

That paper in itself offered avenues for further exploration numerous enough to base a career on. But Mr Kremer is nothing if not diverse in his interests. His provocative and creative papers, often focused on issues that affect developing countries, include models of elephant survival, AIDS transmission and tax reform.

Another producer of fine work on the fringes is Edward Glaeser of Harvard, who has developed and tested theoretical models that explain why cities exist and what determines their size. In the manufacturing era, high transport costs were an important reason for concentrating things in cities; in the modern economy, gains from information overspills matter more. He has meticulously analysed urban phenomena from the cost of urban segregation to blacks to the social costs of rent control. He is now working on models to explain why some people go to church.

Casey Mulligan, in Chicago, made an early name for himself with similar forays into what might normally be seen as sociological questions. His doctoral dissertation, supervised by Mr Becker, modelled altruism between generations. He found that social factors, such as parents' work ethic, contribute far more to inequality than financial constraints do. His more recent work has moved back towards mainstream subjects, but with novel twists: together with Mr Becker, for instance, he has developed models that try to show why an inefficient tax system may be better than an efficient one. (In essence, because more tax revenue means more socially inefficient spending.)

The empirical strikes back
The two other researchers whose non-mainstream work stands out –

Steve Levitt of Chicago and Caroline Hoxby of Harvard) – epitomise another shift in the profession: towards the increasingly creative use of empirical analysis. A decade ago, organising statistics and running regressions was enormously time-consuming and empirical economists could make a name simply by collating and analysing large data-sets. Today, sophisticated software packages allow graduate students to run regressions in a few minutes on their personal computers. Data of all descriptions are easily accessible online. As a result, economists need ever more imagination to do empirical work that shines. Today's top papers use ingenious models to analyse new subjects and find creative techniques to test their validity.

One of the biggest problems of empirical economics is the difficulty of distinguishing causality from correlation. In recent years economists have used increasingly sophisticated techniques to avoid this. The trick is to find an "instrumental variable" which can act as a proxy for one variable in a statistical analysis, but which is clearly unrelated to the others. Mr Levitt and Ms Hoxby are both experts at this, and have carried their expertise with them beyond the traditional borders of economics.

One of Mr Levitt's papers looks at the relationship between imprisoning people and cutting crime. Looking at the raw data (in the upper part of Chart 9.8 overleaf) it is pretty hard to see much of an effect due to increased levels of incarceration. And one can imagine *a priori* reasons why increased incarceration could add to, rather than reduce, violent crime (look at the prisons as training schemes). Mr Levitt cut through this by finding a variable which clearly has an impact on incarceration but which is hard to link directly to crime rates: litigation over prison overcrowding. The lower part of Chart 9.8 shows that in places where litigation is filed (and prison populations fall) crime clearly rises. Another paper clarified the link between the number of police officers and crime rates by looking at how crime varied over the electoral cycle; it turns out to fall in election years, when police numbers swell.

Ms Hoxby has used similar empirical techniques in the field of education. Although it is hotly contested in the education establishment, many people believe that America's poor school quality has something to do with the power of teachers' unions. Difficulties in pinpointing causality, however, have made this thesis tricky to prove; it is not unreasonable to suggest that poor school quality could prompt unionisation. By tracking changes in legislation which affected union power directly, Ms Hoxby showed that reductions in the power of teachers' unions both lowers spending per pupil and results in better

299

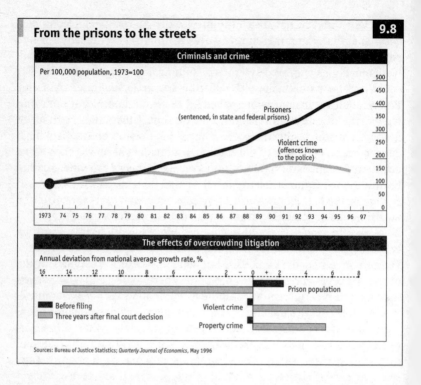

From the prisons to the streets 9.8

Criminals and crime

Per 100,000 population, 1973=100

Prisoners
(sentenced, in state and federal prisons)

Violent crime
(offences known
to the police)

1973 74 75 76 77 78 79 80 81 82 83 84 85 86 87 88 89 90 91 92 93 94 95 96 97

The effects of overcrowding litigation

Annual deviation from national average growth rate, %

16 14 12 10 8 6 4 2 – 0 + 2 4 6 8

Prison population

Before filing
Three years after final court decision

Violent crime

Property crime

Sources: Bureau of Justice Statistics; *Quarterly Journal of Economics*, May 1996

student performance. Looking at the relation between quality and parental choice, which is higher where there are more school districts, and aware that poor quality might be a force that actually created new districts, she used the number of rivers in different places as a proxy (when school districts were first laid out, they tended to follow natural boundaries). This study showed a link between choice and performance.

Theory becomes applied

These five economists illustrate both today's economic imperialism and the trend towards a mingling of theory and empirical work. Other top young researchers have remained more clearly in a single camp. Glenn Ellison of MIT is widely regarded as one of the brightest theorists of his generation. He has made his name with highly sophisticated theoretical work in game theory and in models of the learning process. But, in keeping with today's trend towards mingling theory and numbers, he has also written impressive empirical papers. His work with Judith Chevalier [now at Yale School of Management] suggests that young mutual-fund managers are fired more quickly for bad performance than older ones: hence they are more susceptible to herd-like behaviour.

Other theorists build models to understand politics. Wolfgang Pesendorfer, for instance, an applied theoretical economist at Princeton University, together with Timothy Feddersen of the Kellogg School of Management, has come up with an intriguing theory about why people choose not to vote on particular items on a ballot-sheet. The traditional economist's explanation for not voting is that it is costly to vote, but that hardly applies if you are already in the ballot box. Instead, Mr Pesendorfer suggests that there is a "swing voter's curse" analogous to the "winner's curse" familiar from the economics of auctions.

Almost by definition, everyone participating in an auction wants to win, and everyone except the winner believes the prize to be worth less than it eventually goes for. So a naive bidder, if he wins, is most likely paying too much: this is his curse, and it is best avoided by underbidding. On some issues voters face a similar curse, and analogous reasoning suggests that, if they consider themselves ill-informed, they can avoid it best by abstaining.

While most of the top young economists are taking their tool-boxes to the territory of other social sciences, there is a subtle countercurrent under the surface. The small school of behavioural economists is gaining in influence; its attempts to loosen the assumptions about self-interested, rational individuals that underpin mainstream economic models are being taken more seriously. Taking their cue from psychology, these economists take seriously what every layman knows: that people don't always behave in selfish or even rational ways.

For many years behavioural economics languished at the fringes of the profession. In recent years, under the influence of pioneers such as Dick Thaler of Chicago, that has changed. Behavioural economists have begun to incorporate quasi-rational phenomena (such as difficulties people have behaving as they say that they want to, or the weight they give to idealised views of the world that they know do not apply) into formal mathematical models, and they have started to test them empirically using real-world data.

Two young economists epitomise this trend. Matthew Rabin, at the University of California, Berkeley, is widely recognised as a leading behavioural theorist. He specialises in incorporating the behavioural phenomena observed by psychologists into formal models. His work on fairness, in particular, has caused a considerable stir within the profession. David Laibson from Harvard is another name to watch. He has concentrated on the psychology of saving and developed the idea of "hyperbolic discounting", where individuals have a lower discount rate for events far into the future than for closer times. If people applied constant discount rates when they made their decisions about retirement, for example, they would end up saving about the right amount. By and large, though, they don't, which Mr Laibson takes to mean that they use a different rate for events far off than for those near to. His empirical work has shown that this framework helps explain actual saving patterns better than traditional models; it also suggests that government policies that "lock in" retirement saving (through special retirement accounts) may help overcome the self-control problem.

These researchers will probably have far less immediate impact in the real world than their predecessors in 1988. It will take time for criminologists, sociologists and educationalists fully to appreciate the insights of economics, and it may also be a while before the economists understand all the subtleties of the regions they are moving into. Furthermore, the areas these new economists are entering have their policy implications, by and large, at a local rather than national level. That does not bode well for international fame.

But this generation of young economists will make its mark on the discipline. As young faculty in top American universities (many already have tenure), their work will influence coming generations of graduate students. The erosion of traditional barriers within economics and the increased meshing with other disciplines will continue. In years to come it will not only be hard to distinguish empirical economists from theorists; it may also be hard to disentangle economics from other strands of social science. And contact with the rest of the social sciences could in time filter all the way back to the heart of economics, providing new understandings of humans and their behaviour that, when formalised, could provide a new set of economic tools that surpasses those of rational expectations. Today's young researchers may not be changing much economic policy, but they are helping to revitalise economics.

Notes

1   Published by Worth Publishers, 4th edition, 1999.
2   Published by Dryden Press, 4th edition, 1998.
3   *Quarterly Journal of Economics*, 1993.

Endnote

Since this piece was written in 1998, the established stars continued to prosper. Paul Krugman secured a column on the opinion pages of the *New York Times*; Gregory Mankiw served as chairman of the White House's Council of Economic Advisers before returning to Harvard University, where Larry Summers was president until his resignation in 2006. Jean Tirole has served on the French prime minister's Council of Economic Analysis, and his work has also influenced antitrust thinking and policy.

As this piece predicted, the boundaries of economics have become more nebulous. Of the young stars identified in the piece, Steve Levitt has perhaps shone most brightly, thanks to his popular book, *Freakonomics* (HarperCollins, 2005). But his peers have also assumed prominent places in the economics firmament.

The material on pages 243–303 was first published in *The Economist* between February 1999 and April 2005.

Index

Page numbers for charts are indicated in italics.

A

accounting standards 141, 222
acquisitions
    and booms 59
    and investment banks 147
Aeon 128
Afghanistan 289
Africa
    and ISI 18
    weak growth and persisting
        poverty 21
    see also individual countries
African National Congress 292
ageing society 63, 112, 127
aggregate demand 33
Ahearne, Alan 129
aid
    bilateral 291
    food 248
    foreign 236, 285-7
    foul-ups 288
    fungible aid money 292
    how to make it work 288-93
Alchian, Armen 190
Alesina, Alberto 291, 296
Allfinanz see bancassurance
AMD 118-19
American Airlines 250
Amsterdam
    exchange 137
    market in tulip options 160
anchor effect 279
annuities 150
    variable 154
anti-competitive behaviour 33
anti-monopoly laws 253
antitrust authorities 33, 235
antitrust thinkers 249-56, 303

Aozora Bank 130
Argentina
    capital-importing (19th century)
        204
    current-account deficit 77
    debauched currency 173
    debt 38
    financial crisis (2001-02) 77, 197,
        220
    and the Washington consensus
        38
Aristotle 160
asbestos 154
Ashanti Goldfields 162
asset-price bubbles 177, 190, 191, 192,
    195
assets
    financial 135, 138, 140, 141
    real 135
    risky 145
AT&T (American Telephone &
    Telegraph) 158, 252, 255
auction theory 264, 301
Australia
    capital-importing (19th century)
        204
    consumer spending 62
    current-account deficit 69
    debt stock 78
    a net debtor 74
    property prices 64
    variable-rate mortgages 65
Austria: corporate tax 115

B

Bagehot, Walter 178
balance of payments 69
    crises 72, 77
    US 67, 82
bancassurance 146-7
Bangladesh 87

Bank Credit Analyst 64
bank deposits 140
Bank of England 175, 178, 180
Bank of Japan 121, 122, 145, 175–6, 192
Bank of Mexico 175
Bank of Sweden 178
bankers 137
banking sector size 141
bankruptcy 141, 144, 159, 165, 223
banks 143–72
   agricultural cooperative 146
   in ancient Egypt 137
   assets 143–4, 146, 146, 147
   at the heart of the clearing
     system 143
   and bad loans 103, 217
   bancassurance 146–7
   borrowing from abroad 75
   branches 148
   collapse of 145, 215, 216
   commercial 147, 148, 150
   competition 39, 146
   connected lending 216, 222
   and corruption 223
   deposits and loans 138, 143
   emergence of modern banking
     143
   failures 39
   "forbearance" 217
   fragility of deposit-taking banks
     39, 202
   in Germany 115
   investment 147, 148
   liabilities 143, 144
   loans 20, 150, 205, 210, 212
   a mixed bank 146–8
   nationalisation 146
   privately owned 146, 178, 225
   regional 131
   regulation of 144–6, 222, 225, 227,
     228
   retail 146
   risk of bank runs 39, 145
   in South Africa 247
   state-owned 146, 225
   top five banks' share of total
     bank assets 147
   universal 147, 149

   well-developed banking systems
     141
   and zombies 126, 128, 129
Barings 164–5
Barnes, Martin 64
Barro, Robert 187
Basel Accord 145
basic balance 101
Bauer, Peter, Lord 236, 285–7
Baumol, William 116
Bayer 115
"beauty parades" 152
Becker, Gary 297
beef ban 45–6
behavioural economics 284, 301–2
behavioural finance 282–3
Belgium: green taxes 273
Belgrade 175
Benartzi, Shlomo 283
Bergsten, Fred 85
Berlin Wall 156
Bernanke, Ben viii, 195
beta 170
Bhagwati, Jagdish 17, 18
Black, Fischer 164
Black Death 92–3
black market 247
Blake, Jonathan 254
Blanchard, Olivier 108, 109
Blinder, Alan 194, 195
BMW 119
boardroom changes 172
Bodie, Zvi 139
Bolivia 296
bond funds 151
bond markets 77, 81, 139, 156, 157
bond yields 89, 92, 158
bonded labour 21
bonds 135, 147, 149
   covenants 159
   definition 157
   government 150, 156, 157, 158, 182,
     198
   "junk" 158
   municipal 158
   of related agencies 158
   US Treasury 80, 99, 100, 157–8,
     173

booms 59, 60, 64, 65
booms and busts 39, 91, 177, 189
Bootle, Roger 92
Bork, Robert 253
borrowing
    corporate 38–9
    government 38, 40, 41, 228
Botswana 290–91
Brash, Don 185
Braun, Ludwig Georg 113
Brazil
    and America's outward FDI 11
    debt 38
    exports 17
    financial crises (1999 and 2002)
        197
    and the Russian financial crisis
        220
Bretton Woods monetary system 72,
    163, 178
    revived 98, 99–100
Britain
    banks' returns 146
    capital exported from (19th
        century) 204
    and China's economic growth 97
    consumer spending 62
    and fall in private-sector net
        saving 60
    GDP 17
    pensions 152
    property prices 64
    variable-rate mortgages 65
    yield curves 183, 183
British Airways 250
Brookings Institution 186
Buchanan, James 243
budgets
    and current-account deficit 74–5
    deficits 38, 40, 100, 110, 111
Buffett, Warren (the "Sage of
    Omaha") 67, 68
Building Industry Federation
    (Germany) 115
building societies 138
Bulgaria 296
Bundesbank 175, 180
Burda, Michael 116

Bush, George W. 55, 62, 76, 266
business cycles 56–9
businesses
    and competition 6, 9
    moving production to a lower-
        wage area 8–9
    profits as sole interest 6
    reputation for quality and fair
        dealing 6
    see also companies;
        multinationals

C

Caballero, Ricardo 59
Canada
    and America's outward FDI 11
    capital-importing (19th century)
        204
    current-account deficit 71, 77
    a net debtor 74
Canon 127
capital
    attracting the right sort of foreign
        capital 222–7
    definition 156
    flows from rich to poor countries
        204–9
    foreign 38–9, 82, 197
    inflows 16, 99, 101
    migration of 27, 28
    mobility 30, 31
    return on 34, 35, 93, 107
    scarcity of 15, 34, 35
    stock of 34, 35
    volatile portfolio 75
capital account 69, 72
Capital Asset Pricing Model (CAPM)
    170
capital controls 72, 101, 137, 198, 228,
    296
capital gains 63, 65, 111
Capital One 143
capital-account liberalisation 228
capital-account surplus 69
capitalism ix, 7, 8, 25, 32, 135
    and downturns 56
    European 103
    global 27

laissez-faire 49
mixed-economy 49
and stockmarkets 156
caps 162, 163
car insurers 154
carbon dioxide 269, 270, 273, 274
carbon tax 50
Carrefour 128
cars, petrol-driven 269
Carville, James 100
Case, Karl 64
cashflow 169
central bankers viii, 92, 174, 175, 177, 189, 191
central banks 93, 122, 123, 144, 145, 173–95
    Asian 100
    China 88
    and debt deflation 61
    deliberate attempts to burst a bubble 192
    efforts to head off trouble before it happens 195
    foreign 80
    independence 175–6, 179, 180
    and inflation 185, 187, 188
    lax monetary policies 63
    one main weapon of 192
    power of 175, 176
    and recessions 56, 57
    respect for 176
    role of 33, 176, 177, 178
    and the US current-account deficit 81
Centre for Progressive Regulation (CPR) 266, 267
Challenger space shuttle 298
charities 248
Charlottesville, Virginia 275–6, 277
cheque accounts 139
Chevalier, Judith 301
Chicago Board of Trade (CBOT) 161, 162, 163
Chicago Board Options Exchange 164
Chicago Mercantile Exchange: International Monetary Market 163
Chicago school 251–3, 254, 255

child labour 21
Chile: taxes on inflows of foreign money 198, 230
Chiluba, Frederick 289
China 87–102
    boom of 1993–94 90
    educated workforce 95
    exports 17, 18, 87, 88, 90, 100–101, 102
    FDI recipient 90, 95, 213
    GDP 90, 94, 96
    genuine wealth creation 89, 91
    good infrastructure 95
    growth 89, 90, 91, 94–7
    ICOR 95, 96
    imports 90, 101
    income 24, 95, 97
    industrial revolution ix
    integration consequences 92–3
    investment 89, 95–6
    and Japan 90, 94, 96, 103
    labour 87, 90, 91, 94–5, 98
    migration to coastal cities 87
    and multinationals 87, 90
    open economy 95
    private sector 95
    property prices 64
    rapid industrialisation and urbanisation 96
    relationship with the US 87–8, 98–102
    savings rate 95
    stock exchanges 156
    yuan pegged to the dollar 88, 90, 98, 101, 102
    yuan revaluation issue 101–2
CHIPS (Clearing House Interbank Payments System) 139
Chirac, Jacques 137
Christian Democrats (Germany) 119
Christian Social Union (Germany) 119
churn 135
Citigroup 161
City of London 135
civil society 49
clearing houses 161–2
Cline, William 13

Clinton, Bill 100
Coase, Ronald 241–2
Coca-Cola 250
coffee prices 248
cold war 181, 288
colonialism 286
commercial paper 139
Commerzbank 147
"common banker" effect 221
communism, collapse of 296
companies
    cost-cutting 120
    debtor 159
    and governments 26–7
    political influence 27
    "zombie" 124–31
    see also businesses;
        multinationals
comparative advantage 259
competition
    and advanced technology 249
    banks 39, 146
    and developing countries 6, 9
    and firms' reputation for quality
        and fair dealing 6
    in Germany 115
    in internet access 255
    in Japan 130
    and Microsoft 240
    perfect 295
    price 250
    tax 30
    telecommunications 241
competition policy 251
computers, computing 107, 137, 240,
    250, 257
concentration ratios 240
Congo 288–9
connected lending 216, 222
consumer spending 62–3
consumer-price index 188, 190
consumer-price inflation 189, 190,
    192
contestability 240, 252
Continental Baking 250, 251
contracts
    and cross-border trade 30
    enforcement 141, 286

    forward 160
contributions 150
Corn Laws viii
corporate borrowers 38–9
corporate governance 149, 224
corporate social responsibility 6, 49
corruption 7, 19–20, 27, 214, 222, 223,
    225, 229, 245, 289, 291
cost-benefit analysis 266–8
Council of Economic Analysis
    (France) 303
coupons 157
credit 137
    regulation 33
    risk 144, 161, 162
    short-term 143, 210
credit cards 139, 148
credit lines 143, 144
credit-card operators 143
creditworthiness 140, 141, 158
crime and imprisonment 299, 300
crime rate 110
Cripps, Stafford 178
cross-border bank finance 213–14
cross-border equity finance 214
currency
    debauching the currency 173
    floating 226
    US 77
current-account balances 70, 70, 73
current (checking) accounts 69, 70,
    72, 143, 163
current-account deficits 67, 69–75, 89
    analysing 71, 71
    and net foreign purchases of US
        securities 80, 80
    US deficit and foreign central
        banks 81
    see also under United States

D

Daiei 126, 127–8, 130, 131
Daimler-Chrysler 115
Daly, Kevin 106
database marketing 143
de Soto, Hernando 41
de-unionisation 13
deadweight loss 238, 238, 239

debt
  deflation 61
  and the economy 56
  fixed-rate 144
  foreign 76
  household 62
  insupportable 37, 38
  and mistakes in financial markets
    201–2
  refinancing 198
  short-term bank 38, 212, 221
  and the US 60
  variable or floating rate 144
debt crises (1980s) 204
debtor companies 159
decision science 278
defined-benefit plans 153, 153
defined-contribution plans 153, 153
deflation 89, 121, 122, 125, 177, 187, 192
demand-management policies 58
democracy 7, 8, 28, 29, 51
  in Asia 171
  globalisation v democracy 34–6,
    199
  and the IMF 43
  political 33
  and the Washington consensus
    37
  and the WTO 43, 44, 46
Deng Xiaoping 94
Denmark
  green taxes 273
  ratio of imports to national
    income 25
  taxation 25, 26, 27
deposit-insurance schemes 39, 58,
  145
deposits
  bank 138, 143, 147, 150
  floating-rate 144
  supermarket chains 147
Deppe, Hans 119
deregulation 37, 41, 229, 252
derivatives 135, 137, 139, 140, 160,
  161, 162
  exchange-traded 161
  interest-rate 163
  and risk 164–6

  volume traded 165
Deutsche Bank 84, 98, 147
devaluation 69, 247
developing countries
  and capital 15
  and competition 6, 9
  economic growth 41, 51, 94
  and emissions 269
  employment 4, 6, 8–9
  exports 17–18, 49
  gains-from-trade issue 15–16
  GDP 207
  and globalisation benefits 15
  growth helps the poor 20–21, 21
  imports 18
  and outward FDI 11
  and rich countries' trade rules 48
  wages in 4, 6, 8, 9, 16, 22–4, 23
  and the Washington consensus
    37–8
  wealth creation 285
DIHK (German federation of
  chambers of commerce and
  industry) 113
discount rate 170, 182
disintermediation 147
diversification 170, 171
dividends
  level of 167–8
  payments to foreign investors 70
  taxation of 31
DIW (German Institute for
  Economic Research, Berlin) 117
Dobson, Wendy 207–8
Doe, Samuel 288
Dollar, David 16, 291, 292
Dooley, Michael 98, 99
dotcom bubble 91, 201
Dow Jones Industrial Average 104,
  191
Dresden 118, 119
Dresdner Bank 147
drug companies 44, 280, 281
dynamic programming 194
dysflation 121, 124

E
earnings yield 168, 169

East Asia
  banking crises 146
  borrowing 39
  dependence on bank lending 142
  exports 83, 90
  fastest-growing emerging
    economies 290
  growth helps the poor 20–21
  slump (1997–98) 20, 38, 57, 85, 99,
    137, 200, 205, 208, 212, 216, 217,
    219, 220, 226
  unprecedented prosperity 33
  and the Washington consensus
    38
East Asian tigers 16, 18, 20
Easterly, William 289–90
eastern Europe: privatisation 245
econometrics 16–17
economic growth
  in China 89, 90, 91, 94–7
  in the developing world 41, 51,
    94, 213
  and financial development 141
  helps the poor 20–21, 21, 49
  and inflation 184–5, 186, 187
  and investment of savings 285
  sustaining 177
  and trade 16–17, 18, 20
  and US imports 83–4
  and volatility 59
economic instability 38, 58, 59
economic isolationism x, 28
economic liberalisation 29
economic stability 56, 58, 193
economics
  the brightest young economists
    236, 294–303
    economic imperialism 297–8
    theory becomes applied
      300–302
  and the environment 236
  a powerful aid to policymakers
    235–6
economies
  closed 10, 31, 35, 67, 71–2, 199, 202,
    291
  market-based 33, 237
  national 33

open 10, 31, 35, 67, 72, 72, 95, 291
  poor 10
  rich 10
  stabilisation 41
economies of scale 9
Economist, The viii-ix, 81, 121, 178,
  197, 198, 228, 236, 294
education
  as an equalising force 13–14, 49
  in Germany 117
  and skilled workers 33
  spending 9
  support of 50
  teachers' unions 299–300
efficiency 237, 238, 238
Egypt
  aid to 288
  ancient 137
electoral cycle 296
Ellison, Glenn 300–301
emissions-trading scheme 269–71
empirical economics 299
employment 258, 258
  displaced rich-country workers 8,
    9, 10
  help in changing jobs 14
  higher-paid 11, 12
  and inflation 186
  lower-paid 12
  "mini-jobs" 117
  and outward FDI 8, 11–12
endangered species 44
endowments 150, 153
energy, wasteful use of 48
Enron collapse 148
environment
  protection 49, 50
  standards 4
equity cultures 149
equity funds 151
Ethiopia 290, 292
Eurex 164
Eurobonds 158
Euronext.liffe 161, 164
Europe
  birth rates 112
  capitalism 103
  consumer spending 62

economic and monetary union 118
GDP 105, 108, 112
immigration rates 112
labour force 112
leisure 108, 109, 111, 112
pensions 104, 112
productivity 103, 106–9, 111
return on capital 107
savings rate 111
slowdown 200
total employment 106
unemployment 103, 112
and the US 105–112, 106, 108
welfare system 112
working hours 108–9, 112, 261–2
European Central Bank (ECB) 175, 185
European Union 266
ban on hormone-treated beef from the US 45–6
broadcasting 255
competition in internet access 255
farmers' subsidies 248
and inadvertent obstacles to trade 30
outvoting of individual governments 45
regulatory excess 266, 268
union wide emissions-trading regime 271
exchange controls 228, 291
exchange rates
competitive 37
fall in 84
fixed 72, 98, 178
floating 178, 229
frozen 247
market 96
risk 200
speed of shifts 85
trade-weighted 99, 100, 100
volatile 163
exchanges 161, 164, 165
exports
Chinese 17, 18, 87, 88, 100–101, 102
and the current account 70
of developing countries 17
"export pessimism" theory 16, 17–19
and ISI 19
and outward FDI 11, 12
US 11, 12, 67, 82–3, 83, 90
externalities 239, 241–2

F
fairness 301–2
farm goods 49
Faust, Matthias 114
FDI (foreign direct investment) 15, 210–214, 224
banking-sector 225
cannot flee at short notice 38
and China 90, 95, 213
and corruption 222, 229
creates rather than displaces exports 11, 12
does not need to be serviced 38
drawbacks 210–211
and employment 8, 11–12
goes mostly to rich countries 11, 11
may set back development 16
rise of 212, 212
and taxation 31
US returns on 78–9
and the Washington consensus 37
western multinationals 20
Feddersen, Timothy 301
Federal Agency for Jobs (Germany) 116–17
federal funds rate 181, 182
Federal Open Market Committee 175
Federal Reserve viii, 55, 57–8, 61, 62, 82, 84, 89, 90, 145, 175, 176
electronic game 194
and the federal funds rate 181–2
and inflation 182, 185
and interest rates 181, 191–2, 195
monopoly on supply of bank reserves 181
responsible for bank supervision 178
role of 190

set up in 1913 178
Federal Reserve Bank of Cleveland 193
Federal Trade Commission (FTC) 251
FedWire 139
Feldstein, Martin 186
financial autarky 198
financial centres 135, 136
financial crises 48, 137, 215–21
  falling standards 216–18
  is it infectious? 220–21
  overborrowing syndrome 218–20
financial deregulation 62, 176
financial innovation 137
financial liberalisation 37, 213, 215–16, 218
financial regulation 48
financial revolution 176
Financial Services Agency (FSA) 122
financial system
  allocates and reallocates wealth 135
  matches savers with entrepreneurs 135
  opprobrium heaped on 136, 137
  role in a modern economy 137–42
Finland: green taxes 273
first world war x
fiscal conservatism 229
fiscal discipline 37, 41
fiscal policies 33, 228, 229
Fisher, Irving 174
"floor" 163, 164
Folkerts-Landau, David 8, 99
food
  chemicals in 44
  taxes 40
foreign aid
  and the current-account balance 70
  developing countries' dependence on 38
  and western governments 50
foreign direct investment see FDI
foreign-exchange reserves 198
foreign-ownership restrictions 3
forwards 161, 162

France
  agricultural cooperative banks 146
  banks' returns 146
  capital exported from (19th century) 204
  and China's economic growth 97
  corporate tax 115
  economic reform 112
  GDP per hour 108
  pensions 152
  property prices 64, 111
  universal banks 149
  working hours 108
Frank, Robert 267
Frankel, Jeffrey 16
fraud 33, 165
Freund, Caroline 77, 82
Friedman, Milton 184, 285, 287
Froeb, Luke 251
fuel taxes 40, 273
Fukui, Toshihiko 122
Fullerton, Don 275–7
fund managers 152–3, 163
futures contracts (futures) 137, 139, 162
futures options 162

G
G7 countries 25, 192
G8 debt relief plan 292
game theory 253, 300
garbage pricing 236, 275–7
Garber, Peter 98, 99
Gates, Bill 26–7
GATT see General Agreement on Tariffs and Trade
GDP 258, 290
  China compared with US 94
  and global stock of financial assets 138
  and inflation 186
  and living standards 34
  losses from banking and currency crises 208, 208
Gelos, Gaston 223
General Agreement on Tariffs and Trade (GATT) 44, 45, 46

General Electric 27
General Motors 143
George III, King 87
Germany 113–19
  Agenda 2010 104, 113, 114
  banks 115, 146, 179
  Betriebsrat (workers'
    representative) 114
  building firms 115
  capital exported from (19th
    century) 204
  chronic underachievement ix,
    103, 105
  competition 115
  economic reform 112
  exports 90
  Federal Agency for Jobs 116–17
  federal power structure 118
  GDP 108, 113
  "grand-coalition" government 119
  Hartz Commission 116
  hyperinflation 179, 180
  inflation rate 179, 180
  investment 68, 117, 118–19
  labour laws 114, 118
  "mini-jobs" 117
  national income 25
  productivity 116
  relocation of businesses 113–14,
    115
  reunification (1990) 113, 118, 180
  surplus 68
  taxation 114, 115
  Turkish migrant workers 70
  unemployment 113
  universal banks 149
  wage restraint 104
  wage subsidies 117–18
  Wirtschaftswunder 114
  working hours 108
  yield curves 183, 183
Gerster, Florian 117
Glaeser, Edward 298
Glass-Steagall Act 148
global warming 269
globalisation
  advocated by businessmen and
    politicians 3

  and developing-country poverty
    4
  a different manifesto 48–51
  earlier era of ix–x
  finance 37–42
    beware foreign capital 38–9
    too big to fail 40–41
    trying to get it right 42
    the Washington consensus
      37–8
  of higher education 297
  is government disappearing?
    25–36
  its critics 5–7
  liberal case for 5
  poor workers in the developing
    countries 15–24
  whether it hurts poor workers in
    the developing countries
      pessimism confounded 17–19
      trade as good for growth 16–17
      the trouble with ISI 19–20
      what fairness requires 22–4
  whether it hurts workers 8–14
    winners and losers 10–12
  the WTO 43–7
GM 139
Godley, Wynne 60, 79
gold standard 178
Goldman Sachs 96, 107, 297
Goldstein, Morris 101, 102
goods
  cheap 87, 88
  finished 11
  intermediate 11
  pollution in making some goods
    239
  prices 93, 199
  public 239, 241, 242
Gordon, Robert 110
governments
  accountability 50
  and aid 292
  allowable emissions 269–70
  and central banks 175, 180
  and companies 26–7
  curb on government power 29
  democratic 29

developing countries 19, 20
and globalisation 5, 25–6, 50–51
heavy borrowing by 38
influence of corporate interests 48
interventions by 5, 7, 243
the limits of 27–9
oppression by 28
and public-choice theory 243–4
and recessions 56
redistribution by 243
and retirement-saving schemes 282, 283, 284, 302
and social policies 35–6
spending 58, 243
taking responsibility for their policies 42
and taxation 25, 26, 50–51, 243
unreliable servants of the public interest 7
grabbing hand model 244, 245
Graham, Edward 23–4
Great Depression 39, 55–8, 137, 188, 189, 204
Great Fire of London (1666) 155
green taxes 272–4
greenhouse gases 269–72
Greenspan, Alan viii, 106, 141–2, 176, 189, 191, 195
Grossman, Sanford 296
growth managers 151

H
Hahn, Robert 266, 267
Hambrecht, Jürgen 114
Hamlet (Shakespeare) 137
Hammour, Mohamad 59
Hartz Commission 116–17
Harvard University 295, 296, 298, 299, 302, 303
Hausman, Jerry 250
Hayami, Masaru 122
Hayek, Friedrich 56, 285
health care 29, 104, 127
health spending 33
hedge funds 151–2
hedge ratio 164, 166
hedging 162

helping-hand model 243
Herfindahl-Hirschman Index 249–50
Hertz, Noreena 26
Hicks, Sir John 140
home bias 280
home heating systems 269, 270
Hong Kong 156
Hooper, Peter 84, 85
"hot money" 224
housing
bubble 64
house prices 55, 61–6, 65, 92, 111, 174
mortgages 64–5
Houthakker, Hendrik 83
Hoxby, Caroline 299–300
HSBC 147
Hufbauer, Gary 207–8
human rights 28
Hungary: current-account deficit 69
hyperbolic discounting 302
hyperinflation 179, 180
hysteresis 58

I
IBM 139, 161
ICOR *see* incremental capital output ratio
IG Bau 116
IG Metall 116
illegal dumping 276
IMF *see* International Monetary Fund
immigration 83
skill distribution 259–60
and unemployment 257
as an unequalising force 13
import tariffs 3
import-substituting industrialisation (ISI) 18, 19–20
imports
cheap 257, 259
Chinese 90, 101
and the current account 70
and developing countries 18
and outward FDI 11, 12
US 67, 82–5, 83, 98

income 223
  aggregate incomes 35, 36
  corporate 31
  cushioning losses 50
  income gap between US and
    Europe 108
  inequality 13
  national 26, 27
  redistribution of 28
  see also wages
incremental capital output ratio
  (ICOR) 95, 96
India
  aid 293
  child labour 21
  exports 17
  fall in infant mortality 290
  foreign investment in 213
  income 290
  and ISI 18
  missed opportunities 20
  separation from the international
    economy 20
  wages 95
Indonesia 208
  and America's outward FDI 11
  currency 85
  lending boom 216
  wages 24
industrial organisation 249
Industrial Revolution 10, 87, 140
infant mortality 290
inflation ix, 41, 61, 65, 89, 92, 93, 99,
  101, 123, 163, 173, 175, 176, 177, 179,
  180, 182, 184-8, 228, 246
  asset-price 190-91
  consumer-price 189, 190, 192
  costs 185-6
  falling 185
  and growth 184-5, 186, 187
  high 185
  is a bit of inflation good for you?
    185-8
  minimising 286
  rising 185, 194, 195, 248
  and savings 187
  and taxation 186
  and unemployment 184, 195, 260

  zero 186, 187, 188
information
  asymmetric 141, 263-5
  on borrowers' creditworthiness
    140, 141
  global flow of 29
  greater disclosure of financial
    information 222
  importance of 239-40
initial margin 161
initial public offerings (IPOs) 157
innovation 56
Institute for International Economics
  23
institutional investors 149-55
  assets 149, 151
  collectivist individualism 152-4
  growth at the expense of banks
    149
  power over company
    management (US) 149
instrumental variables 299
Insurance Act (1601) 155
insurance companies 140, 149, 153
intellectual property, protection of
  48
interbank market 143
interest payments to foreign
  investors 70
interest rates
  and asset prices 191
  cuts 55, 57, 58, 61, 110, 185
  fixed 163
  floating 163, 210
  high 90
  long-term 296
  low 62, 64, 89, 92, 99, 100, 189
  rise in 64, 72, 72, 79, 89, 90
  set by the Fed 181
  short-term 182, 296
  volatile 163
  zero 121
International Monetary Fund (IMF)
  20, 37, 38, 40-41, 42, 77, 82, 96, 123,
  208, 209, 219, 222, 226, 227, 228,
  230, 289, 291
  criticism of 40, 42, 43, 50, 295
internet 3

Interstate Bakeries 250, 251
investment
　　boom 77
　　by local companies 15
　　competition for inward
　　　investment 33
　　and economic instability 59
　　and education 33
　　high rates of 94
　　long-term 140
　　misdirected 129
　　portfolio 15, 79
　　returns on investment in the
　　　developing world 15
investment consultants 152
investment risk 154
investment trusts 151
Iraq 120
Ireland
　　property prices 64, 111
　　working hours 109
ISI *see* import-substituting
　industrialisation
Israel 280, 288
IT
　　investments in 129
　　revolution 91
Italy
　　green taxes 273
　　pensions 152
　　property prices 111
　　working hours 108
Ito-Yokado 128, 129

J
Japan 104, 120–32, 200
　　agricultural co-operative banks
　　　146
　　and America's outward FDI 11
　　bad loans 124–5, 129, 130, 131
　　banks 130, 144, 145, 146
　　and China 90, 94, 96, 103
　　chronic underachievement ix, 103
　　comatose economy about to
　　　revive 120–21
　　companies' cost-cutting 120
　　debt ratios 123, 124
　　deflation ix

　　dependence on bank lending 142
　　and fall in private-sector net
　　　saving 60
　　financial crisis (1989) 126, 127, 137,
　　　189, 190, 192
　　GDP 96, 120
　　government net debt 122, 123
　　health care 127
　　import restrictions 70
　　Japan's problems diagnosed 121–2
　　low growth 123–4, 127
　　manufacturing 18
　　mergers 130, 131
　　monetary policy 122–3, 192
　　post-war growth 96
　　postal system 132
　　price rises ix
　　productivity 129, 129
　　profit increases 131, 131
　　prolonged credit crunch 142
　　public-works projects 123, 124
　　regional banks 131
　　service industries 126–32
　　stockmarket 120, 121
　　surplus 73
　　unprecedented prosperity 33
　　working hours 262
　　youth unemployment 125, 125
　　"zombie" companies 124–31
Japan Telecom 130
Jarass, Lorenz 115
Jerram, Richard 127
job-protection laws 107
job-sharing 260, 262
Johnson, Karen 84, 85

K
Kahneman, Daniel 278–81
Kashyap, Anil 124, 129
Kaunda, Kenneth 289
Kellogg School of Management 301
Kenya 288, 291–2, 293
Keynes, John Maynard 173, 174
Keynesian thought 295
Kim Il Sung 288
King, Mervyn 187
King, Stephen 60
Kinnaman, Thomas 275–7

"KiwiSaver" scheme 283
Klein, Benjamin 190
Koizumi, Junichiro 122–5, 131–2
Kraay, Aart 16
Kremer, Michael 298
Krueger, Anne 227
Krugman, Paul 83, 296, 303
Kyoto environment conference (1997) 269
Kyoto Treaty (2005) 271

L
labour
    bonded 21
    child 21
    in China 87, 90, 91, 94–5, 98
    demand for 11
    in developing countries 16
    in Europe 112
    low-skilled/unskilled 12, 13, 13, 87, 93, 104, 259
    mobility 30, 32
    part-time workers 107, 260
    skilled 12, 13, 13, 23, 27, 28, 33, 259
    strict hiring-and-firing laws 58
    temporary workers 107
labour-market reforms 58, 59
Laibson, David 302
laisser-faire 5, 40
Larsen, Flemming 190
Latin America
    debt crisis (1980s) 38, 78, 146, 200, 202
    education abroad 292
    and ISI 18
    and the Russian financial crisis 220
Lau, Lawrence 101
law of diminishing returns 204, 240
law of large numbers 154–5
Lawson, Nigel 75
Lawson doctrine 75
Lawsons 129
LDP (Liberal Democratic Party) (Japan) 123, 125
Leeson, Nick 165
leisure 108, 109–110, 112
Lenin, Vladimir Ilyich 173

leverage 165, 201, 255
Levine, Ross 141
Levitt, Steve 299, 303
Liang, Hong 96
liberalism x
Liberia 288
life assurance 147
life insurers 150, 153, 154, 155
LIFFE see Euronext.liffe
lighthouses 241
liquidity 33, 42, 136, 161, 184
    capital-market 142
    crisis 145
    domestic 90
    excess 99
    increased 140
    market 223
    stockmarket 141
Litan, Robert 255–6
living standards
    and leisure time 109
    and productivity-cutting policies 34, 35
    rise in 9, 12
    US v Europe 108, 110
    and wages in developing countries 23
Lloyd's of London 154
loans
    bank 20, 150, 205, 210, 211
    longer-term 144
    non-performing 217, 225
    to poor countries 15
Lockheed-Martin 254
London International Financial Futures and Options Exchange (LIFFE) see Euronext.liffe
Long-Term Capital Management 57
Louvre Accord 192
low-income countries see developing countries
LTCM hedge fund 85
Luddites 10, 257
"lump of labour" fallacy 18, 235, 257–60, 262
"lump-of-trade" fallacy 18
Luxembourg 27

M
Macartney, Lord 87
McKinnon, Ronald 218, 219
McKinsey & Company 279
McKinsey Global Institute 135
McNamara, Robert 278
macroeconomic data 223, 224
macroeconomic policy 223, 224, 228
macroeconomic stability 222, 229
Magee, Stephen 83
Malaysia 285
  exports 17
  imposes exchange controls 228
  lending boom 216
Mali 71, 288
Mankiw, Gregory 296, 303
Mann, Catherine 81, 83, 87
Mannesmann 118
manufacturing
  labour-intensive 18
  US 59, 88, 98
margin 143
marginal productivity 22–3
market efficiency 171, 237, 238, 239
market failure 237, 239–42
market mechanism 237
market power 249, 250, 251, 255, 256
market-suppressing controls 19–20
markets 237–42
  asset 190, 200–201
  bond 77, 81, 139, 156, 157
  capital 75, 76, 82, 140–43, 147, 150, 156, 159, 201, 202, 219, 227
  closure of 4, 7
  contestable 240, 252
  credit 60
  definition 156
  and democracy 28
  efficiency 33
  emerging 198
  equity 156
  foreign-exchange 139, 160
  as a form of exchange 3
  forward 160
  free 285
  globalisation 33
  a high regard for 5
  and human rights 28

  and international companies 7
  labour 106
  legitimacy 33
  limits of 5
  money 139
  and NGOs 7
  stock 77
  suspicion of 48
  swaps 161
Marquez, Jaime 84, 85
Marra, David 130
Marris, Stephen 86
Marsh, David 118
Martin, Bill 59
Martin, William McChesney 190
Massachusetts Institute of Technology (MIT) 295, 298, 300
Matif 164
maturity transformation 144
Maxwell, Robert 152
MBNA 143
Mellon, Andrew 55, 58
mergers 172, 249, 250–51, 250
  blocked 254
  and booms 59
  and investment banks 147
  Japan 130, 131
Merkel, Angela viii, 104, 119
Merton, Robert 139, 164
Mesopotamia 137
Metallgesellschaft 162
Mexico
  and America's outward FDI 11
  bungled devaluation 69
  and Chinese unskilled labour 87
  current-account deficit 75
  exports 17
  financial crisis (1994) 77, 85, 197, 200, 205
  wages 23–4
microeconomics 296
Microsoft 26–7, 240, 249, 254–5
middle-income countries: wages paid by affiliates 23, 23
Mill, John Stuart 241
Miller, Geoffrey 192
Miller, Merton 159

Mirrlees, James 263–5
Mitsubishi Tokyo Financial Group
(MTFG) 126, 130, 131
Mizuho 130
Modigliani, Franco 159
Mogae, Festus 291
Moi, Daniel arap 291–2
monetarism 285
monetary policy
dealing with asset prices 189
improving the standard of 229
Japan 122–3, 192
and prices 193
and uncertainty 191
US 89, 90, 101, 102, 110, 195
"money illusion" 189
money market 139
money purchase schemes 153
monopoly 239, 240, 242, 251
Moody's Investors Service 130, 159
Moore, John Hardman 136
Morris, Derek 253
mortgage refinancing 65
mortgages 64–5, 92, 111, 137
Mozambique: aid 288, 293
Mugabe, Robert 235, 246, 247, 291
Mulligan, Casey 298
multinationals
affiliates 11, 12, 23
campaign to hobble them 21, 22
and China 87, 90
and profit 6, 7, 20, 21, 23
and subsidies 49
and taxation 49
and third-world development 20
wages in developing countries 6,
16, 22, 23
see also businesses; companies
Münchhausen, Baron 116
mutual funds 137, 138, 140, 143, 149,
150–52, 150
close-ended 150, 151
open-ended 150–51

N
NAIRU (non-accelerating inflation
rate of unemployment) 184, 185,
261, 262

Namibia 247
Napoleon Bonaparte 94
NASDAQ 253
national borders 30
National Bureau of Economic
Research (US) 19
nationalisation 146
natural monopolies 240–41
natural resources 48, 49, 50
neo-liberalism ix, x, 248
net complements 11
Netherlands
agricultural co-operative banks
146
green taxes 273
pension funds 149
Netscape 255
network effects 255
"New Classicists" 295
new product launches 172
New York Earth Summit (1997) 272
New York Stock Exchange 156–7
New York Times 303
New Zealand
consumer spending 62
"KiwiSaver" scheme 283
property prices 64
NGOs (non-government
organisations) 6, 7, 50
Nordic aid 291
North American Free-Trade
Agreement (NAFTA) 8
North Korea 28, 288
Northrop Grumman 254
Norway: green taxes 273, 274
NTT 130

O
Obstfeld, Maurice 85
OECD (Organisation for Economic
Co-operation and Development)
19, 25, 31, 236, 274
Jobs Study 258, 262
Office Depot 251
oil prices ix, 89
oil shocks 163
Okada, Motoya 128
Olsen, Mancur 243

O'Neill, Jim 80, 85
O'Neill, Paul 76
open-market operations 181, 182
options 139, 160, 161, 162, 164
Osaka 160
output
    actual 185, 185
    gap 185
    potential 185, 185
    and recessions 58
outsourcing 90
outward orientation 19
overborrowing 218–19, 220, 226
overdrafts 143, 144
Oxfam 248

P
P&C insurers see property and
    casualty insurers
Pakistan 20
PartnerRe 279
paternalism viii
payments, clearing and settling 139
pension funds 137, 138, 140, 149–50,
    150, 151
pensions 104, 112, 147, 152–3
PepsiCo 250
perestroika 237
"perfect competition" 239
Pesendorfer, Wolfgang 301
Peters, Jürgen 116
Phelps, Edmund 184
Phillips, Bill 184
Phillips curve 184
Pierer, Heinrich von 114
Poland: "shock therapy" economic
    reforms (1990) 295
political right 41
politicians 6, 235
    attitude to globalisation 3
    and big companies 27
politics
    democratic 49
    special-interest 49
    voting 301
pollution
    costs 49
    emissions-trading scheme 269–71

in making some goods 239
taxes 50, 236, 272–4
poor countries see developing
    countries
population growth 286–7
populism viii
portfolio
    flows 211, 212
    investment 15, 212, 212
Posen, Adam 124, 179
post-Chicago school 253
poverty
    and aid 288–93
    developing-country 4
    and economic stabilisation 41
    growth helps the poor 20–21, 21,
        49
    policies to relieve 50
power plants 269, 270, 274
PPP (purchasing power parity) 96
Prasad, Eswar 102
premiums 150
prestiti 156
price controls 246
price stability 175, 177, 179, 188–91,
    193
price/earnings (p/e) ratio 159, 168,
    169
prices
    asset 103, 189–92, 201, 224
    average 185
    coffee 248
    cuts 9
    equity 62–3, 219
    "fair" 248
    fall in 121, 187, 188, 192
    goods 93, 199
    import 84
    and ISI 19
    land 87
    low 253, 254
    oil ix, 89, 170
    and pollution costs 49
    property 55, 61–5, 65, 92, 111, 174,
        192
    relative 84, 185
    and scarcity of natural resources
        49

share 60, 63, 92, 167, 171, 189, 192
world 90
primary market 157
Princeton University 301
private sector
financial deficit 60–61
growth in China 95
net saving 60
privatisation 37, 132, 244, 245
process innovation 257
Procter & Gamble 128, 164
product innovation 257
productivity 32, 57, 257, 258
growth 192, 193, 195, 259
Japanese 129, 129
marginal 22–3, 94–5
productivity-cutting policies 34, 35
and public spending 33–4
rising 187
US vs Europe 103, 105–6, 107
and welfare policies 34, 35
profitability 146, 252
profits
businesses' sole interest 6, 7, 20
cutting 84
fall due to productivity-cutting policies 34, 35
and moving production to a lower-wage area 9
rise in 131, 131
and stricter regulation of international business 6
taxes on 31, 32
windfall 37
"profits before people" 28
property and casualty (P&C) insurers 154, 155
property rights 41, 141, 223, 229, 286
proprietary trading 147
protectionism viii, 10, 99
public finance principles 229–30
public health 50
public spending 9, 33, 40, 41, 50
public-choice theory 243–4

Q
quasi-interest rate 79

quotas 19, 230

R
R&D announcements 172
Rabin, Matthew 301–2
ratings agencies 159
"rational expectations" theory 295
Reagan, Ronald 77, 285
real wealth
creating 63
and house prices 62–3
recessions 57–61
avoiding 56
the dark side of the boom 60–61
economy-wide 39
following financial crises 137
and interest rates 187
should we learn to love recessions? 57–8
United States 55
reciprocity 46
recycling 277
regulatory authorities 33
Reichsbank 180
Reserve Bank of New Zealand 175
Resona 125
retirement-saving schemes 282–4
rich countries
current-account deficits 69
displaced workers 8, 9, 10
and globalisation benefits 15
trade rules 48
Rio de Janeiro Earth Summit (1992) 272
Ripplewood 130
risk
credit 144
and derivatives 164–6
exchange rate 200
and false sense of security 189
interest-rate 144
investment 154
political 206
pooling of 140
poor decision-making 278–81
portfolio 170
and return 170
shares 168, 170, 171

Rodrik, Dani 17, 25–6, 27, 32–3
Rogers, Will 178
Rogoff, Ken 85–6
Romer, David 16
Roosevelt, Theodore 137
Rosenberg, Michael 84
Rueff, Jacques 99
Russia 171, 296
    aid 293
    corruption 245
    financial crisis (1998) 85, 197, 220
    see also Soviet Union

S
Sachs, Jeffrey 16, 295–6
safety nets 28
Sainsbury 147
Salop, Steven 253
Samuelson, Paul 241
"Saturday Night Special" 175
Saudi Arabia 17, 288
"Save More Tomorrow" programme 283
savings
    pooling of 139–40
    and the US 60, 64
savings accounts 137, 143
savings-and-loan (thrifts) industry 138, 144
Scandinavia: banking crises 146
scanner data 250–51
Scholes, Myron 164
Schröder, Gerhard viii, 104, 113, 118, 119
Schumpeter, Joseph 56, 57, 59
"Seattle stomp" 276
secondary market 157
securities 156
    bought by the Fed 181, 182
    fixed-income 157
    and mutual funds 138
    and open-market operations 181, 182
    prices 140
    purchase of unsold securities 147
    standard 139
    volume of trading 138, 138
    yield curves 183, 183

Seiyu 129
self-interest 5, 243
Sen, Amartya 3, 287
September 11th attacks, 2001 280
service industries, Japanese 126–32
Seven-Eleven Japan 129
share valuation 159, 167, 168
shareholders 159
shares 140
    definition 158
    prices 60, 63, 92, 167, 171
    and risk 168, 170, 171
    US 80, 137
Shell 170
Shiller, Robert 64
Shimada, Haruo 125
Shinada, Naoki 129
Shinsei Bank 130
Shleifer, Andrei 296
    and Vishny, Robert 243–5
Singapore 230
Singapore Airlines 170
SMFG 130
Smith, Adam 5, 237
Social Democrats (Germany) 119
social insurance 26, 33
social justice 40
social policies 35–6
social programmes 28, 33
social services 40
social spending 35
socialism 48
sociology, economics in 297
Softbank 130
Software AG 114
software spending 107
Son, Masayoshi 130
Soto, Marcelo 211
South Africa 247, 292
South Korea
    becomes a world-ranking industrial power 19
    capital-account liberalisation 228
    current-account deficit 73
    exports 17
    financial crisis (1998) 197, 218
    GDP per person 96

growth 96
"merchant banks" 217
non-performing loans 217
a poor country in the 1950s 18
US predictions 18–19
South-East Asia: financial crisis
(1997) 197
"sovereign bankruptcy" 227
Soviet Union
aid from 288
and markets 237
totalitarianism and economic
isolation 28
see also Russia
Spain
cajas (savings banks) 146
consumer spending 62
property prices 64, 111
variable-rate mortgages 65
spot rate 161
spread 143
Srinivasan, T.N. 17, 18
Standard & Poor's 159
Staples 251
statism x, 245
Steiner, Viktor 119
Stiepelmann, Heiko 115
Stiglitz, Joseph 42
stockmarket 139
bubble (1990s) 174
capitalisation 141, 157, 157
collapse (2000–01) 55
communist criticism of 156
crash (1987) 145, 166
liquidity 141
Stolpe, Manfred 117
straddles 162
student loans 137
subsidies 75, 248
curbs on 37, 41, 291
ending 40, 50
extra 49
and rich countries 48
subsistence farming 94–5
sulphur dioxide 269, 271, 273–4
Summers, Larry 295, 303
supply and demand 199, 237–8,
238

surplus 67, 68
capital-account 69
China 101
consumers' 238–9
current-account 69, 73
Japan 73
producers' 238
trade 70, 73, 101
Sutton, Willie 143
Svensson, Jakob 292
swaps 139, 160, 161, 162
currency 161, 163
interest-rate 161, 163, 164
swaptions 162
sweatshops 4, 6, 16, 20, 21
Sweden
and fall in private-sector net
saving 60
green taxes 273, 274
taxation 25, 26
Swiss National Bank 175

T
Taiwan 17, 96
Takenaka, Heizo 124, 125
Taliban 289
tariffs 19
taxation 25–6, 26, 27–8, 29, 286
corporate 31, 32
cuts 55, 62
and governments 25, 26, 50–51,
243
green taxes 272–4
and immobile labour 32
incentive compatible tax system
264
increased 40
indirect 31
an inefficient system 298
and inflation 186
and multinationals 49
the mystery of the missing tax
cut 30–32
OECD tax mix 31
pollution 50, 236
on profits 31, 32
and public spending 33
tax reform 37

and working hours 109
technology
    and competition 249
    and cross-border trade 5
    and distance 30
    its importance in widening
        inequality 13
    making more with less 10
    new 257, 258, 259
    protection of workers displaced
        by 50
    and rapid economic growth 94,
        187
    rapid technological change 12, 193
    and unemployment 257, 258
    winners and losers 10
telecommunications 137, 240–41
television broadcasting 241
Tesco 128, 147
Texas Instruments 164
textiles 49
Thailand
    and America's outward FDI 11
    current-account deficit 69
    fall in infant mortality 290
    finance companies 217
    income 290
    lending boom 216
Thaler, Richard 283, 301
Thatcher, Margaret, Baroness 119,
    285
Tirole, Jean 296, 303
"too big to fail" 39, 40–41
totalitarianism 28
Toyota 127
trade
    both sides able to gain from 15
    and economic growth 16–17, 18, 20
    and employment 8, 9–10
    its relative unimportance in
        widening inequality 13
    liberal 47
    mercantilist view of 46–7
    static gains from 9
    and the Washington consensus
        37
    and the WTO 43–4
trade agreements 47

trade balance 84
trade barriers
    lowering 46, 83, 199
    in poor countries 15
    and wages 6
trade deficits viii, 73, 82, 83, 192
trade liberalisation 218
trade policy 50
trade surplus 70, 73
trade unions 16, 116
training 262
    as an equalising force 13–14, 49
    in Germany 117
    in poor countries 206
transfers 75
transparency 223, 224, 224, 230
trust funds 152
Tullock, Gordon 243
Turkana nomads (Kenya) 288
Turkey: financial crisis (2000–01)
    197, 220

U
UFJ Holdings 126–7, 128, 130, 131
Uganda 293
unemployment viii, 257–62, 258
    above the NAIRU 185
    benefits 104, 117
    cyclical increases in 58
    in the euro area 103, 112
    in Germany 113
    and inflation 184, 195, 260
    and working hours 261, 261
    youth unemployment in Japan
        125, 125
Unilever 128
unit trusts see mutual funds
unit-linked policies 154
United States
    aid from 288
    balance of payments 67, 82
    banks and capital markets 142
    banks' returns 146
    booms and busts (late 19th
        century) 91
    budget deficit 100, 110, 111
    capital-importing (19th century)
        204

Chinese imports 87, 88, 90
consumer borrowing 55, 60, 61, 62
consumer spending 62, 89, 111
crime rate 110
currency 77, 84–6
current-account deficit 60, 67, 69–75, 85, 86, 89, 98, 100, 107, 110
  blame the budget 74–5
  the highest in the country's history 76–7
  not necessarily bad 69–72
  why it is hard to turn around 82–4
debt stock 78, 79, 79
dotcom bubble 91, 201
and the euro area 105–112, 106, 108
and European ban on hormone-treated beef 45–6
excessive debt 60
exports 11, 12, 67, 82–3, 83, 90
failure to provide adequate health care 29
fixed-interest mortgages 64–5
fragile economic recovery 200
GDP 94, 105, 107, 108, 110
Great Depression 39, 55–8, 137, 188, 189, 192
house prices 55, 61–6, 65, 92, 111, 174
immigration 83, 260
imports 25, 67, 82–5, 83, 98
industrialisation 91
institutional investors 149
interest rate cuts 55, 57, 58, 61, 110
investment by 205
investment in 68
"jobless recovery" 91
and the Kyoto Treaty (2005) 271
local government 245
manufacturing 59, 88, 98
monetary policy 89, 90, 101, 102, 110, 195
mutual fund ownership 150, 152
as a net debtor 78, 78
net foreign liabilities 205

outward FDI 11, 11, 78–9
payments volume 139, 139
pensions 104, 152, 153, 153
the price of profligacy 76–81
  borrowing binge 76–7
  lack of enthusiasm for US assets 80–81, 82
private-sector deficit 60–61, 60
private-sector wages and salaries 62, 63
productivity 103, 105–6, 111
prosperity 33, 55
raises funds abroad at an increasing pace 68
rapid technological change 12
recession (2000–01) 55, 57, 62, 89
relationship with China 87–8, 98–102
remarkable success of the economy (1990s) 29
retirement-saving schemes 282–3
return on capital 107
savings rate 60, 63, 100, 111, 205
savings-and-loan (thrifts) industry 144
share ownership 80, 137
stock and bond markets 77
taxation 25
total employment 106
trade deficit viii, 192
wealth illusion 63, 89, 91, 92
working hours 108, 109–110, 262
world's biggest net creditor 73
University of California, Berkeley 301
University of Chicago 297, 299, 301
  principles for competition policy 251–2
Uruguay 26–7
  financial crisis (2001–02) 197
Uruguay Round of trade talks 44
US Department of Justice 251, 254
US Treasury 38, 57–8, 295
  bonds 80, 89, 92, 99, 100, 157–8, 173

V
value added 26, 27, 95

value managers 151
variation margin 162
Venezuela 24
Verheugen, Günter 266, 268
vertical restraints 253
Vickrey, William 263-5
"Vickrey auction" 265
Vietnam 95, 293
Vietnam war 278
Vishny, Robert see Shleifer, Andrei
visible-trade balance 70, 71
Vodafone 118
volatility 58, 59, 162-3, 166, 170, 171,
    202
Volcker, Paul 175, 176
Volkswagen 260

W
wages
    cuts 186-7
    in developing countries 4, 6, 8, 9,
        16, 22-4, 23
    and displaced rich-country
        workers 8, 10
    in eastern European countries
        115
    and economic growth 21, 21
    fall in 12, 34, 35, 186, 187
    flexible 262
    lagging behind inflation 65
    local 23, 23
    minimum wage 13, 262
    nominal 193
    real 65, 186
    relative 259
    rich-country workers 8, 9
    rise in 12
    subsidiaries 117-18
    and trade barriers 6
    US private-sector wages and
        salaries 62, 63
    see also income
Wal-Mart 128, 129, 148
Wall Street, New York 135, 168, 170,
    189, 190, 279, 297
Warner, Andrew 16
Warren-Boulton, Frederick 254

Warsaw Stock Exchange 156
Washington consensus 37-8, 41
water charges 40
Wei, Shang-Jin 223
welfare
    benefits 104
    policies 34, 112, 243
    spending 9, 33
welfare state 26, 28, 32
Werden, Greg 251
West Africa 285
Western Europe 11, 33
Wharton Business School 296
White House
    Council of Economic Advisers
        303
    Office of Management and
        Budget 268
Whitman, Walt ix
"will of the people" 28
Williamson, John 37
wire transfers 139
Wolfers, Justin 58-9
working hours 108-110, 112, 260-62,
    261
World Bank 19, 37, 38, 161, 285, 286,
    291, 293, 295
    criticism of 40, 41, 42, 50
world growth 89, 91
World Trade Organisation (WTO)
    43-7, 50, 95, 203
    and democracy 43, 44, 46
    principal role 45
world wide web 29
WTO see World Trade Organisation

Y
Yahoo! Japan web portal 130
Yale School of Management 301
yield curves 183, 183

Z
Zambia 289-90, 290, 291
Zervos, Sara 141
Zimbabwe 235, 246-8, 291
Zitzelsberger, Heribert 115
"zombie" companies 124-31